FOUNDATIONS OF FAITH

ROBERT O. WAHL, D.MIN.

NE✗GEN®

Building the New Generation of Believers

COOK COMMUNICATIONS MINISTRIES
Colorado Springs, Colorado • Paris, Ontario
KINGSWAY COMMUNICATIONS LTD
Eastbourne, England

FOUNDATIONS OF FAITH

NexGen® is an imprint of
Cook Communications Ministries
Colorado Springs, CO 80918
Cook Communications, Paris, Ontario
Kingsway Communications, Eastbourne, England

FOUNDATIONS OF FAITH
© 2006 by The Resource Connection, Inc.

First Printing, 2006
Printed in the United States of America
1 2 3 4 5 6 7 8 9 10 Printing/Year 10 09 08 07 06

Cover design: BMB Design
Interior Design and Maps: Paul Segsworth Design

ISBN-13: 978-0-7814-4380-7
ISBN-10: 0-78144-380-6

Dedication

Dedicated to my devoted wife, Frances, and daughter, Beverly, whose steadfast encouragement was the stimulus for completion of this project, and to my Ministery Associate, Sonya Neal, who spent countless hours at the computer typing and arranging these materials.

—Bob Wahl

Foundations of Faith

Contents and Outline of the Course

Welcome

...to the *Foundations of Faith* series. It is our prayer that by learning together we will continually grow in our knowledge of God and in our effectiveness as His witness in the world.

The following pages represent the cumulative efforts of many who have studied the depth of wisdom in God's Word and the realities of the world around us. We immerse ourselves in that river of knowledge and understanding, grateful for the legacy of those who have gone before us, and worshipping the one and only true God, the source of all wisdom.

> My son, if you accept my words and store up my commands within you, turning your ear to wisdom and applying your heart to understanding, and if you call out for insight and cry aloud for understanding, and if you look for it as for silver and search for it as for hidden treasure, then you will understand the fear of the LORD and find the knowledge of God. For the LORD gives wisdom, and from his mouth come knowledge and understanding.
>
> —Proverbs 2:1-6

Course Objectives

Completing *Foundations of Faith* will help you:

• Feel at home in your Bible. You will know how it all fits together, how the people and events fit into history, and "who came after what" in the order of events. The Bible will no longer be such a formidable and incomprehensible book. You will have a renewed hunger to read and marvel at its astounding truths and prophecies.

• Understand why and when the various denominations came into being and how they differ from one another.

• Distinguish truth from error and understand what is meant by the terms "cult" and "occult."

• Develop skill in understanding the culture we live in and effectively sharing the Christian message to people characterized by a twenty-first century "postmodern" mindset.

• Know what to say when people ask questions like, "How do you know there is a God?" "How do you know the Bible is true?" "Are miracles really possible?" "Why do you believe in creation?".

Certificate of Completion

Upon completion of this course you will receive a certificate in recognition of your achievement. As a graduate, you become part of the *"Foundations of Faith* alumni family," having established friendships that continue for many years into the future.

Important!

Before you begin teaching this series, please review the following explanations, guidelines, and suggestions:

1. This manual includes both lesson material for students and an instructor's guide for each lesson. Be sure to read both before designing your lesson plans. Make sufficient copies of the student material for your class and distribute them at least one lesson prior to the class lesson.

2. The Leader section pages include a column of information to the left and a column on the right where you can make notations or reminders of visuals you plan to use in class. Some suggested reminders and visuals are already inserted in these columns as examples.

3. You will need the following equipment to effectively teach this course:
   • A chalkboard or whiteboard
   • Maps including Mesopotamia (modern Iraq), Israel, Egypt, Asia Minor (modern Turkey), the regions of Paul's missionary journeys, and Europe. These could be either classroom maps or overhead transparencies if you have access to an overhead projector. A globe may be useful in the first lesson.

4. The goal of the first unit ("Surfing the Bible") is for students to be able to tell the story of the Bible in three minutes or less. It is important they tell the story with reference to a map. From the first lesson, demonstrate this by pointing to a map and repeating the sequence of names learned to that point (from Adam to Joseph in Lesson 1. Add Moses in Lesson 2, etc.). The entire story is written in the Student section (Lesson 7) as an example, but it is essential that students learn to do this from memory. This places the entire Bible in chronological order and greatly enhances future Bible study.

We ask students to tell this story in three minutes or less so they can stay on the "high road" and see the "big picture," rather than become entangled in detail. Seeing this overview of Bible history is the great strength of this unit. Bible students seldom have an opportunity to see the overall picture—the "grand sweep" of Bible history. They need to see that the 66 books of the Bible are *one story*—the story of God's creation, man's sin, and God's plan of redemption.

5. Inform students that they should read the lesson material for each lesson before class. The obvious exception is the first class because most students will probably not receive their material before the course begins. Lesson 1 is designed as a review of the material you present in class, but beginning with Lesson 2, the students should study the material and complete the assignments prior to class. There is minimal homework. The curriculum is designed for busy people. The heart of learning takes place in the classroom as you present the material and guide the interaction of class members.

6. Your teaching will be greatly enhanced by the background information on some of the topics not frequently studied. We suggest you browse all the way through this manual and begin some study now in subjects you will teach in upcoming lessons. The units on church history, apologetics and especially postmodernism will be enriched by additional reading on your part. You may already have a background in these subjects or have resources available. If not, we suggest the following:
   • For church history: *Church History in Plain Language* by Bruce Shelley (Word Publishing).

- For apologetics: *The Case for Christ, The Case for Faith,* and *The Case for a Creator*, by Lee Strobel (Zondervan). *I Don't Have Enough Faith to be an Atheist*, by Norma L. Geisler & Frank Turek (Crossway Books).
- For Postmodernism: *The Death of Truth,* by Dennis McCallum (Bethany House Publishers).

For background information when teaching Unit I, "Surfing the Bible," we suggest *The New Unger's Bible Dictionary* (Moody Press) or a similar comprehensive dictionary of the Bible.

These are just suggested resources. You, your pastor, or church librarian may have additional suggestions. An expanded list of apologetics resources appears in Lesson 19.

7. You may wish to enhance your teaching with an occasional video presentation. If so, we have found the following videos fit the designated lesson topics well:
- For Lesson 2 in the Bible survey unit: "The Exodus Revealed, Search for the Red Sea Crossing." This video gives evidence of Israel in Egypt and documentation for the Red Sea crossing.
- For Lesson 10 in the church history unit: "The Inquisition," a documentary by The History Channel.
- For the church history unit in general: "History of Christianity," a series by Dr. Timothy George of Beeson Divinity School. This is a six-part overview of church history with a Leader's Guide and Student Worksheets.

Since these videos will no doubt be longer than you have time for in class, you will need to preview them and use just the portion of each video that is pertinent to your topic.

In addition to your local Christian bookstore, a good source for videos is Gateway Films / Vision Video, P.O. Box 540, Worcester, PA 19490-0540, 1-800-523-0226, www.visionvideo.com

8. Each of the seven units has an objective as a goal for students to reach when they complete the unit. Teaching toward that objective will give you direction, enhance student learning, and adequately prepare students for the next unit. The objectives are:

Unit I To tell the entire Bible story, with reference to a map, in three minutes or less.

Unit II To trace the origin and development of two or more denominations and define their distinctives and differences.

Unit III In one sentence each, to summarize biblical doctrine of the nature of God, person of Christ, and means of salvation.

Unit IV In two or three sentences each, to defend belief in the existence of God, the deity of Christ, His resurrection, and the trustworthiness of Scripture.

Unit V To evaluate a belief system by applying the "Five-Point Test of Truth."

Unit VI To compare and contrast characteristics of modern and postmodern culture and describe the impact of postmodern culture on the church.

Unit VII To set a personal goal for improvement in discipleship.

May the Lord richly bless you in your teaching ministry!

About the Author

Robert O. Wahl is the founder of The Resource Connection, Inc., a provider of educational materials and training programs for churches and individuals. Dr. Wahl began The Resource Connection in response to the alarming number of people he has observed becoming vulnerable to false teachings and alternative religions because they are not grounded in solid biblical teaching. Part of his duties with The Resource Connection include teaching ministry lectures and courses on a wide array of topics designed to help people mature in their faith as well as their biblical knowledge. Some topics include Understanding Islam, Creation Theories, Principles of Church Leadership, and Defending Your Faith. Dr. Wahl is also the founder of Church Educational Ministries, Inc., is a member of the Cañon City Ministerial Association, is a coordinator, presenter, and exhibitor at the Christian Ministries Convention in Denver, Colorado, and has seen several articles published in *Moody Magazine* and *Sermon Builder Magazine*. Dr. Wahl holds a D.Min. and M.Div. degree from Denver Seminary and a degree in history from Wheaton College. He has four grown children and currently resides in Cañon City, Colorado with his wife Frances.

UNIT

I

Surfing the Bible

LESSON

Genesis

Equipment Needed

1) Chalkboard or whiteboard.
2) Maps showing Mesopotamia, Canaan, and Egypt.
3) Globe, if available.

Teaching Supplies Needed

1) Copies of Genesis Quiz (page 23).
2) Copies of student lessons 1 and 2 to distribute to the class.

---

1. Introduce yourself. Write your name on whiteboard.

2. Have class members briefly introduce themselves.
Ask them to state their name and one fact about themselves. The one "fact" can be anything—their favorite food, pet peeve, where they grew up, etc. The purpose is to slow the process so students can write the names and connect with fellow class members.

3. Introduce the course:
   • Review objectives. Explain procedures and teaching/learning style (informal, interactive, non-threatening, seeking truth as a team of equals). Mention your role as a "gate keeper," meaning you are responsible to make sure everyone has an equal opportunity to participate in class discussion. You will sometimes have to limit one or more student's "speeches" so others will have an opportunity to participate.
Ask that no one feel offended by this. It's your responsibility to be a gatekeeper, and it's essential to good discussion.
   • Review the "Table of Contents" page that lists the topics for each lesson.
   • Describe homework expectations.

> **Note:** For your own background information on the patriarchs, we suggest reading the entry for each person in *The New Unger's Bible Dictionary* or similar reference.

Lecture

1. Define "Genesis" (Beginning). Refer to the list of things that began in Genesis (the opening paragraph on the first page of their student handouts). Have students underline each.

2. Show the location of Mesopotamia, Canaan, and Egypt. Relate Mesopotamia to modern Iraq, and share any information you have about the area. Current interest in Iraq will make this easier. Class members may already have information from the media or other sources to share.

Margin notes:

Write your name on board.

Ask students to turn to the Introduction portion of their handouts and follow along as you explain the objectives, expectations, and content outline.

Genesis - "Beginning"

Use overhead or free-standing maps to identify locations. Pass a globe around classroom if you have one, and show or mark the location of Mesopotamia, etc.

On Board:
Adam—2
Noah—6
Abraham—12
Isaac—21
Jacob—25
Joseph—37

Abraham—2,000 B.C.

3. Introduce the names of the six patriarchs. Define "patriarch" (the head of a family or clan, the originator of a line of descent). Point out the advantages of memorizing these names (basic to all of Scripture, quick reference when seeking information about them, simple and easy familiarity with the content of Genesis.)

4. Tell the story of each patriarch, using the best story-telling technique possible. Make it lively, interesting, and colorful. Ask students to remember Abraham's date—approximately 2,000 B.C. Be sure to include everything in the lecture that is tested in the "Genesis Quiz." Refer to the Family Tree chart in the student manual, page 29, as you tell the stories.

Note: With regard to the date of creation and the length of creation days, explain that the Bible does not give a date. Limit discussion on this issue by pointing out that an adequate examination of this question would require more time than is available in a survey course of this kind. However, it should be noted that Christians, all of whom have respect for the authority of Scripture, disagree on this issue. Some hold to a young earth (6,000 to 10,000 years old and literal twenty-four-hour creation days). Others hold to an old earth (millions? billions? of years) and understand the "days" to be long periods of time. Still other theories are proposed, including the "gap theory," which proposes a long period of time elapsed between Genesis 1:1 and 1:2, after which the earth was "recreated" in six twenty-four-hour days.

I. Adam

Point to Mesopotamia (Iraq) on the map.

A. The Garden of Eden
1. Possibly located in Mesopotamia
2. Adam & Eve's sin—Stage set for drama that unfolds throughout the Bible. This attitude of rebellion is called sin, affects the entire human race, and separates man from God.
3. The rest of the Bible is the story of God bringing man back into fellowship with Himself.
B. Acts of mercy
1. Kept from tree of life (Gen. 3:22-24) Was this an act of mercy? What would life be like if we lived forever in bodies affected by sin? The Bible doesn't say, but it's a great discussion question.
2. Clothed with skins (symbolic of sacrificial life given to cover sin)
3. Gen. 3:15—Redeemer to come from the human race (offspring of the woman) and will "crush" Satan's head.
C. Adam's children
1. Cain and Abel
2. Seth is father of the godly line
3. The pattern in Genesis is to follow the main line of the family, break away for peripheral lineage, then return to the main line.
4. Seth's line
• Longevity (Methuselah—969 years)
• Enoch—Transported to heaven without dying.

II. Noah

Point to location of Mt. Ararat on the map.

A. Righteous— "...found favor in the eyes of the LORD" (Gen. 6:8)
B. Major climatic and human longevity changes associated with the Flood.
C. Location of Mt. Ararat

D. "Second father of human race"

E. Migration of Noah's children and their families:

    1. Shem: Arabian Peninsula, Syria, Assyria, Persia, and the Orient

    2. Ham: Mesopotamia, Egypt, Africa

    3. Japheth: North and West

F. Tower of Babel

Show migrations of Noah's descendants on map.

III. Abram/Abraham

A. Father of the nation through which the Messiah would come. Previously (Gen. 3:15), God said the Savior would come from the human race. Now the prophecy is narrowed to the nation descending from Abraham through Isaac (Gen. 12:1-3; 17:15-21; 21:12).Through this nation God will bring blessing to "all peoples on earth" (Gen. 12:3).

B. Ur—Abraham's hometown

    1. Began approx. 5,000 to 6,000 B.C.

    2. At its height about 3,100 B.C.

    3. Sumerians: Highly intelligent. Libraries, cultural centers, schools, irrigation, flood control systems, canals

    4. City water and sewer systems (canals that carried fresh water into the city and other canals carried sewage out.)

    5. A wealth of information about Ur is available on the Internet. Do a search of "Ur of the Chaldees."

Point to the location of Ur on the map.

Refer to the Bible Lands map, page 30, and Family Tree chart, page 29 in the Student section.

C. Went with father to Haran

    1. Same name as brother. Coincidental?

    2. "Haran" means "road."

    3. Father, Terah, died at Haran.

D. Received call

    1. Read Genesis 12:1-5

    2. Note promises

E. Trace route

    1. About 600 miles around "Fertile Crescent"

    2. Jerusalem already there (Salem). Note visit by Melchizedek.

F. Relationship to Lot

G. Sodom and Gomorrah

H. Chapter 15—Promise reconfirmed

    1. Still childless

    2. Promise: His descendants would be numberless, like the stars. (Today we know the stars can't be counted. At that time the Babylonians thought there were about 3,000 stars).

    3. Fire and smoke between animals. This was an ancient rite to confirm a promise.

    4. Fulfillment delayed (15:13-16) — 400 yrs. Note God's mercy and patience.

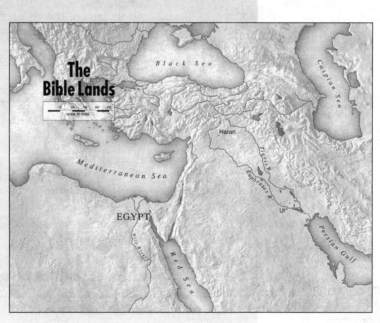

I. Significance of Abraham in the Bible story:

    1. The geography of the Bible story moves to Canaan.

    2. Abraham's descendants are identified as the nation through whom the Messiah will come.

    3. Abraham is the father of both Israel and Arab nations.

J. Abraham lived about 2,000 B.C. Ask students to memorize that date.

Refer to Family Tree chart, Page 29 in the Student section.

Abraham—2,000 B.C.

Point to Haran on map.

Refer to the Family Tree chart, page 29 in the Student section, as you tell the story of Jacob, Laban, Rachel, and Leah.

IV. Isaac

A. Note how the sacrifice of Isaac is a picture (type) of Christ's sacrifice—(God sacrificing His only son). Some scholars think even the place of sacrifice may be the same or nearby.

B. Search for wife
   1. Back to Haran
   2. Rebekah, cousin Bethuel's daughter
   3. Note one generation behind Nahor's family because of Abraham's age when Isaac was born. (Refer to Family Tree chart, page 29 in the Student section.)

V. Jacob

A. Name means "heal catcher" or "supplanter"
B. Deceived his father and brother
C. Mother, Rebekah, feared Esau would kill him, so told Jacob to return to Haran to marry.
D. Story of Laban, Rachel, and Leah
E. Return—Esau meets with 400 men.
F. Night of prayer—wrestled with angel—renamed "Israel" — "Wrestler with God."
G. Significance of Jacob—every descendant of Jacob is now part of the chosen nation.

VI. Joseph

A. Favorite of his father
B. Story of sale into slavery
C. His life divides into three major periods: "The pit, the prison, and the palace."
D. New Pharaoh
E. Type of Christ. Despised by his brothers, sold to the Gentiles, went ahead to prepare salvation for those who caused his suffering.

FAMILY TREE CHART

Genesis Chapter

2 — Adam — Cain / Abal
Seth
Enoch
Methuselah
6 — Noah
Shem — Ham / Japheth
Cush / Canaan
Nimrod
Terah
Haran / Nahor
Lot / Bethuel
12 — Abraham — Rebekah / Laban
Ishmael
21 — Isaac — Leah / Rachel
25 — Esau — Jacob
37 — Reuben, Levi, Dan, Gad, Issachar, Joseph, Benjamin
Simeon, Judah, Naphtali, Asher, Zebulon
Lineage of Christ — Ephraim / Manasseh

Demonstrate tracing the patriarchs on an overhead or classroom map.

Summary

The book of Genesis takes the story from the grandeur of the Garden of Eden and sinless perfection to the misery of a "coffin in Egypt" (the concluding words of the book—50:26).

Practice

Make enough copies of the Bible Lands map on page 29 so you will have extra maps available for students to practice tracing the stories of Adam, Noah, Abraham, Isaac, Jacob, and Joseph on the map.

Review

If time permits, administer the quiz over Genesis. Explain that this is not a "test." It is just a fun way for each student to see how much he has learned in this lesson.

No one will see the papers. Students do not hand them in to be graded. When all students have completed the quiz, discuss each question and give the correct answer.

The correct answers are:

1)	a	5)	c	9)	c
2)	b	6)	a	10)	c
3)	b	7)	b	11)	a
4)	c	8)	a	12)	c

Assignment

Tell students to look over Lesson 2 materials in preparation for next week, but to spend most of their time reviewing what they learned about the patriarchs in Lesson 1 and memorizing the names of the six patriarchs in order.

Genesis Quiz

1. The patriarch who lived about 2,000 B.C. was

   a. Abraham
   b. Noah
   c. Joseph

2. The patriarch who was renamed "Israel" was

   a. Joseph
   b. Jacob
   c. Abraham

3. A good place to start looking for the story of Abraham would be

   a. Genesis chapter 6
   b. Genesis chapter 12
   c. Genesis chapter 21

4. According to the Bible, the date of creation is

   a. 10,000 B.C.
   b. 4,004 B.C.
   c. unknown

5. The events of the first eleven chapters of Genesis took place in the region of the modern country of

   a. Israel
   b. Iran
   c. Iraq

6. Europeans are probably descendants of Noah's son

   a. Japheth
   b. Ham
   c. Shem

7. Abraham's hometown was

   a. Jerusalem
   b. Ur
   c. Babylon

8. The name, "Mesopotamia," means

   a. between the rivers.
   b. beyond the mountains.
   c. in the garden.

9. The "miracle child" born in his parent's old age was

   a. Jacob
   b. Joseph
   c. Isaac

10. In Old Testament chronology,

    a. Joseph lived before Ishmael
    b. Jacob lived before Isaac
    c. Noah lived before Abraham

11. Try some more Old Testament chronology:

    a. Sarah lived before Rachel
    b. Japheth lived before Methuselah
    c. Rebekah lived before Shem

12. The patriarch most closely related to Egyptian government was

    a. Abraham
    b. Jacob
    c. Joseph

LESSON

Genesis

The word, "Genesis," means "beginning." This first book of the Bible tells about the beginning of the universe, the beginning of life on earth, the human race, sin, God's plan of redemption, and the beginning of the nation of Israel. It is foundational to the entire Bible. You might say the "plot" for the entire Bible story is described here, and the rest of the Bible is much more understandable to someone who has a knowledge of Genesis.

The Place

The Bible story begins in Mesopotamia. "Mesopotamia" means "between the rivers," and refers to the region betweens the Tigris and Euphrates Rivers (modern Iraq). Refer to the Bible Lands map on page 30 to identify these locations. The Garden of Eden was located somewhere in this region and the families of Adam and Noah lived here.

Also on this map identify the location of modern Israel, sometimes referred to as Canaan or Palestine. During Abraham's lifetime, Bible geography moves from Mesopotamia to Canaan.

A third region of importance in the Bible story is Egypt. Egypt has much literal and symbolic significance in Scripture.

The People

We ask you to memorize only a few things in this course. Please memorize the following names in order. When you have done so, you will have not only an outline of the book of Genesis, but you will also be able to comprehend a huge section of Bible history in chronological order. The names are:

Adam	Isaac
Noah	Jacob
Abraham	Joseph

You may want to write these names on a 3 x 5 card and carry it with you for a few days. Keep saying these names as you go about your activities. Remembering them in order will help you in all your subsequent Bible study.

If you have the six names memorized and want an additional challenge, we suggest you go one step further and memorize a number after each name. The numbers are the chapters in the book of Genesis that record the story about each of these personalities. When you study your Bible or participate in a group discussion and want to refer to something in the life of one of these men or their families, you can turn directly to the appropriate passage. You will know, for example, that Noah and his family are described in Genesis 6 to 11. The names and beginning chapters are:

Adam: 2	Isaac: 21
Noah: 6	Jacob: 25
Abraham: 12	Joseph: 37

These six men are called "Patriarchs," meaning "fathers, rulers, or founders of families or tribes." By tracing the lives of these six patriarchs we will observe the beginning of the nation of Israel and God's plan of redemption that continues through the rest of the Bible. The book of Genesis describes the human problem (sin), and the rest of the Bible tells how God is solving the problem. The story ends in Revelation, where the work of Christ completely resolves the problem.

The Story

Genesis begins with the creation event. Critics of the creation record in chapters 1 and 2 claim the accounts are "unscientific." However, this description of the beginning of the universe has repeatedly been shown to be incredibly accurate. After studying the Genesis account of creation for eighteen months, Dr. Hugh Ross, a renowned astrophysicist, concluded he was "unsuccessful in finding a single provable error or contradiction. . . . All of the scientific and historical evidences I had collected deeply rooted my confidence in the veracity of the Bible and convinced me that the Creator had indeed communicated through this holy book."[1]

We will study these issues of the truth of the biblical account in Session 21. Today's lesson focuses on tracing the origin of human history through the families of the six patriarchs: Adam, Noah, Abraham, Isaac, Jacob, and Joseph.

Adam

The Bible story begins in the land of Mesopotamia, the area between the Tigris and Euphrates Rivers, roughly the location of modern Iraq. Somewhere in this region God planted the Garden of Eden and placed the first human family there.

The sin of Adam and Eve marked the beginning of what is sometimes called "the human problem." As a result of that original sin, the entire human race is adversely affected. Both human nature and the environment suffer because man is in rebellion against God and separated from Him. God exiled Adam and Eve from the Garden of Eden and did not permit them to partake of the Tree of Life. The results of sin soon became apparent in Adam's family. Adam's son, Cain, killed his brother, Abel, out of jealousy. The rest of the Bible relates how God made it possible for sinful man to be brought back to a holy God. The book of Revelation is the story of God restoring to the faithful all that was lost in Genesis.

Genesis traces the "family tree" of each patriarch, following the "main line" of each and gives us a brief account of the most prominent people in it. From Adam to Noah, people apparently had a very long life span, the longest of whom (Methuselah) lived 969 years! Several theories try to explain the sudden change in life span after the flood. Some suggest that drastic changes in climate and other earth conditions shortened human longevity.

Noah

The events in Noah's family also take place in Mesopotamia. Whether the Flood was universal or covered only the area of human habitation is hotly debated among Bible scholars and will probably not be resolved in our lifetime. The point at issue, however, is that all human life perished except Noah and his family, so Noah literally became "the second father of the human race."

The families of Noah's sons spread out from Mesopotamia in three different directions. Japheth's family went west and north to become the ancestors of European people. Shem's family went east and south into the Arabian Peninsula and what became known as Syria, Assyria, and Persia. Ham went into Mesopotamia, Egypt, and Africa.

The human family attempted to stay together with a common language and unified human religion with a grand tower "to reach to the heavens," but God dispersed the human family from the Tower of Babel. He confused the people's speech so they would spread out over the earth and not develop a unified false religion.

Abraham

The story of Abraham is critical to understanding the flow of Bible history and the development of the nation of Israel. Abraham is the first patriarch we can date with any degree of certainty. We ask you to remember only two dates in this entire course. This is the first. Abraham lived about 2,000 B.C.

Abraham's story begins in the splendid ancient city of Ur. From here God called him to "go to the land I will show you" (Gen. 12:1). Trace on the Bible Lands map (page 30), Abraham's journey from Ur, north along the Euphrates Valley to Haran, around the loop of the "Fertile Crescent," and down the Mediterranean shore to Canaan. In Abraham's lifetime the focus of Bible geography shifted from Mesopotamia to Canaan, with occasional excursions into Egypt.

Names of people in Genesis begin to compound at this point, and to "keep it all straight," you may want to refer frequently to the Family Tree chart on page 29.

The significance of Abraham in the Bible story cannot be overemphasized. Some of the important things about Abraham include:

• The shift in geography mentioned above.

• Abraham is the first individual God picked out of the stream of humanity and announced He would do something special with his descendants.

• Abraham is highly regarded by each nation descended from him, both Israeli and Arab.

Isaac

Isaac was Abraham and Sarah's "miracle child." He was born when they were very old. The touching story of Abraham's willingness to offer Isaac as a sacrifice is not only significant in showing Abraham's faith, but also a beautiful "type" (a person, thing or event that represents or symbolizes some other person, thing, or event) of the crucifixion of Christ, God's only Son given to us. Many Bible scholars think Abraham offered Isaac on or near the mountain where Jesus died.

Isaac returned to Haran to find a wife, in obedience to his father's instructions, and married Rebekah, the granddaughter of his uncle Nahor (see Family Tree chart, page 29).

Jacob

"Jacob" means "heel catcher," or "supplanter," a name Jacob aptly deserved. Born clutching the heel of his older twin brother Esau, Jacob persisted by intrigue and deceit until he finally supplanted his brother and inherited the birthright. He learned some difficult lessons, however, and later in life God changed his name to "Israel," meaning "wrestler with God." Other Hebrew scholars translate "Israel" variously as "having power with God," "God's wrestler," or even "ruling with God."

Jacob is the only descendant of Abraham whom God specifically chose to be the father of a special nation, Israel. In Scripture, the nation of Israel is most often called "the children of Israel," and occasionally "the children of Jacob." Frequently the simple terms "Israel" or "Jacob" are used to refer to the nation.

Jacob married Leah and Rachel, daughters of Laban (see Famly Tree chart, page 29). The twelve sons of these marriages became the heads of the tribes of Israel.

Joseph

In contrast to his father, Joseph exhibited incredibly noble character. His high moral standards, gentleness, patience, faithfulness, and perseverance have been recognized as exemplary and unsurpassed in human conduct.

Joseph is truly a "type" of Christ. He was his father's favorite son, was rejected by his brothers, sold for twenty shekels of silver, and unjustly accused and persecuted. Nevertheless, he became the savior of his family and ultimately of his nation.

When his brothers sold him into slavery, Joseph was taken to Egypt. Consequently, the geography of the Bible story moved to Egypt. When, finally, Joseph revealed his identity to his brothers, he invited them and his father to come to Egypt and take up residence in Goshen, the choice pastureland of Egypt. All was well until after Joseph's death, when a new ruler ascended the throne of Egypt and forced the sons of Israel into slavery.

When Joseph's father, Jacob, finally learned that Joseph was alive, he must have still considered him dead in regard to the family inheritance. Bypassing Joseph, he placed his blessing on Joseph's sons, Ephraim and Manasseh. Consequently, there is no tribe of Joseph, but there are tribes of Ephraim and Manasseh. You would think, then, that there should be thirteen tribes. However, the tribe of Levi did not receive a land inheritance because its sons were to serve as priests throughout all twelve tribes. Therefore, the land was divided among twelve tribes.

In reviewing this lesson, we suggest you repeat the names of the six patriarchs and trace their adventures on the map: Adam and Noah in Mesopotamia, Abraham traveling from Ur around the "Fertile Crescent" to Haran and Canaan, Isaac and Jacob in Canaan, and finally Joseph in Egypt.

Along with the beautiful story of man's creation in the image of God, Genesis tells the sad story of man's fall into sin and the consequences. Note that the story starts with the blessing and joy of the Garden of Eden, and ends "in a coffin in Egypt" (Gen. 50:26).

FAMILY TREE CHART

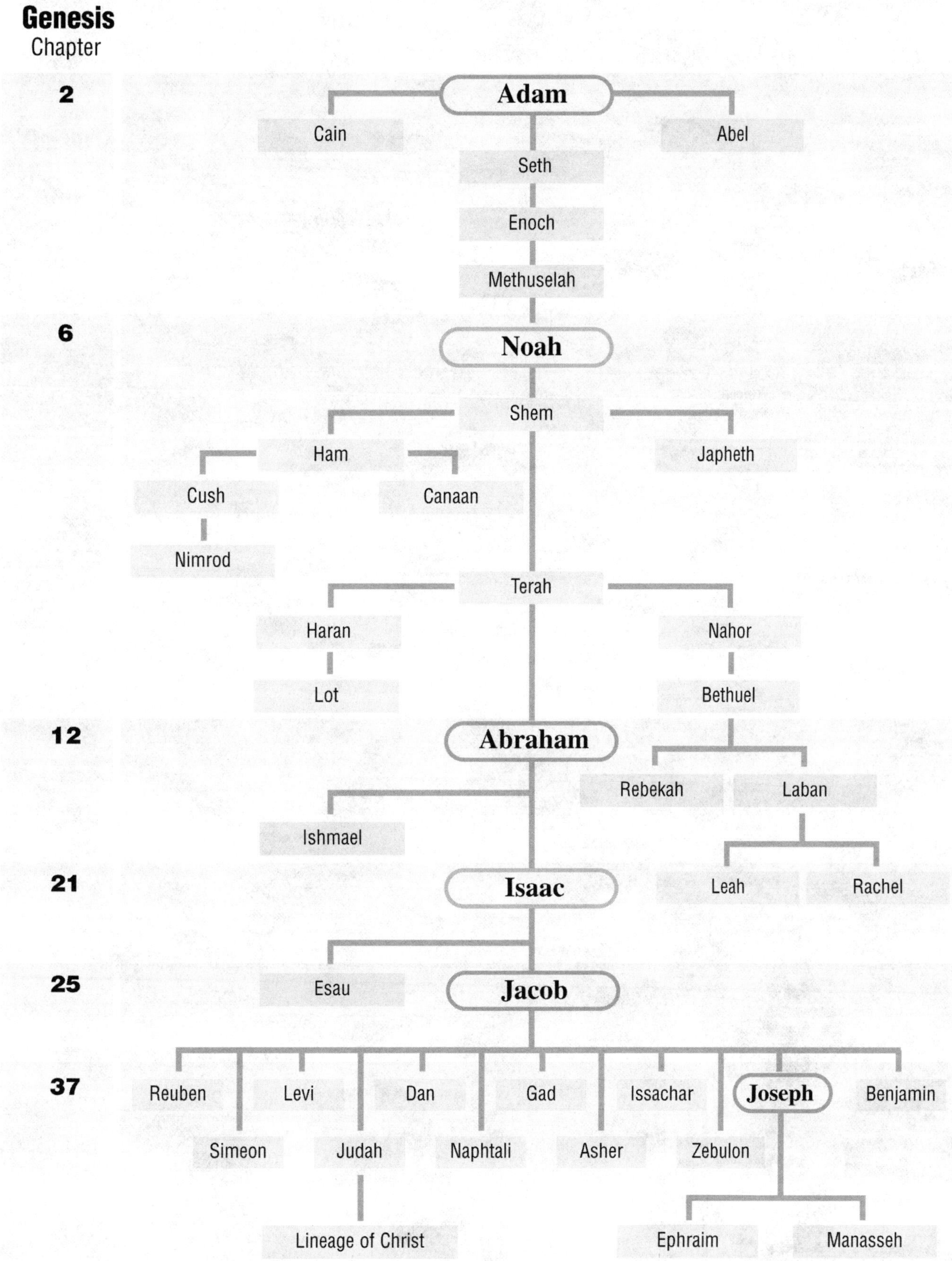

Genesis
Chapter

2

Adam

Cain — Abel

Seth

Enoch

Methuselah

6

Noah

Shem — Japheth

Ham

Cush — Canaan

Nimrod

Terah

Haran — Nahor

Lot — Bethuel

12

Abraham

Rebekah — Laban

Ishmael

21

Isaac

Leah — Rachel

25

Esau — **Jacob**

37

Reuben — Levi — Dan — Gad — Issachar — **Joseph** — Benjamin

Simeon — Judah — Naphtali — Asher — Zebulon

Lineage of Christ

Ephraim — Manasseh

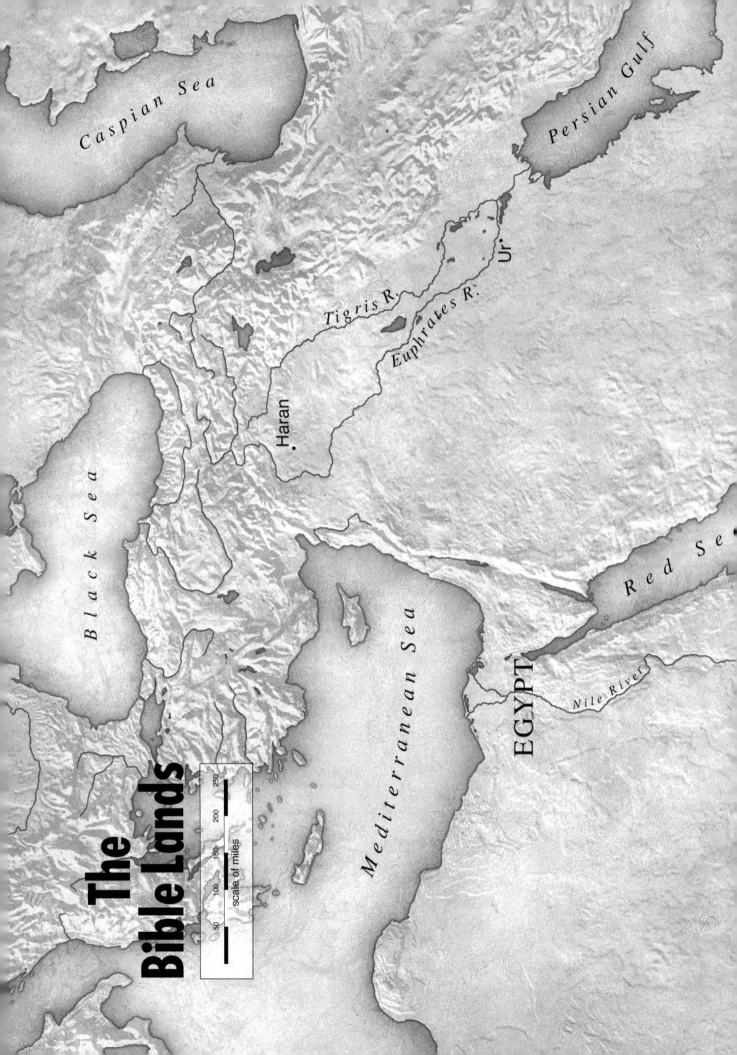

Caspian Sea

Persian Gulf

Tigris R.

Euphrates R.

Ur

Haran

Black Sea

Red Sea

Mediterranean Sea

EGYPT

Nile River

The Bible Lands

250

200

150

100

50

scale of miles

LESSON 2
The Exodus

Equipment Needed

1) Overhead projector and screen maps or classroom maps of Old Testament world showing Abraham's journey and the Exodus route to Sinai.

Teaching Supplies Needed

1) Maps, as indicated.
2) Copies of student lesson 3 to distribute to the class.

Review

Use the Genesis Quiz if you didn't use it in Lesson 1.

Lecture

Introduction

1. The story of Genesis is a downward spiral from the perfection of the Garden of Eden to a "coffin in Egypt" (Gen. 50:26).

2. From this low point, God began to lead His people upward. The first step in this upward journey was toward an earthly kingdom. The books of Exodus, Leviticus, Numbers, and Deuteronomy are the beginning of this part of the story, as God molds and fashions this new nation—the nation through which all the earth would be blessed.

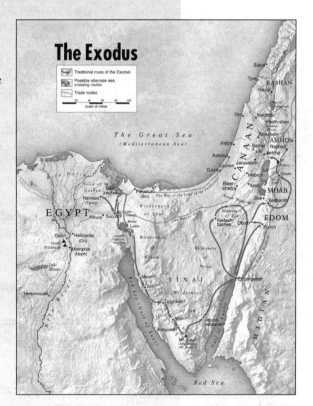

Locate Midian on map.

I. The Call of Moses

A. His early life in Egypt—Learning about Egyptian government and practice from "the inside."
B. Escape after murder of Egyptian. Trace his route to Midian.
C. Residence in Midian with Jethro
D. Burning bush incident
E. Moses' reluctance and role of Aaron

II. The Plagues and the Passover

A. Misery of the people—slavery

B. Review ten plagues.

C. The Passover—Discuss symbolism. Ask for student response to "A Point to Ponder" about the Passover in the Student section, page 36.

D. Consecration of the firstborn

III. The Exodus

Refer to map in Student section.

A. Trace the traditional route.

B. Explain: Actual route uncertain. Several alternate routes have been suggested. Some recent discoveries suggest the crossing may have been at the Gulf of Aqabah and that Mt. Sinai was in northwest Midian (modern Saudi Arabia).

C. Significance of separation from Egypt and finality of Red Sea crossing. "Baptized into Moses" (See 1 Cor. 10:1-2. Their "baptism" in the Red Sea sealed their decision. There was no turning back).

IV. The Wilderness

A. Other events en route to Sinai
   1. People complaining
   2. Manna (the word means: "what is it?")
   3. Quail
   4. Jethro's visit and helpful advice
B. The events at Mt. Sinai (Exod. 19–Num. 10:10)
   1. The call of God (Exod. 19:3-6) —a holy nation
   2. The Ten Commandments
   3. Laws of health and sanitation
   4. Highly organized (Num. 2)
   5. The appointment of the Levites to take the place of the firstborn, as dedicated to the Lord (Num. 3:5-13)
   6. Many instructions about sacrifices, festivals, and general laws governing the nation.
   7. Details of the tabernacle arrangement and construction. This is rich with symbolism. Have students turn to the diagram of the tabernacle (page 38) and ask for suggestions of the symbolic meaning of the tabernacle arrangement. Some possible symbols might include:
      a) One door—Christ is the only way.
      b) The first item of furniture is the altar. The beginning of anyone's journey into the presence of God is to accept the sacrifice of Christ.
      c) The laver indicates cleansing. The one who gives his/her life to Christ is cleansed by the Holy Spirit.
      d) The menorah and the table of shewbread represents Jesus, the "Light of the World" and the "Bread of Life."
      e) The altar of incense was nearest the veil, behind which was the ark of the covenant, representing the presence of God. The pleasing aroma of the incense filtered into the Holy of Holies, just as the prayers of the saints ascend into the very presence of God. (See Ps. 141:2.)
      f) And perhaps many other symbols your students will suggest.

Locate Kadesh-barnea on map.

C. Resume journey
   1. Kadesh-barnea—The spies and the sin of unbelief
   2. Forty years wandering in wilderness
   3. Water from rock—Moses' sin & punishment
   4. Edom refused passage Numbers 20:14-21 (Edomites are relatives—descendants of Esau.)

5. Story of Balaam and Balak in Moab—Numbers 22—24 (The Moabites were descendants of Lot's oldest daughter.)

D. Arrival at Mt. Nebo
   1. View of land of promise
   2. Death of Moses
      a) End of an era: "The age of Moses"
      b) Moses is known as "the lawgiver of Israel"
   3. Joshua appointed as Moses' successor.

Ask for student response to "A Point to Ponder," page 37 of the Student section.

Locate Mt. Nebo on map.

Review

Ask students to trace the Bible story from Genesis (Adam) to Mt. Nebo on their maps, noting the spiritual significance of the effects of sin and the beginning of God's plan of redemption. Be sure they name each of the primary individuals as they trace the story: Adam, Noah, Abraham, Isaac, Jacob, Joseph, and Moses.

LESSON 2
The Exodus

The Bible books relating to this session are Exodus, Leviticus, Numbers, and Deuteronomy. These four books, together with Genesis, are sometimes called "The Five Books of Moses," referring to the Mosaic authorship. You will also find them called the "Pentateuch," which simply means "five books."

Exodus means "going out." This book describes the departure of the Israelites from Egypt.

Leviticus is about the laws of the Levites, the spiritual leaders of Israel.

The book of **Numbers** is so named because it begins with God's telling Moses to "number" the people. It means to take a census. The book is rich with details about Israel's 40-year journey through the wilderness.

> **Hint:** If you haven't already done so, this is a great time to memorize the books of the Bible in order. Knowing the Bible books in order will help immensely when you look up a reference in the Bible.

Deuteronomy means "the second law," so called because it is the record of Moses repeating all the law to his people before he died and just before the people entered the Promised Land.

Moses was the significant personality of this period. He lived 120 years, and his life divides evenly into three sections. The first forty years he lived in Egypt as part of the royal family. The middle forty years he was an exile shepherding sheep in the deserts of Midian. He didn't know it, but God was equipping him, first with knowledge of the courts of Egypt, then with familiarity with the desert, so he could effectively lead the Israelites out of Egypt and beyond during his final forty years.

This lesson divides into four topics:

1) The call of Moses
2) The Plagues and the Passover
3) The Exodus
4) The Wilderness

The Call of Moses

As a result of being rescued from the river by Pharaoh's daughter while he was still an infant, Moses grew up in the royal family of Egypt. Witnessing an Egyptian beating one of the Hebrew slaves, he killed the Egyptian and fled to Midian, where he worked as a shepherd for forty years at a ranch owned by Jethro, a priest and prince of Midian. Moses eventually married Jethro's daughter Zipporah.

While in Midian, Moses came face to face with God at the burning bush, recorded in Exodus chapter 3. God called him to go back to Egypt to free His people. Read Exodus 3 and 4 for the exciting details.

The Plagues and the Passover

Moses and his brother Aaron confronted Pharaoh. God gave Moses several miraculous signs to convince Pharaoh that the true God sent him, but the signs failed to persuade the hard-hearted Pharaoh. Consequently, God sent ten horrible plagues on the nation of Egypt.
The ten plagues were:

1) Water turning to blood.

2) The Nile River teeming with frogs that crawled into homes and even into the royal palace.

3) Dust turning into gnats that covered people and animals.

4) Swarms of flies filling the air and invading homes.

5) Disease killing the domestic animals of Egypt. (However, no animals owned by Hebrews died.)

6) A fine dust over the whole land. When it landed on people or animals, it caused painful boils.

7) The worst hailstorm in Egyptian history (but there was no hail in Goshen where the Hebrews lived).

8) The worst invasion of locusts in Egyptian history, so thick that the ground was black with them. They ate everything left from the hailstorm and filled the houses of the Egyptians.

9) Darkness so thick it could be felt. No one was able to leave home for three days (but there was light in the Hebrews' homes).

10) The Angel of Death came to every home not protected by blood over the doorposts. The firstborn of every family in Egypt died.

Following the tenth plague, Pharaoh gave permission for the Hebrew slaves to leave Egypt. Read Exodus 12 for the thrilling story of Passover night. The Angel of Death saw the blood on the doorposts of the homes of the Hebrews, so he "passed over" those homes and did not take the life of the firstborn. God commanded His people to observe the Passover perpetually. When Jesus instituted the Lord's Supper the night before His crucifixion, He was observing Passover with His disciples.

"A Point to Ponder"

What "connection" do you see between the Passover in Egypt, the Lord's Supper observed by Christians, our salvation, and the work of Christ on the cross? Write a one- or two-sentence response. Be prepared to share your thoughts with the class.

The Exodus

The Exodus from Egypt is among the most awesome events in all of Israel's history. Exodus 12—14 tells the story, a story so exciting it has been repeated in drama, monologue, and sermons for thirty-four centuries! Read these passages and imagine yourself part of that throng of possibly two million slaves marching out of Egypt. Then read the worshipful song of Moses and his sister, Miriam (Exod. 15:1-21), celebrating the event.

The Wilderness

God led the people of Israel through the wilderness to Mt. Sinai, where He gave them the law, which included the miraculous writing of the Ten Commandments. At Mt. Sinai, Israel's "government" was established with God as king. The remainder of Exodus and most of Leviticus and Deuteronomy detail the laws by which the people were to be governed and justice determined. The book of Numbers provides interesting details about experiences in the wilderness travel and the incredible organization involved in the logistics of moving so many people.

Become familiar with the map of the Exodus on page 39. Note the route of the Exodus, and the locations of Mt. Sinai, Kadesh-barnea, Edom, and Moab. The exact route of the Exodus is uncertain. Recent research suggests the route and the location of Mt. Sinai may be different from what has traditionally been accepted.

The time spent at Mt. Sinai was crucially important for the people because it was here that God fashioned a disorganized crowd of slaves into a nation governed by laws and characterized by freedom. Also at Mt. Sinai God gave Moses the design of the tabernacle, the place God would meet with the representative of His people and where the people would assemble to offer sacrifice and worship. The tabernacle design carried through into the temple that was built much later. See page 38 for a diagram of the tabernacle design. The arrangement of the tabernacle and its furniture has much symbolic significance.

Arriving at the southern tip of Canaan, the people lost faith in God's ability to lead them in victory over the inhabitants of the land. They sent spies into the country, probably to build some assurance. But when the spies returned after 40 days, all but Caleb and Joshua were convinced they couldn't stand against such formidable enemies. So the people refused to invade the land. As a result of their lack of faith (actually rebellion), God sentenced them to 40 years wandering in the wilderness—a year for every day the spies were in Canaan. The story unfolds in Numbers 13 and 14.

Enemies and hardships confronted Israel throughout their forty-year journey, but God came to their rescue each time. Sometimes, He brought judgment in response to their rebellion and unbelief. Eventually, however, the Israelites arrived at Mt. Nebo, the staging area for their conquest of the Promised Land. Here, just before his death on Mt. Nebo, Moses repeated the law for the people with specific instructions to follow it when they enter the land.

Review

Now go back to the Bible Lands map on page 30 (or a copy of it). On the map, trace the story of Adam, Noah, Abraham, Isaac, Jacob, Joseph, and Moses. Keep reviewing this over and over. Doing so will help you to "put it all together."

A Point to Ponder

Some Bible students consider the slavery and eventual escape from Egypt, the wilderness experience, and the arrival at the Promised Land to be a "type," or picture of a Christian's spiritual experience. Do you agree? If so, what symbols or parallel experiences do you recognize? What would Egypt symbolize? Mt. Nebo? The warfare along the route? The Promised Land?

Think about it and write a paragraph-long response. Be prepared to share your thoughts with the class.

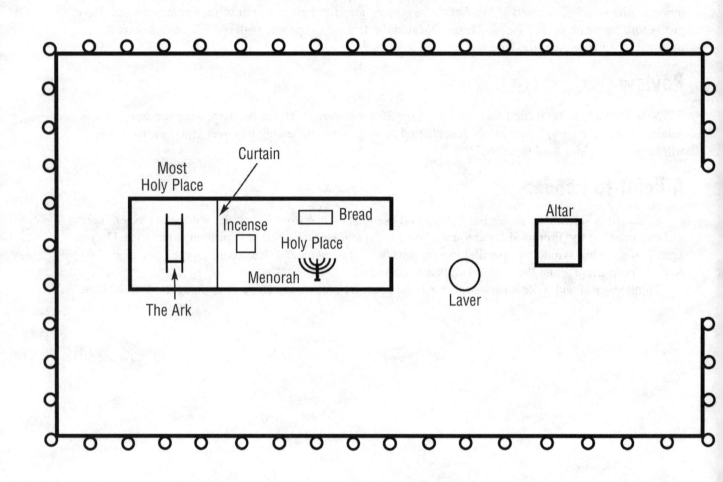

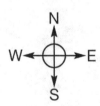

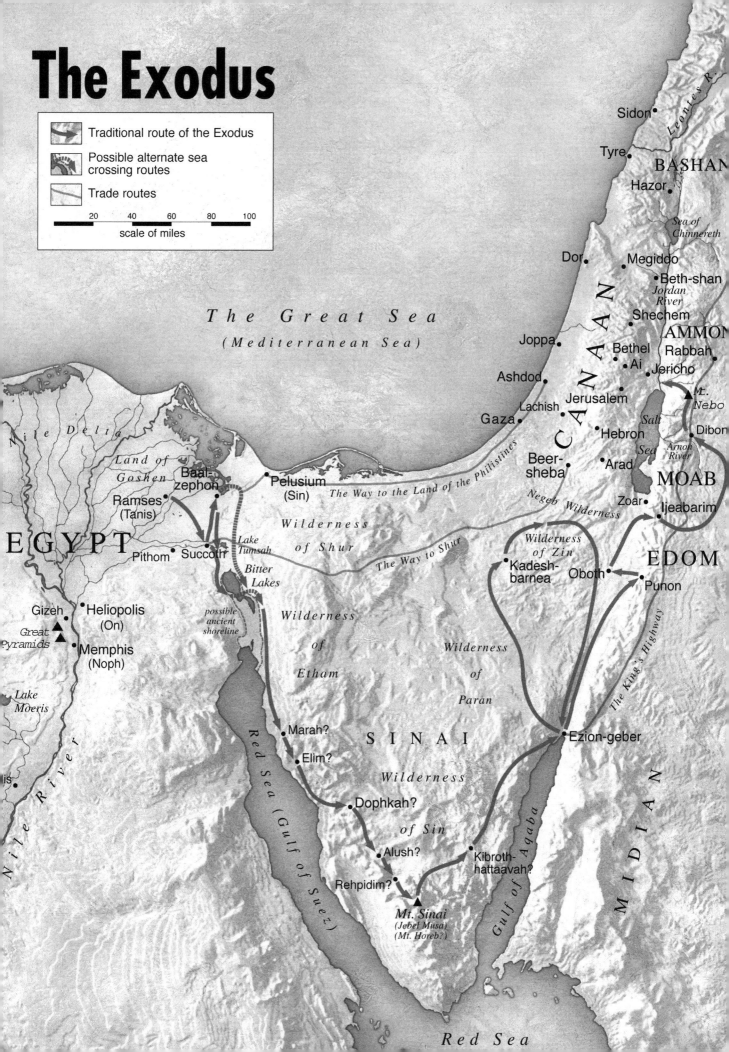

The Exodus

Traditional route of the Exodus

Possible alternate sea crossing routes

Trade routes

20   40   60   80   100
scale of miles

The Great Sea
(Mediterranean Sea)

Leontes R.

Sidon

Tyre

BASHAN

Hazor

Sea of Chinnereth

Dor

Megiddo

Beth-shan

Jordan River

Shechem

AMMON

Joppa

Bethel   Rabbah

Ashdod   Ai   Jericho

Jerusalem   *Mt. Nebo*

Lachish

Gaza

Salt Sea

Hebron   Dibon

Beer-sheba   *Arnon River*

Arad

Negeb Wilderness   Zoar   MOAB

Ijeabarim

Nile Delta

Land of Goshen

Baal-zephon

Pelusium (Sin)

The Way to the Land of the Philistines

Wilderness of Shur

Wilderness of Zin

EDOM

Ramses (Tanis)

Pithom   Succoth

Lake Timsah

The Way to Shur

Kadesh-barnea   Oboth

Punon

EGYPT

Bitter Lakes

possible ancient shoreline

Wilderness of Etham

Wilderness of Paran

The King's Highway

Gizeh   Heliopolis (On)

Great Pyramids

Memphis (Noph)

Lake Moeris

Nile River

Red Sea (Gulf of Suez)

Marah?

Elim?

SINAI

Wilderness of Sin

Dophkah?

Alush?

Rehpidim?

Mt. Sinai (Jebel Musa) (Mt. Horeb?)

Kibroth-hattaavah?

Ezion-geber

Gulf of Aqaba

MIDIAN

Red Sea

LESSON 3

The Conquest, Judges, and United Kingdom

Equipment Needed

1) Overhead Projector or classroom maps.

Teaching Supplies Needed

1) Transparency or classroom maps of Palestine, preferably showing the division of land by tribes and the topography of Palestine.
2) Copies of student lesson4 to distribute to the class.

Review

1. Adam through Moses

Trace Adam through Moses on map.

Inform the class of the goal at the conclusion of this unit, which is that each student will be able to tell the entire Bible story in three minutes or less, tracing it on a map. At that time (Lesson 7) the class will divide into pairs and tell the story to each other. Demonstrate this two or more times in this lesson (From Adam through Moses at the beginning of the class, and through Solomon at the end of the class) and during each lesson remaining in this unit.

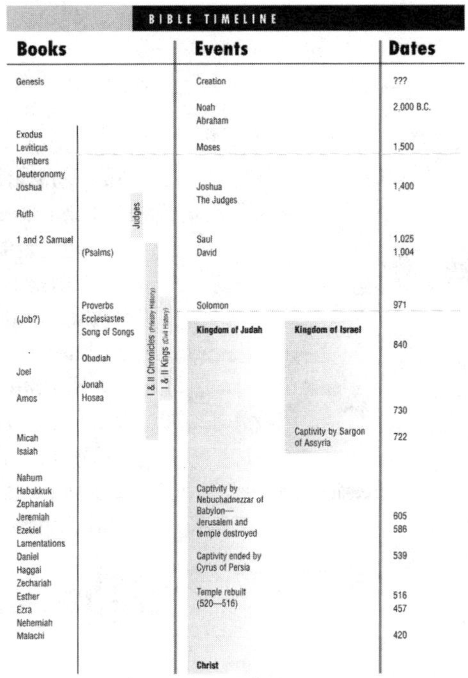

BIBLE TIMELINE		
Books	**Events**	**Dates**
Genesis	Creation	???
	Noah	2,000 B.C.
	Abraham	
Exodus	Moses	1,500
Leviticus		
Numbers		
Deuteronomy		
Joshua	Joshua	1,400
	The Judges	
Ruth		
1 and 2 Samuel	Saul	1,025
(Psalms)	David	1,004
	Proverbs	Solomon	971
	Ecclesiastes	
(Job?)	Song of Songs	Kingdom of Judah Kingdom of Israel	
			840
	Obadiah		
Joel			
	Jonah		730
Amos	Hosea		
		Captivity by Sargon of Assyria	722
Micah			
Isaiah			
Nahum		Captivity by Nebuchadnezzar of Babylon—	
Habakkuk			
Zephaniah			605
Jeremiah		Jerusalem and temple destroyed	586
Ezekiel			
Lamentations			
Daniel		Captivity ended by Cyrus of Persia	539
Haggai			
Zechariah			
Esther		Temple rebuilt (520—516)	516
Ezra			457
Nehemiah			
Malachi			420
	Christ		

(Judges — vertical label)
(1 & II Chronicles (Priestly History) — vertical label)
(1 & II Kings (Civil History) — vertical label)

Lecture

Introduction
1. Call attention to the Events chart on page 48 of the Student section. Suggest that students refer to this chart frequently to keep events in chronological order.

2. Locate Mt. Nebo.

3. Describe the topography of Palestine, pointing out the four major regions:

4. The "Maritime Plain" along the western coast is a rich agricultural region with a gentle upward slope from the Mediterranean coast to the central mountains.

5. The Central Highlands is a ridge of hills usually 2,000 to 3,000 ft. in elevation, some reaching nearly 4,000 ft. An international trade route followed the top of this ridge connecting the various cities in central Canaan. Jerusalem is on this ridge at an elevation of about 2,600 ft.

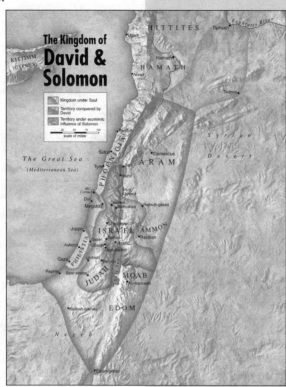

Point to Mt. Nebo on the map.

6. The Jordan Valley is a deep rift along a major fault line. The Jordan River follows this fault and empties into the Dead Sea, the lowest body of water on earth. The surface of the Dead Sea is 1296 ft. below sea level, and the sea is about 1,300 ft. deep. Note the sharp difference in elevation from Jerusalem to the Dead Sea, a distance of less than fifteen miles.

7. The Eastern Plateau is sometimes called "The Bread Basket of Palestine." This is a large, fertile plateau around 3,000 ft. in elevation.

8. Because of this stark variety of elevation, topography, and rainfall, Palestine has an extremely varied climate for its size. It includes snow-capped peaks, fertile valleys, deserts, forests, rocky dry hills, and plains.

I. The Conquest

A. Joshua takes command
B. Crossing the Jordan and the capture of Jericho
1. The manna stopped when the people crossed the Jordan.
2. Rahab received the spies, hid them, and helped them escape. The "scarlet cord" was her sign of faith in the God of Israel, and her faith saved her life. It is symbolic of faith in Christ as the means of salvation. (Ask for student response to the question about the "scarlet cord" on page 45 of the Student section.)
C. The Central Campaign—Capture of Ai
1. First attempt unsuccessful because of "sin in the camp" (Josh. 7)
2. The capture of Ai intercepted the international trade route and effectively cut the territory in half, separating enemy tribes in the north from those in the south. A strategy of "divide and conquer."
3. The Gibeonite deception (Josh. 9)
D. The Southern Campaign (Josh. 10)
E. The Northern Campaign (Josh. 11)
1. Israel's first war against horses and chariots
2. Joshua's genius in surprise attacks and swift movements
F. Land divided among the tribes.

Map showing division of tribal lands

II. The Period of the Judges (Book of Judges)

A. There was no king or central government. "Everyone did as he saw fit" (Judges 17:6)
B. Kept slipping spiritually—Key phrase in book: "The Israelites did evil in the eyes of the LORD" (2:11; 3:7, 12; 4:1; 6:1; 10:6; 13:1).

C. Whenever the nation fell into sin, a foreign power conquered it, and it went through the "cycle" again.

D. There were extended periods of peace during this time. For example, the story of Ruth takes place during the period of the Judges, and it seems to be set in a time of peace. However, the purpose of the book of Judges is to emphasize the results of disobedience. Therefore, it is a "bloody book."

E. Samuel's ministry began during the latter part of the period of the Judges and extended into the United Kingdom period. Samuel was a bridge between the time of the judges and the time of the prophets. He was both judge and prophet in Israel.

Refer to chart, Cycle of Judges in the Student section, page 49

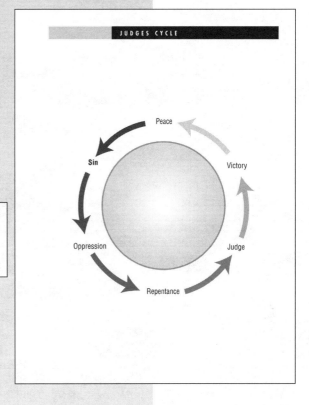

III. The United Kingdom (Monarchy)

A. Demand for a king—Samuel the pivotal figure.

B. Three kings during this period. Ask students to remember them in chronological order: Saul, David, and Solomon.

Tell students to memorize the date for David—1,000 B.C.

C. Saul united the tribes under one central government. Later in life he became melancholy and insanely jealous of David.

D. David—The most significant ruler in Israel, whose kingdom is to be forever (Check the references in the Student section.)

1. David brought the ark of the covenant to Jerusalem.
2. He intended to build the temple, but God did not allow him to do so because David was a man of war. So he stockpiled materials for his son, Solomon, to do the actual building.

E. Solomon
1. Magnificence, luxury (2 Chron. 9:13-28)
2. Built the temple
   a) Prayer of dedication—1 Kings 8
   b) Note reference to "when they sin…" and the results of that sin. (8:46-51). Prophetic?
3. Disobedient: Many wives, huge numbers of horses and chariots, great wealth, and dabbled in idolatry—all forbidden by God (Deut. 17:17; 1 Kings 11:1-13)

Review

Ask students to trace again the Bible story on a map, beginning with Adam, but now including the Conquest, period of Judges, and the United Kingdom with the kings, Saul, David, and Solomon.

LESSON 3

The Conquest, Judges, and United Kingdom

When Moses and the people of Israel arrived at the top of Mt. Nebo, they could enjoy a commanding view of the Land of Promise stretching out before them to the west. It must have been an impressive sight to the wilderness traveling, battle-weary refugees. Below them was the Jordan Valley and Dead Sea. Beyond this valley and river lay the Judean hills and mountain range, stretching to the hills of Galilee to the north with groves of olive trees and green valleys. The Hebrews probably couldn't see it from Mt. Nebo, but beyond the mountains was the fertile "Maritime Plain," gently sloping to the Mediterranean coast, rich with vineyards and fruit trees. Vast differences in climate and vegetation in different regions and altitudes of this small country make this a most unusual land.

The three periods of Bible history encompassed by this lesson extend from about 1400 B.C. to 922 B.C., and include the dramatic events of the Hebrew invasion of Canaan, the period of the Judges when there was no central government, and the establishment of the monarchy. The Bible books describing these events include Joshua, Judges, Ruth, 1 and 2 Samuel, 1 and 2 Kings, and 1 and 2 Chronicles. Also during this time Psalms, Proverbs, Ecclesiastes, and the Song of Songs were written. It was a rich period of development for the nation of Israel, culminating in the height of power and riches under kings David and Solomon.

To help keep this historic period straight, we have prepared an Events chart (page 48). It correlates events with Bible books and dates. You may want to consult the chart frequently as you survey the rest of the Old Testament.

The Conquest

Joshua followed Moses in leadership of the new nation and received his marching orders directly from God. You will want to read Joshua 1—11 for the story of the Hebrews' conquest of this territory. It started with the miraculous crossing of the Jordan River and the capture of Jericho. Jericho, the first city captured, was to be offered up to God. The Hebrews were to take nothing of value from it. However, it didn't turn out exactly that way. As you read this passage you will notice the "sin of Achan" (chapter 7) that caused the nation much grief. Also note the role of Rahab. Do you see any important symbolism in the "scarlet cord" (Josh. 2:17-18) the spies told Rahab to display? It is sometimes said that a "scarlet cord" weaves its way all the way through Scripture.

The conquest involved three major campaigns, each of which demonstrated Joshua's military genius:

The Central Campaign was intended to control the international trade route that followed the high mountain ridge north and south across the area. Gaining control of this trade route divided the tribes of the north from the ones in the south and made conquest easier. The capture of Ai accomplished this objective. It also put the "fear of God" into the inhabitants of the city of Gibeon. Read about the Gibeonites' response in Joshua 9 and about Joshua and the Israelites' serious error.

The Southern Campaign was fought against the "Amorite League" that attacked Gibeon for what they considered to be treason by the Gibeonites. Joshua's strategy of surprise attacks and swift movements are evidenced here, as he completely defeated these kings. However, he had some significant help! God caused the sun to stand still to provide Joshua some additional time to complete the battle.

The Northern Campaign was against a huge confederacy of kings that gathered at Hazor. The story is in Joshua 11. The military assembly is described as "a huge army, as numerous as the sand on the seashore" (11:4). In this battle the Hebrews, for the first time, faced horses and chariots.

Upon learning about this coalition of kings gathering in the north, Joshua marched his army from Gilgal (central Canaan) to Hazor (more than seventy miles) and performed an early morning preemptive strike. Before his army attacked, however, Joshua sent commandos ahead to "hamstring" the horses, effectively neutralizing the enemy's military advantage of horses and chariots. For good measure, the Hebrews also burned the chariots.

The northern campaign completed the conquest of the territory, but unfortunately, there were still large areas of the country not completely conquered. Consequently, Israel constantly endured harassment from these native residents.

Following the conquest, the captured lands were divided among the twelve tribes, each autonomous within its own assigned territory.

The Period of the Judges (Book of Judges)

For approximately 400 years after the conquest, no central government existed in Israel. The various tribes had some internal organizational structure, but it was often ineffectual. "In those days Israel had no king; everyone did as he saw fit" (Judg. 17:6). The plan was for God to be their king, but the general disobedience to the will of God caused the actual outcome to be virtual anarchy.

Judges describes seven invasions by surrounding nations. Each invasion is introduced with the phrase, "the Israelites did evil in the sight of the LORD." Their sin was followed by invasion and oppression, after which they repented, and God raised up a "judge." These judges were political/military leaders who delivered the people from bondage to a foreign power and provided leadership in the period of peace that followed. See the Cycle of Judges (page 49) for an illustration of this continual cycle. The nation went around this circle seven times! The invading nations and the judges raised up to deliver them were:

1) Mesopotamia — Othniel
2) Moab — Ehud
3) Canaan — Deborah
4) Midian — Gideon
5) Civil war — Abimelech
6) Ammonites — Jephthah
7) Philistines —Samson

The book of Judges describes some gruesome experiences, largely because Israel was in rebellion against God and suffered the consequences. However, during the periods of peace, there were some good and prosperous times. The book of Ruth was written in this time, and the events surrounding Ruth describe a time of apparent political tranquility and peace. In fact, scholars tell us that of the approximately 400 years encompassing the period of the judges, there were about 200 years of peace.

A very important individual, Samuel, began his ministry near the end of this period. Samuel served as a bridge between the judges and the prophets, being both. The Israelites approached Samuel and demanded a king because they were convinced their problems stemmed from the fact that surrounding nations have kings but the tribes of Israel do not. They failed to recognize that their problem was spiritual, not political. At first resistant to the idea, Samuel, after receiving permission from God, finally agreed to the demand. God led him to a young man, Saul, whom he anointed as Israel's first king.

The United Kingdom (Monarchy)

The "United Kingdom" period was the height of prosperity for Israel. Three kings ruled during this time: Saul, David, and Solomon. Saul brought the kingdom together under central leadership and gained victory over surrounding enemies. Unfortunately, his personal life ended in ruin.

David, the much loved king of Israel received the promise from God that his kingdom will endure forever (2 Sam. 7:16) and that the Messiah will come from his family (Isa. 11—Jesse was David's father). In a previous study we saw how God said the Messiah would come from the human race (Gen. 3:15). Later He narrowed it down to the nation descended from Abraham through Isaac (Gen. 12:2-3; 17:19-22; 21:12; 26:1-6). Now God identified the actual family—the family of David—from which the Messiah will fulfill God's promise of blessing to the nations.

David was the author of most of the Psalms. His many skills and administrative abilities were awesome. He was deeply devoted to the Lord but also fell into grave sin. He wanted to build a permanent house of worship to replace the tabernacle, but God would not allow it because David was a man of war. It was left to David's son, Solomon, to build the magnificent temple, but David began to stockpile materials for it.

Under Solomon's reign the kingdom achieved its maximum size and magnificence. See the map of the Kingdom of David and Solomon (page 50) for some idea of the geographical size of the kingdom. The luxury and wealth of his kingdom is described in 2 Chronicles 9:13-28. Be sure to read that passage and try to imagine what the kingdom must have been like. Unfortunately, in spite of God's evident blessing, Solomon disobeyed God by having many wives, building up a huge army of horses and chariots, and accumulating much wealth. The sad result of those sins will be evident in the next lesson.

Books	Events	Dates
Genesis	Creation	???
	Noah Abraham	2,000 B.C.
Exodus Leviticus	Moses	1,500
Numbers Deuteronomy Joshua	Joshua The Judges	1,400
Ruth		
1 and 2 Samuel	Saul	1,025
(Psalms)	David	1,004
Proverbs Ecclesiastes Song of Songs	Solomon	971

Judges

I & II Chronicles (Priestly History)

I & II Kings (Civil History)

	Kingdom of Judah	Kingdom of Israel	
(Job?)			
			840
Obadiah			
Joel			
Jonah Hosea			
Amos			730
Micah		Captivity by Sargon of Assyria	722
Isaiah			
Nahum Habakkuk Zephaniah	Captivity by Nebuchadnezzar of Babylon—Jerusalem and temple destroyed		
Jeremiah			605
Ezekiel			586
Lamentations			
Daniel	Captivity ended by Cyrus of Persia		539
Haggai			
Zechariah			
Esther	Temple rebuilt (520—516)		516
Ezra			457
Nehemiah			
Malachi			420
	Christ		

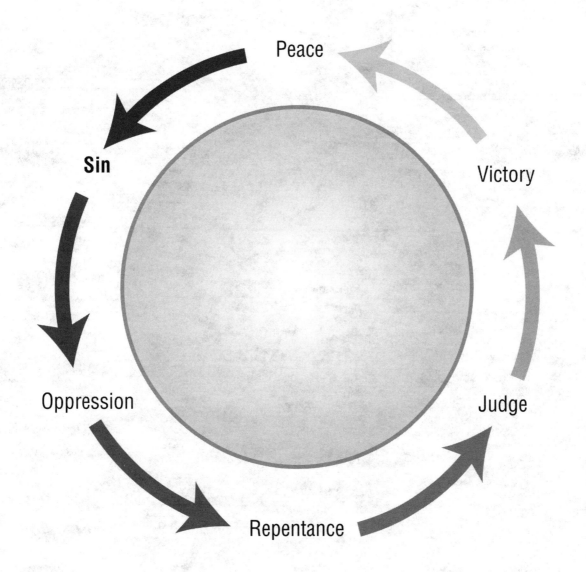

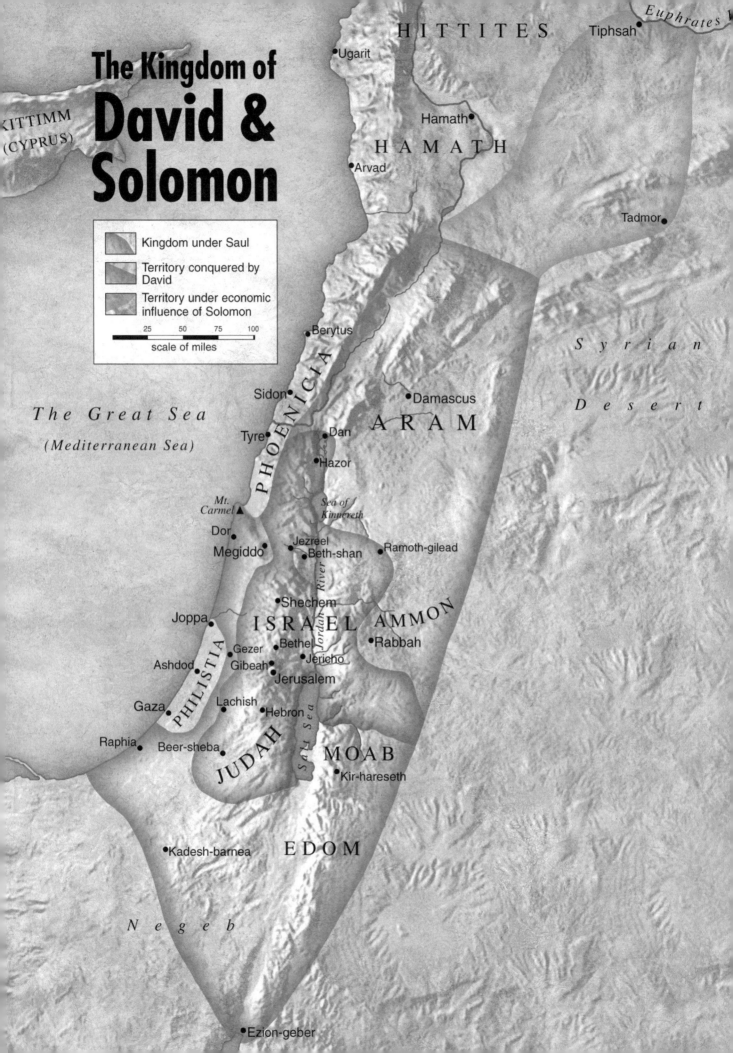

The Kingdom of David & Solomon

Kingdom under Saul

Territory conquered by David

Territory under economic influence of Solomon

25   50   75   100
scale of miles

HITTITES

Euphrates

Tiphsah

Ugarit

Hamath

HAMATH

Arvad

Tadmor

XITTIMM (CYPRUS)

Berytus

Syrian

Desert

Sidon

Damascus

ARAM

PHOENICIA

Tyre

Dan

Hazor

The Great Sea

(Mediterranean Sea)

Mt. Carmel ▲

Sea of Kinnereth

Dor

Jezreel

Megiddo

Beth-shan

Ramoth-gilead

Shechem

Joppa

ISRAEL

AMMON

Jordan River

Gezer

Bethel

Rabbah

Ashdod

Gibeah

Jericho

PHILISTIA

Jerusalem

Gaza

Lachish

Hebron

Salt Sea

Raphia

Beer-sheba

MOAB

JUDAH

Kir-hareseth

Kadesh-barnea

EDOM

Negeb

Ezion-geber

LESSON 4

The Divided Kingdom, Captivity, and Restoration

Equipment Needed

1) Whiteboard or chalkboard.
2) Classroom maps showing Israel, Assyria, and Babylonia.

Teaching Supplies Needed

1) Copies of Old Testament Quiz (page 55).
2) Copies of student lesson 5 to distribute to the class.

Review

Trace on map: Adam, Noah, Abraham, Isaac, Jacob, Joseph, Moses, Joshua, Saul, David, Solomon.

Lecture

Introduction
Call attention to the Chronology of Kings of Assyria, Babylonia, and Persia chart in the Student section (page 59). Inform students they should keep this chart in their manuals as a helpful reference in linking Bible events to political history. During this time of the Divided Kingdom, Captivity, and Restoration, Israel was interacting with numerous nations around them.

1. Tell the story of revolt and division. Refer to the map in the Student section, and relate the story of the revolt in 1 Kings chapter 12. The nation was now divided between the ten tribes to the north—the "Northern Kingdom," known as "Israel," and the two tribes to the south, the "Southern Kingdom," known as "Judah." The term, "Jew," developed during this time in reference to a resident of Judah.

2. "The age of the prophets." Briefly review the long list of prophets during this period of Old Testament history.

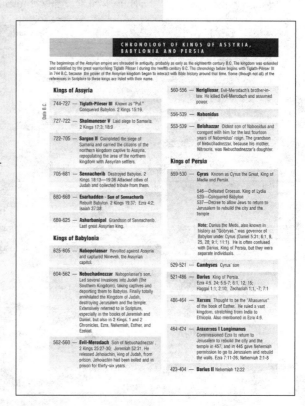

CHRONOLOGY OF KINGS OF ASSYRIA, BABYLONIA AND PERSIA

The beginnings of the Assyrian empire are shrouded in antiquity, probably as early as the eighteenth century B.C. The kingdom was extended and solidified by the great warrior/king Tiglath Pileser I during the twelfth century B.C. The chronology below begins with Tiglath-Pileser III in 744 B.C. because the power of the Assyrian kingdom began to interact with Bible history around that time. Some (though not all) of the references in Scripture to these kings are listed with their name.

Kings of Assyria

Date B.C.

744-727 — **Tiglath-Pileser III** Known as "Pul." Conquered Babylon. 2 Kings 15:19.

727-722 — **Shalmaneser V** Laid siege to Samaria. 2 Kings 17:3; 18:9

722-705 — **Sargon II** Completed the siege of Samaria and carried the citizens of the northern kingdom captive to Assyria, repopulating the area of the northern kingdom with Assyrian settlers.

705-681 — **Sennacherib** Destroyed Babylon. 2 Kings 18:13—19:36 Attacked cities of Judah and collected tribute from them.

680-669 — **Esarhadden - Son of Sennacherib** Rebuilt Babylon. 2 Kings 19:37; Ezra 4:2; Isaiah 37:38

669-625 — **Ashurbanipal** Grandson of Sennacherib. Last great Assyrian king.

Kings of Babylonia

625-605 — **Nabopolassar** Revolted against Assyria and captured Nineveh, the Assyrian capitol.

604-562 — **Nebuchadnezzar** Nabopolassar's son. Led several invasions into Judah (the Southern Kingdom), taking captives and deporting them to Babylon. Finally totally annihilated the Kingdom of Judah, destroying Jerusalem and the temple. Extensively referred to in Scripture, especially in the books of Jeremiah and Daniel, but also in 2 Kings, 1 and 2 Chronicles, Ezra, Nehemiah, Esther, and Ezekiel.

562-560 — **Evil-Merodach** Son of Nebuchadnezzar, 2 Kings 25:27-30; Jeremiah 52:31. He released Jehoiachin, king of Judah, from prison. Jehoiachin had been exiled and in prison for thirty-six years.

560-556 — **Neriglissar** Evil-Merodach's brother-in-law. He killed Evil-Merodach and assumed power.

556-539 — **Nabonidus**

553-539 — **Belshazzar** Oldest son of Nabonidus and coregent with him for the last fourteen years of Nabonidus' reign. The grandson of Nebuchadnezzar, because his mother, Nitrocris, was Nebuchadnezzar's daughter.

Kings of Persia

559-530 — **Cyrus** Known as Cyrus the Great, King of Media and Persia.

546—Defeated Croesus, King of Lydia
539—Conquered Babylon
537—Decree to allow Jews to return to Jerusalem to rebuild the city and the temple

Note: Darius the Mede, also known in history as "Gobryas," was governor of Babylon under Cyrus (Daniel 5:31; 6:1, 9, 25, 28; 9:1; 11:1). He is often confused with Darius, King of Persia, but they were separate individuals.

529-521 — **Cambyses** Cyrus' son

521-486 — **Darius** King of Persia. Ezra 4:5, 24; 5:5-7; 6:1, 12, 15; Haggai 1:1; 2:10; Zechariah 1:1, -7; 7:1

486-464 — **Xerxes** Thought to be the "Ahasuerus" of the book of Esther. He ruled a vast kingdom, stretching from India to Ethiopia. Also mentioned in Ezra 4:6.

464-424 — **Araxerxes I Longimanus** Commissioned Ezra to return to Jerusalem to rebuild the city and the temple in 457; and in 445 gave Nehemiah permission to go to Jerusalem and rebuild the walls. Ezra 7:11-26; Nehemiah 2:1-8

423-404 — **Darius II** Nehemiah 12:22

Refer to the Events Chart on page 48 of the Student section.

3. Refer to the chart, Chronology of Kings of Judah and Israel, (page 60). Most of the kings in both kingdoms were evil and ungodly. Jeroboam and successive kings of Israel tried to prevent their citizens from traveling to Judah to worship, so Jeroboam set up idols at Bethel and Dan as centers of worship (1 Kings 12:25-33). There was little cooperation between the two kingdoms—mostly treachery and war. At one point Athaliah, the daughter of King Ahab and Jezebel (of Israel), ruled Judah for six years and attempted to kill all of David's descendants. She would have succeeded if it had not been for "Aunt Jehosheba," who hid the one survivor, one-year-old Joash (Jehoash). He ascended to the throne at age seven. The exciting story is in 2 Chronicles 22:10—23:21 and 2 Kings chapter 11.

CHRONOLOGY OF KINGS OF JUDAH AND ISRAEL

Saul
David
Solomon

Date B.C.	Judah	Israel
922	Rehoboam Abijah Asa	Jeroboam I
901		Nadab Baasha Elah Zimri Omri
873	Jehoshaphat	Ahab Ahaziah
849	Jehoram Ahaziah (Athaliah) Jehoash (Joash)	Jehoram Jehu
815	Amaziah	Jehoahaz Jehoash
783	Uzziah Jotham Ahaz	Jeroboam II Zachariah Shallum Menahem Pekahiah
732	Hezekiah Manasseh Amon Josiah Jehoahaz Jehoiakim Jehoiachin Zedekiah	Pekah Hoshea (722) Fall of Samaria
(586)	Fall of Jerusalem	

4. Destruction of the Northern Kingdom of Israel occurred in 722 B.C. by the Assyrians and the deportation of many of the citizens to Assyria. Israel was repopulated by Assyrian immigrants. The mixed race that developed in Israel was known as "Samaritans."

Refer to classroom or overhead map showing Assyria and Israel.

5. Destruction of the Southern Kingdom of Judah took place by Nebuchadnezzar in 586 B.C. He destroyed the city and the temple and took the residents captive to Babylon. Refer to the book of Lamentations—Jeremiah's description of the city of Jerusalem after the Babylonian invasion. Also, ask students to respond to Psalm 137, their assigned reading. Jewish refugees in Babylon wrote this psalm. Some of the horrors of the last days of the Southern Kingdom are described in Jeremiah chapter 52.

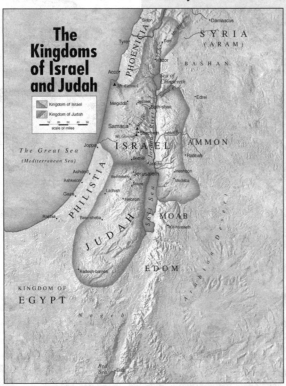

The Kingdoms of Israel and Judah

Kingdom of Israel
Kingdom of Judah
scale of miles

6. Ezekiel was one of the refugees. He wrote his prophecy from Babylon.

7. Daniel was one of the captives. He knew of Jeremiah's prophecy that the Captivity would last seventy years, and he was probably expecting the coming of the Messiah and the fulfillment of the prophecies about God's coming kingdom of peace at the end of the seventy-year Babylonian captivity. In response to his prayers, God revealed an awesome prophecy indicating a long period of time is still to intervene before God's kingdom arrives. He even revealed to Daniel the succession of Gentile empires still to come. Have students turn to Daniel, chapters two and seven, and chart the prophecy on the chalkboard. Tell the exciting story of Nebuchadnezzar's dream and its interpretation (Dan. 2).

Chapter 2	World Kingdom	Chapter 7
Head of gold	Babylonia	Lion
Chest & arms of Silver	Medo/Persia	Bear
Belly of bronze	Greece	Leopard
Feet of Iron and clay	Rome	"Terrifying Beast"
"The Rock"	Christ's Kingdom	"Son of Man"

Write the chart to the left on the chalkboard. If you're good at making drawings, you may want to attempt a drawing of the "enormous, dazzling statue." (Dan. 2:31)

These prophetic images are amazingly descriptive of each of these world kingdoms. Point out how the chest and arms of silver represent the two nations of the Medo-Persian Empire, and the bear turning on its side represents the Persians gaining dominance over the Medes. Also, the leopard (its speed) is so descriptive of Alexander the Great's rapid conquest of huge amounts of territory. Even today the remnants of Rome (our legal system, governmental systems, architecture, etc.) like "iron mixed with clay," no longer hold together as an empire, but the "ghost of Rome" is still very much present. The two legs of the image represent "East" and "West" in the heritage of Rome (Western Europe and America on the one hand, and Eastern Europe central Asia and Russia on the other).

8. Refer to Isaiah 44:28—45:4, the prophecy concerning Cyrus. This prophecy was given nearly 200 years before Cyrus was born! Cyrus was the Persian king who conquered Babylon, "the unconquerable city," and allowed the Jewish captives to return to their homeland and rebuild the city of Jerusalem and the temple.

- The temple was rebuilt and dedicated in 516 B.C., exactly seventy years after its destruction.
- The walls of Jerusalem were rebuilt under Nehemiah's leadership. His principles of leadership are sometimes called the best description of Christian service ever written.

9. The Old Testament record comes to a close at this time, approximately 400 years before the coming of Christ. The 400 years from the last Old Testament prophecy to the birth of Christ are sometimes called the "The Silent Years," or the "Inter-Testament Period." This period, along with the Ministry of Christ, will be the topics of next week's discussion.

Review

Make copies of the "Old Testament Quiz." Distribute it to the class and allow time for students to complete it. Then give the correct answers. Use the "answer time" for discussion about each of the situations surrounding the topics referred to in the questions. Do not collect students' responses because the quiz is not to be graded; it is simply a means whereby each student self-evaluates his or her progress.

Old Testament Quiz

UNIT I

The correct answers are:

1. b   6. b
2. c   7. c
3. a   8. b
4. a   9. b
5. a   10. c

Old Testament Quiz

Circle the letter of the phrase that best completes each statement:

1. The word, "Genesis," means

   a. going out
   b. beginnings
   c. the second law

2. Moses lived before

   a. Abraham
   b. Joseph
   c. Saul

3. At the close of the "wilderness wanderings," the Promised Land was conquered under the leadership of

   a. Joshua
   b. Joseph
   c. Moses

4. The sun stood still during the

   a. southern campaign
   b. central campaign
   c. northern campaign

5. The kingdom of Israel achieved its maximum size and magnificence under the reign of

   a. Solomon
   d. David
   c. Saul

6. The leader of the rebellion that split the nation of Israel into two nations was

   a. Rehoboam
   b. Jeroboam
   c. Jeremiah

7. The patriarch who started in Canaan but moved the Bible story to Egypt was

   a. Moses
   b. Abraham
   c. Joseph

8. The great "wall builder of Jerusalem" was

   a. Ezra
   b. Nehemiah
   c. Cyrus

9. The Northern Kingdom was destroyed and its citizens taken captive by

   a. Nebuchadnezzar of Babylon
   b. Sargon of Assyria
   c. Belshazzar of Babylon

10. The period of Israel's history sometimes called "The Age of the Prophets" was

   a. the Exodus
   b. the Conquest, Judges, and United Kingdom
   c. the Divided Kingdom, Captivity, and Restoration

LESSON 4

The Divided Kingdom, Captivity, and Restoration

At the death of Solomon, his son Rehoboam ascended to the throne. The people petitioned him for a reduction in the heavy tax burden. Rehoboam's older and more experienced advisors told him to grant the people's request, but his younger and less experienced advisors told him to ignore the request and actually raise taxes. Rehoboam followed the advice of his younger advisors, causing a revolt. Under the leadership of Jeroboam, ten tribes revolted against Rehoboam and established their own kingdom, known as "Israel," or the "Northern Kingdom." The remaining tribes, Benjamin and Judah, retained Jerusalem and are known as the Kingdom of Judah, or the "Southern Kingdom." First Kings chapter 12 tells the sad story of the tearing apart of the kingdom. The map of the kingdoms of Israel and Judah (page 61) shows the division of the territory.

This period in the nation's history is sometimes also called "the age of the prophets," because God raised up many outstanding individuals to proclaim His Word to the people. As we noted in last week's lesson, Samuel served as a "bridge" between the judges and the prophets, functioning as both. Following Samuel's time and during the Divided Kingdom, prophets and kings took center stage in Israel's leadership. Many Old Testament books came from the pens of these prophets.

We usually think of a prophet as someone who foretells the future; and some of these prophets did so. But the basic meaning of prophet is someone who proclaims the will of God to His people. Notice on the Events Chart (page 48), the long list of prophets, and their writings during this Divided Kingdom period.

Four of the prophets (Daniel, Jeremiah, Isaiah, and Ezekiel) are called "major prophets" because of the length of their writings. Sometimes Jeremiah, Isaiah, and Ezekiel are also called "Prophets of the Trinity," because each seems to speak from the standpoint of one of the persons of the Trinity. Jeremiah, the "Prophet of the Father," thundered the message: "Thus saith the Lord…." Isaiah, the "Prophet of the Son," gave remarkable prophecies about Jesus with amazing detail about His birth, life, and crucifixion—some 700 years before Jesus was born! Ezekiel, the "Prophet of the Spirit," made at least twenty-five references to the Spirit in his prophecies and told of the mysterious work of the Spirit in making even "dry bones live."

The two kingdoms existed separately, each with its succession of kings. Note the Chronology of Kings of Judah and Israel Chart on page 60. It lists the succession of kings in each kingdom with their dates.

Throughout this time foreign nations were threatening Israel and Judah, particularly Babylonia, Assyria, and Egypt. The prophets kept warning the people that if they did not repent of their sinful conduct, God would once again allow foreign powers to overcome them. This, in fact, happened to the Northern Kingdom in 722 B.C. when Sargon of Assyria invaded and destroyed the Northern Kingdom's capital of Samaria and took many of the people captive to Assyria. Sargon also colonized Israel with immigrants from Assyria who mixed with the population of Israel that had remained behind. This "mixed race" became known as Samaritans and was much despised by the "true Jews" during the time of Jesus.

Meanwhile, the people in the Southern Kingdom of Judah felt smug and safe because surely God would not allow them to be conquered. After all, they possessed the holy city of Jerusalem and were descendants of Judah, through whom God promised special blessing. In spite of Jeremiah's stern warnings, they continued in their sinfulness and refused to repent. Consequently, God allowed the Babylonians under Nebuchadnezzar to invade and conquer them in 586 B.C. The people of Judah were taken captive to Babylon, exactly as Jeremiah predicted. In the book of Lamentations, Jeremiah lamented the destruction of Jerusalem. **Read Psalm 137** and feel the grief of the captives in Babylon. Among the captives were Ezekiel and Daniel.

Jeremiah had prophesied that the captivity would last seventy years and the nation would be restored (Jer. 29). When the seventy years were almost completed, Daniel interceded for his people, looking forward to the fulfillment of God's kingdom on earth. God responded to Daniel with remarkable information about the future. He told Daniel, in essence, that his people would, indeed, return to their land but many more years would pass before God fulfilled His kingdom purposes and eradicated evil. He gave Daniel an outline of Gentile kingdoms still to come.

God prepared a military ruler to invade and conquer Babylon and told of his arrival 200 years before his birth (Isa. 44:28—45:4). His name was Cyrus, and he allowed the captives to return to their land. The dramatic account of their return and the rebuilding of the city of Jerusalem and the temple are in the books of Nehemiah and Ezra. The story of rebuilding the walls of Jerusalem under Nehemiah's leadership has been an inspiration to builders and Christian workers for 2,400 years! **Read the first six chapters of Nehemiah before the next class.** It will help to prep you for class discussion.

Ezra describes the rebuilding of the temple. **Read Ezra 3—6**. The temple was completed and dedicated in 516 B.C., exactly seventy years after it was destroyed! In historical reference, it is known as the "second temple," since it was a restoration of the first temple built by Solomon.

The Old Testament record comes to a close at this time. In the next lesson we will look at the "Inter-Testament Period" and the ministry of Christ.

The beginnings of the Assyrian empire are shrouded in antiquity, probably as early as the eighteenth century B.C. The kingdom was extended and solidified by the great warrior/king Tiglath Pileser I during the twelfth century B.C. The chronology below begins with Tiglath-Pileser III in 744 B.C. because the power of the Assyrian kingdom began to interact with Bible history around that time. Some (though not all) of the references in Scripture to these kings are listed with their name.

Date B.C.

Kings of Assyria

744-727 — **Tiglath-Pileser III** Known as "Pul." Conquered Babylon. 2 Kings 15:19.

727-722 — **Shalmaneser V** Laid siege to Samaria. 2 Kings 17:3; 18:9

722-705 — **Sargon II** Completed the siege of Samaria and carried the citizens of the northern kingdom captive to Assyria, repopulating the area of the northern kingdom with Assyrian settlers.

705-681 — **Sennacherib** Destroyed Babylon. 2 Kings 18:13—19:36 Attacked cities of Judah and collected tribute from them.

680-669 — **Esarhadden - Son of Sennacherib** Rebuilt Babylon. 2 Kings 19:37; Ezra 4:2; Isaiah 37:38

669-625 — **Ashurbanipal** Grandson of Sennacherib. Last great Assyrian king.

Kings of Babylonia

625-605 — **Nabopolassar** Revolted against Assyria and captured Nineveh, the Assyrian capitol.

604-562 — **Nebuchadnezzar** Nabopolassar's son. Led several invasions into Judah (the Southern Kingdom), taking captives and deporting them to Babylon. Finally totally annihilated the Kingdom of Judah, destroying Jerusalem and the temple. Extensively referred to in Scripture, especially in the books of Jeremiah and Daniel, but also in 2 Kings, 1 and 2 Chronicles, Ezra, Nehemiah, Esther, and Ezekiel.

562-560 — **Evil-Merodach** Son of Nebuchadnezzar. 2 Kings 25:27-30; Jeremiah 52:31. He released Jehoiachin, king of Judah, from prison. Jehoiachin had been exiled and in prison for thirty-six years.

560-556 — **Neriglissar**, Evil-Merodach's brother-in-law. He killed Evil-Merodach and assumed power.

556-539 — **Nabonidus**

553-539 — **Belshazzar** Oldest son of Nabonidus and coregent with him for the last fourteen years of Nabonidus' reign. The grandson of Nebuchadnezzar, because his mother, Nitrocris, was Nebuchadnezzar's daughter.

Kings of Persia

559-530 — **Cyrus** Known as Cyrus the Great, King of Media and Persia.

546—Defeated Croesus, King of Lydia
539—Conquered Babylon
537—Decree to allow Jews to return to Jerusalem to rebuild the city and the temple

Note: Darius the Mede, also known in history as "Gobryas," was governor of Babylon under Cyrus (Daniel 5:31; 6:1, 9, 25, 28; 9:1; 11:1). He is often confused with Darius, King of Persia, but they were separate individuals.

529-521 — **Cambyses** Cyrus' son

521-486 — **Darius** King of Persia. Ezra 4:5, 24; 5:5-7; 6:1, 12, 15; Haggai 1:1; 2:10; Zechariah 1:1, -7; 7:1

486-464 — **Xerxes** Thought to be the "Ahasuerus" of the book of Esther. He ruled a vast kingdom, stretching from India to Ethiopia. Also mentioned in Ezra 4:6.

464-424 — **Araxerxes I Longimanus** Commissioned Ezra to return to Jerusalem to rebuild the city and the temple in 457, and in 445 gave Nehemiah permission to go to Jerusalem and rebuild the walls. Ezra 7:11-26; Nehemiah 2:1-8

423-404 — **Darius II** Nehemiah 12:22

Saul

David

Solomon

Date B.C.	Judah	Israel
922	Rehoboam Abijah Asa	Jeroboam I
901		Nadab Baasha Elah Zimri Omri
873	Jehoshaphat	Ahab Ahaziah
849	Jehoram Ahaziah (Athaliah) Jehoash (Joash)	Jehoram Jehu
815	Amaziah	Jehoahaz Jehoash
783	Uzziah Jotham Ahaz	Jeroboam II Zachariah Shallum Menahem Pekahiah
732	Hezekiah Manasseh Amon Josiah Jehoahaz Jehoiakim Jehoiachin Zedekiah	Pekah Hoshea (722) Fall of Samaria
(586)	Fall of Jerusalem	

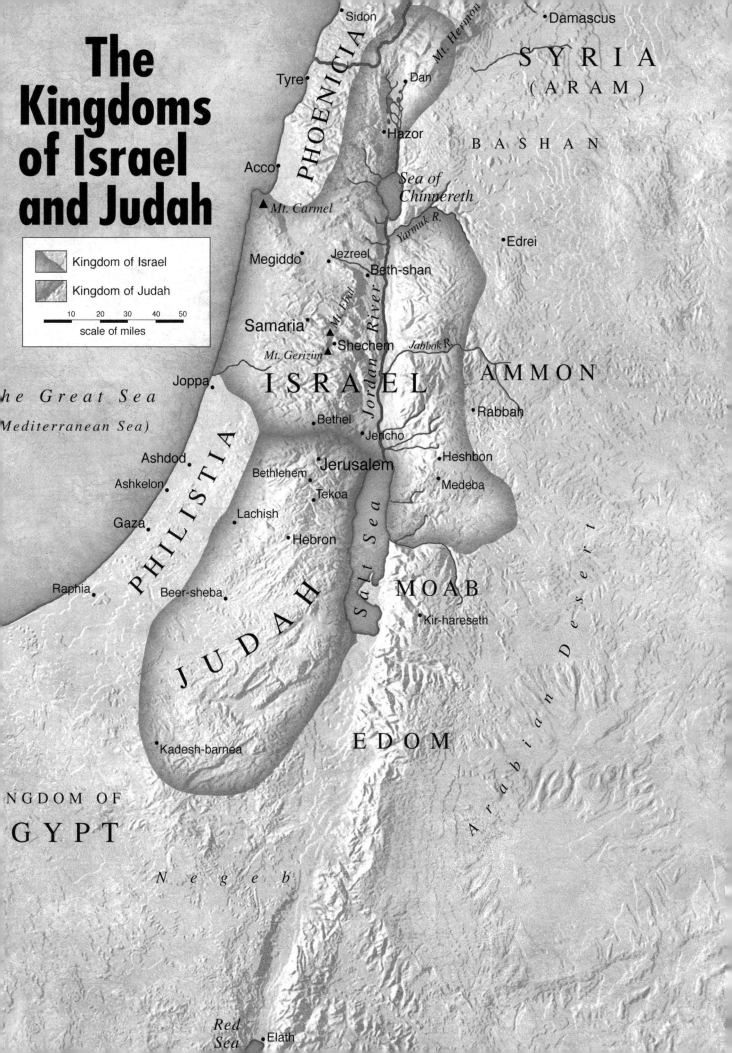

The Kingdoms of Israel and Judah

Kingdom of Israel

Kingdom of Judah

10 20 30 40 50
scale of miles

Sidon

Damascus

SYRIA
(ARAM)

Tyre

Dan

Mt. Hermon

PHOENICIA

Hazor

BASHAN

Acco

Sea of
Chinnereth

Mt. Carmel

Yarmuk R.

Edrei

Megiddo

Jezreel

Beth-shan

Mt. Ebal

Jordan River

Samaria

Mt. Gerizim

Shechem

Jabbok R.

AMMON

Joppa

ISRAEL

Rabbah

Bethel

Jericho

the Great Sea
(Mediterranean Sea)

PHILISTIA

Heshbon

Ashdod

Jerusalem

Ashkelon

Bethlehem

Medeba

Tekoa

Gaza

Lachish

Salt Sea

Hebron

Raphia

Beer-sheba

MOAB

Kir-hareseth

JUDAH

Arabian Desert

Kadesh-barnea

EDOM

NGDOM OF
GYPT

Negeb

Red
Sea

Elath

LESSON 5

The Inter-Testament Period and the Ministry of Christ

Equipment Needed

1) Overhead or classroom maps of Palestine in Jesus' time.

Teaching Supplies Needed

1) Copies of Chronological Events Quiz with answer sheet (pages 66-67).
2) Copies of student lesson 6 to distribute to the class.

Prepare the Chronological Events Quiz by copying the pages at the end of this lesson (one copy for every two students). Cut out each statement and jumble the statements so they're out of sequence. Near the end of this lesson, divide the class into pairs, and ask them to work on arranging these names and events in chronological order, laying them out in a vertical row with the earliest on top, down to the last on bottom. When all the pairs have completed the task, pass out the answer sheets for them to check the accuracy of their work. They will enjoy this exercise. Make it fun!

Several charts are included in the Student section with this lesson. Inform students that the Jerusalem Timeline chart (page 72), the Grouping (or classification) of Old and New Testament Books (page 71), the pictures of the Hanukkah and traditional menorahs (page 69), and the Summary of the Ministry of Jesus (page 70) are simply reference aids.

Lecture

1. Begin the class by reviewing the prophecy of Daniel with focus on the division of the Greek Empire after the death of Alexander. One of the four divisions of Alexander's empire was the kingdom established by Seleucis I, one of Alexander's most capable generals. The kingdom of the Seleucids expanded all the way from Asia Minor (modern Turkey) to India, with its capital at Antioch. After the establishment of Antioch as capital, nearly all the Seleucid kings added the name of this city to their own name and were known as "Antiochus _____."

Since the Bible does not record this period, we are dependent upon secular records, such as those provided by the historian Josephus and the books of 1 and 2 Maccabees. (The books of the Maccabees are part of the "Apocrypha," sometimes called the "Deutro-canonical books" that are included in Catholic Bibles but not recognized as inspired Scripture by most Protestants.)

Antioch and the region of the Seleucid Empire.

2. Antiochus IV, also known as Antiochus Epiphanes, invaded Palestine in route to and from his wars with Egypt. He inflicted incredible bloodshed and misery upon the Jewish people and presided over what has been called the "first thoroughgoing persecution of the Jews for their faith." He was guilty of causing the death of thousands of people and untold misery to thousands more. He called himself "Epiphanes," meaning a manifestation of deity. Among the outrages committed by Antiochus were:

a. He set fires in Jerusalem, tore down its walls and many of its homes.

b. He inflicted the death penalty for observing any Jewish ceremony, including the Sabbath, circumcision and dietary laws.

c. He destroyed Jewish Scriptures.

d. He took women and children captive as slaves and destroyed their homes.

e. He set up pagan altars throughout Israel and commanded Jews to worship his pagan gods and eat swine flesh on penalty of death.

f. As the ultimate blasphemy, he erected a statue of the heathen god, Zeus, in the temple, demanded its worship, and sacrificed a pig on the altar of burnt offering.

3. When the Syrian soldiers came to the little town of Modin, about twenty miles from Jerusalem, and commanded the residents to worship at the heathen altar set up there, an old priest named Mattathias refused to obey. Seeing one of his countrymen sacrifice to this false god, Mattathias couldn't stand it any longer. He rushed to the altar, killed both the Jew worshiping there and the commissioner of Antiochus who was present. He also tore down the altar before escaping to the hills. Mattathias's five sons immediately took up the cause, gathered a rag-

> If you have access to 2 Maccabees, read chapters 5 and 6 for a description of Antiochus' destruction of Jerusalem and Judea.

tag army, and started a guerilla war against the Syrian invaders. The "War of the Maccabees" was on! ("Maccabee" means "hammer.") The Jews changed Antiochus's chosen title, "Epiphanes," to "Epimanes," meaning "crazy."

4. One of the great miracles of warfare took place during the next three and a half years. The Jewish defenders drove the immense, highly disciplined Syrian army (complete with elephants and the "latest" equipment) right out of the country! The temple was cleansed, and on December 25, 165 B.C., the temple was rededicated to the worship of Jehovah. The Hebrew word for dedication is "Hanukkah," and Jews remember this great event to this day in their observance of Hanukkah every December.

5. Many legends surround this historic event, but the best known is the "miracle of the oil." In their haste to reestablish true worship when the temple was cleansed

and the Syrians driven out, the Jews relit the sacred menorah. However, there was only enough sanctified oil for it to burn one day, and it would take eight days to sanctify. It is said that the one-day's supply burned miraculously for eight days until more oil could be sanctified. That is why Hanukkah is observed for eight days and the Hanukkah menorah has eight branches instead of the traditional six branches with a center candle.

Not all scholars agree that the legend is true. Many think a more likely reason Hanukkah is celebrated for eight days is that when the Jews recaptured Jerusalem they may have belatedly observed the Feast of Tabernacles, an eight day festival. The Bible doesn't tell us. The only mention of Hanukkah in the Bible is in John 10:22-23, stating that Jesus attended the festival.

6. Meanwhile, to the west, the city of Rome was flexing its muscles. Expanding its power and influence, Rome grew from an important city to a territorial power, and finally an immense empire. The Romans largely adopted Greek culture and added their administrative and engineering skills to it. Rome systematically extended its sovereignty beyond Italy and Greece and eventually became the undisputed ruler of the western Mediterranean. After defeating Hannibal of Carthage, Roman legions marched into the kingdom of the Seleucids. After a three-month siege, they captured Jerusalem (198 B.C.) and Judah became a Roman province.

7. Depending on the translation you read, Galatians 4:4 seems to imply that Jesus came at just the right time. History certainly corroborates this view. Consider, for example, that at this time:
   a. There was a universal language (Greek) throughout the vast Roman empire, so the good news of the Gospel could be understood by most people in the empire, regardless of their ethnicity.
   b. There was general dissatisfaction with the old gods, and people were hungry for a new spiritual reality.
   c. As a result of being conquered and scattered, Jews were located in almost every major city, and worshiped weekly in their synagogues. These synagogues provided strategic centers for early missionaries to share the good news of the resurrection.
   d. The unified empire of Rome opened travel to many nations formerly restricted by border security. It was almost like traveling from state to state in the United States.
   e. The Romans were highly skilled engineers and their highways stretched hundreds of miles across the empire, making travel the easiest it had ever been. Their engineering genius is still the envy of road builders, and many of their roads continue in use 2,000 years later! The Apostle Paul and others traveled incredible distances on these highways, telling the good news ("Gospel" means "good news") throughout the empire.

At this point we are at the end of the Old Testament and ready to begin a quick survey of the New Testament.

Refer to the chart, Grouping of Old and New Testament Books, page 71 in the Student section. Briefly review and discuss the major divisions of books.

8. The ministry of Jesus is arranged in the Student section by six major periods.

Review each of these in class, referring to a map of Palestine during the time of Jesus and relating it to the map in the student material. Just as with "Adam, Noah, Abraham...etc." in the Old Testament, students should develop the skill of tracing Jesus' ministry on a map. This, then, becomes a continuation of the Old Testament "story," and part of "telling the Bible story in three minutes or less." They should memorize in order:

> Early Judean Ministry
> Great Galilean
> Perean
> Later Judean
> Passion Week
> Resurrection and Ascension

Again, because of the nature of this course, we can't spend much time in details. We want students to see the "big picture." The Summary of the Ministry of Jesus, on page 70, will be helpful to students in any subsequent study of the Gospels. But you will want to point out one or more significant events in each period as mental "hooks" for students to remember the sequence of Jesus' ministry.

Review

Distribute the Chronological Events Quiz
Have students work in groups of two to arrange events in chronological order. Then give each group an answer sheet. Follow up with any pertinent discussion.

Demonstrate "telling the Bible Story in three minutes or less."
Tell the story from Adam through the Ministry of Christ, including the six periods of Jesus' ministry.

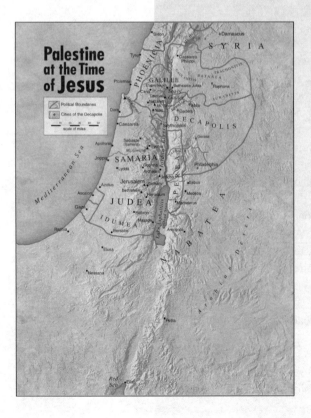

Correct Answers to Chronological Events Quiz

1. Garden of Eden
2. Methuselah
3. The Flood
4. Abraham
5. Isaac
6. Jacob
7. Joseph
8. Slavery in Egypt
9. Ten Plagues in Egypt
10. Passover
11. Crossing the Red Sea
12. Conquest of Jericho
13. Joshua's Long Day
14. Period of the Judges
15. Saul
16. David
17. Solomon
18. The Divided Kingdom
19. Babylonian Captivity
20. Antiochus Epiphanes

Chronological Events Quiz

Garden of Eden	Isaac
The Flood	Jacob
Slavery in Egypt	Joseph
Abraham	Passover
Conquest of Jericho	Ten Plagues in Egypt
Period of the Judges	Joshua's Long Day
Saul	Babylonian Captivity
David	Antiochus Epiphanes
Solomon	Crossing the Red Sea
The Divided Kingdom	Methuselah

LESSON 5

The Inter-Testament Period and the Ministry of Christ

The experience of the restored nation of Judah during the Inter-Testament period was stormy. Surrounding tribes and nations constantly threatened Judah's peace and security.

The greatest threat came from a Syrian ruler, "Antiochus Epiphanes." Epiphanes, a name Antiochus gave himself, means roughly, "God revealed." Many consider him to be a "type" (picture) of the future Antichrist. Daniel 11 appears to be a direct prophecy of the destruction Antiochus brought to the nation of Judah. In verses 36-45 of that chapter Daniel seems to move mysteriously into a prophecy of the coming Antichrist as though Antiochus in some way impersonates him.

Antiochus set up a statue of Zeus in the temple and forced the Jews to worship this false god on penalty of death. He also prescribed death for anyone taking part in any Jewish religious ceremonies, including observing the Sabbath, practicing circumcision, or making traditional sacrifices.

Relief from the Syrian invaders came through the revolt of the Maccabeans, led by a Jew named Judas Maccabeus. Incredibly, this "rag-tag" militia of Judah under Judas's leadership drove the Syrians out of the country. On December 25, 165 B.C., they cleansed the temple and restored true worship. It is claimed that, lacking enough consecrated oil for the menorah in the temple, the menorah nevertheless burned miraculously for eight days until enough holy oil could be consecrated. The Jews celebrate this historic "cleansing of the temple" to this day as "Hanukah," which means "Dedication." The celebration lasts eight days,

Traditional Menorah   Hanukkah Menorah

commemorating the eight days of miraculous light. It is also called the "Festival of Lights." The Hanukah menorah, unlike the traditional menorah, has eight branches (see the illustration on this page).

The following pages provide a list of Old and New Testament books in chart form, an outline of Jesus' ministry, and a Jerusalem Timeline chart. The summary of the ministry of Jesus is a reference you may wish to turn to frequently when reading or studying in the books of Matthew, Mark, Luke, and John. These four books serve as biographies of Jesus. In preparation for the next class session, try to relate the sequence of Jesus' ministry to the map, starting in Judea, then to Galilee, back to Judea, then to Perea, and finally to Jerusalem.

UNIT I

Summary of the Ministry of Jesus

Books of Matthew, Mark, Luke, and John

Early Judean Ministry

Baptism, temptation, trip to Cana, where He performed His first miracle, calling of first disciples, first cleansing of the temple, interview with Nicodemus, visit with Samaritan woman at Jacob's well enroute to Galilee.

> Matthew 3:13—4:11
> Mark 1:9-13
> Luke 3:21—4:13
> John 1:19—4:44

Great Galilean Ministry

Rejection at Nazareth and move to Capernaum, appointment of the twelve apostles, Sermon on the Mount, the "great group of parables," the sending out of the Seventy and the sending out of the Twelve, various miracles, the transfiguration.

> Matthew 4:12—18:35
> Mark 1:14—9:50
> Luke 4:14—9:50
> John 4:45—7:9

Later Judean Ministry

Healing of the blind man on the Sabbath and various other healings, the parable of the Good Samaritan, the Pharisees' attempt to stone Jesus, teachings about His death.

> John 7:10—10:39
> Luke 9:51—19:27 is apparently arranged topically more than chronologically, with a vast amount of information about Jesus' journey from Galilee to Jerusalem, and this section may include events from both the Judean and Perean ministries.

Perean Ministry

Raising of Lazarus, teaching about Jesus' death, encounter with the rich young ruler, healing of two blind men and Bartimaeus, teaching about divorce.

> Matthew 19:1—20:34
> Mark 10:1-52
> John 10:40—11:54

Passion Week in Jerusalem

"Palm Sunday" entrance into Jerusalem, prediction of the destruction of the temple and of Jerusalem, teaching about end-time events, cursing of the fig tree, continued teachings about Jesus' death, various parables, washing disciples' feet, final instructions, the Last supper, the betrayal, arrest, trial, crucifixion, and burial.

> Matthew 21:1—27:66
> Mark 11:1—15:47
> Luke 19:28—23:56
> John 12:1—19:42

Resurrection and Ascension

> Matthew 28:1-20
> Mark 16:1-20
> Luke 24:1-53
> John 20:1—21:25
> Acts 1:1-11

Books of the Old Testament

Books of the Law
Genesis
Exodus
Leviticus
Numbers
Deuteronomy

Books of History
Joshua
Judges
Ruth
1 Samuel
2 Samuel
1 Kings
2 Kings
1 Chronicles
2 Chronicles
Ezra
Nehemiah
Esther

Books of Poetry
Job
Psalms
Proverbs
Ecclesiastes
Song of Solomon
Lamentations
   (Lamentations is sometime classified as
   a book of prophecy and sometimes as a
   book of poetry)

Books of Prophecy
Isaiah
Jeremiah
Ezekiel
Daniel
Hosea
Joel
Amos
Obadiah
Jonah
Micah
Nahum
Habakkuk
Zephaniah
Haggai
Zechariah
Malachi

Books of the New Testament

Biographies of Jesus
Matthew
Mark
Luke
John

History
The Acts of the Apostles
Letters (Epistles)

From	To	Book
Paul	Christians in Rome	Romans
Paul	Christians in Corinth	1, 2 Corinthians
Paul	Christians In Galatia	Galatians
Paul	Christians in Ephesus	Ephesians
Paul	Christians in Philippi	Philippians
Paul	Christians in Colossae	Colossians
Paul	Christians in Thessalonica	1, 2 Thessalonians
Paul	Timothy	1, 2 Timothy
Paul	Titus	Titus
Paul	Philemon	Philemon
?	Hebrew Christians	Hebrews
James	Christians in general	James
Peter	Christians in general	1, 2 Peter
John	Christians in general	1, 2, 3 John
Jude	Christians in general	Jude

Prophecy
The Revelation of Jesus Christ

Date	Event
586 B.C.	Invaded and destroyed by Nebuchadnezzar of Babylon
538 B.C.	Decree of Cyrus allowing Jews to return to Jerusalem and rebuild the temple.
536 B.C.	Temple foundation laid and altar set up.
516 B.C.	Temple finished and dedicated.
445 B.C.	Nehemiah arrives in Jerusalem and supervises rebuilding the walls.
322 B.C.	Alexander the Great conquers Jerusalem.
198 B.C.	Jerusalem is conquered by the Romans and placed in the district of Syria.
165 B.C.	The Maccabean revolt.
63 B.C.	Invaded by the Romans under General Pompey.
54 B.C.	Plundered by Crassus of Rome.
40 B.C.	Sacked by the Parthians.
37 B.C.	Recaptured for Rome by Herod.
A.D. 66	Jewish revolt against Rome.
A.D. 70	Destruction of Jerusalem by the Romans under Titus.

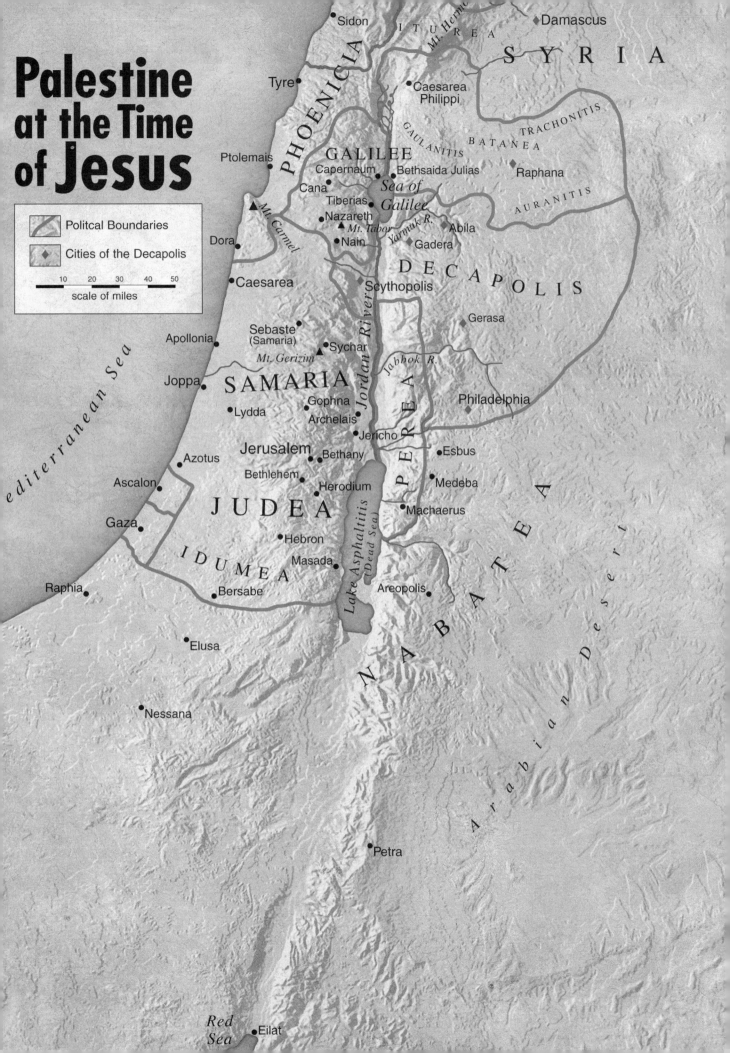

Palestine at the Time of Jesus

Politcal Boundaries
Cities of the Decapolis

10 20 30 40 50
scale of miles

Mediterranean Sea

SYRIA

Damascus

Sidon

ITUREA

Mt. Hermon

Tyre

PHOENICIA

Caesarea
Philippi

TRACHONITIS

BATANEA

Ptolemais

GALILEE

Capernaum

Bethsaida Julias

Raphana

GAULANITIS

Cana

*Sea of
Galilee*

AURANITIS

Tiberias

Mt. Carmel

Nazareth

Mt. Tabor

Yarmuk R.

Abila

Dora

Nain

Gadera

DECAPOLIS

Caesarea

Scythopolis

Jordan River

Gerasa

Sebaste
(Samaria)

Apollonia

Sychar

Mt. Gerizim

Jabbok R.

PEREA

Joppa

SAMARIA

Gophna

Lydda

Archelais

Philadelphia

Jericho

Azotus

Jerusalem

Bethany

Esbus

Ascalon

Bethlehem

Herodium

Medeba

Gaza

JUDEA

Machaerus

Hebron

*Lake Asphaltitis
(Dead Sea)*

NABATEA

IDUMEA

Masada

Raphia

Bersabe

Areopolis

Elusa

Arabian Desert

Nessana

Petra

*Red
Sea*

Eilat

LESSON 6

Paul's Missionary Journeys

Equipment Needed	Teaching Supplies Needed
1) Classroom maps or overhead projector and maps of Paul's missionary Journeys.	1) Copies of student lesson 7 to distribute to the class.

Lecture

This lesson consists of three major sections: Pentecost, Antioch as a Christian center, and Paul's missionary journeys. Some background information appears below for each of these topics as an aide in preparing for the class.

Pentecost

Students are instructed in their reading assignment to read Acts 2 in preparation for this lesson. The Christian community holds conflicting views about the meaning and significance of the Pentecost experience and a student may have an emotional identification with an opposing view. Therefore, it is important, from our perspective, not to identify with any given interpretation, but to carefully and honestly explore the event and encourage students to study the meaning of the event within the context of their own church. The controversy usually centers on the question of whether the Pentecost experience is valid today. Do not allow class discussion to degenerate into a debate. Our purpose is to inform students about what happened in Jerusalem that day and to respect one another's differing interpretations.

All Christians agree Pentecost was an important event. It was the "birthday of the Church" and fulfilled the promise Jesus made in Acts 1:8; John 14:16, 26; 15:26; and 16:7. Some interesting Old Testament background to Pentecost should be mentioned:

1. Pentecost was observed on "the day after the Sabbath," which was Sunday (Lev. 23:15). It was also connected with "new grain," or "first fruits," a fitting symbol of new life in Christ. As the Sabbath looked back to the law (pictured by the last day of the week), Pentecost looks forward to what is ahead in Christ (pictured by the first day of a new week). However, it needs to be mentioned that not all interpreters agree with this view. Some understand "Sabbath" in the Leviticus

passage to refer to a ceremonial Sabbath, not the seventh day of the week.

2. Pentecost is linked directly to Passover, just as the coming of the Holy Spirit is linked directly to the sacrifice of Christ. Fifty days separated the Festival of Passover and the Festival of Pentecost, just as fifty days separated the crucifixion and Pentecost. The meaning of "Pentecost" is "fifty."

Other symbolic significance may be drawn from Pentecost. For example:

1. When the Spirit of God entered the original temple built by Solomon, He did so in a great demonstration of the "glory of the Lord" (2 Chron. 5:13-14). Likewise, when the Spirit departed from that temple before its destruction, the glory of the Lord was again visible (Ezek. 10). At the Acts 2 Pentecost experience, the Spirit of God moved into His "new temple," the heart and body of His people, the church (2 Cor. 6:16).

2. The old temple was preliminary to God's eventual purpose and was therefore centered in Judaism because the Jews were the vehicle through whom God's plan of salvation entered the world. The message of Pentecost, however, was that the new temple was not restricted to Judaism but was for the whole world! This is symbolized by the fact that all these people from so many different nations heard the message in their own language. It served as a prelude to Revelation 5:9 and 7:9. Because the Jews had a difficult time understanding this concept, God gave Peter a special object lesson (Acts 10), and Paul kept preaching that the "dividing wall of hostility" between Jew and Gentile was removed in Christ (Eph. 2:14).

These issues are the major ones we want our students to grasp about Pentecost. Questions such as whether Christians should speak in tongues today are peripheral to our purpose.

Antioch as a Christian Center

Point to both Antioch in Syria and Antioch in Asia Minor on the map.

Remind students the Bible mentions two Antiochs—Antioch in Syria and Antioch in Asia Minor (modern Turkey). The following discussion concerns Antioch in Syria, located about 300 miles north of Jerusalem along the Mediterranean coast. The other Antioch will be included later in this lesson as a destination in Paul's missionary journeys.

After Pentecost the Gospel spread rapidly from Jerusalem, across Judea, Samaria, and Asia Minor. In Jerusalem severe persecution of Christians broke out, some of which Saul (later called Paul) instigated.

Many believers in Jerusalem fled to other areas. The largest concentration of these refugees was in Antioch, where the followers of Jesus were first called "Christians" (Acts 11:26). Antioch became a strong church and a center for missionary outreach. Barnabas, one of the early church leaders at Antioch, enlisted Paul's help after Paul's conversion.

Paul's First Journey
Acts 13:1-14:28

Paul's Missionary Journeys

The information for this section comes from the book of Acts, the full title of which is "The Acts of the Apostles." Luke, a physician, wrote Acts and accompanied Paul and his team during a portion of their missionary travels. He is believed to be the same Luke who authored the Gospel of Luke.

Give the class a brief background of Paul's life prior to his missionary journeys:

1. He was a native of the city of Tarsus (Acts 21:39).
2. He was a "pure" Jew, from the tribe of Benjamin (Phil. 3:5).
3. He was a Pharisee (Acts 23:6).
4. He was a Roman citizen by birth (Acts 22:28).
5. He was well educated (Acts 22:3; 26:24).
6. He participated in the stoning of Stephen (on the wrong side; Acts 7:57-58).
7. He persecuted Christians fiercely (Acts 9:1-2).
8. He was dramatically converted to Christ (Acts 9).
9. After his conversion, he spent time "sorting things out," spending considerable time in the Arabian Desert, in Jerusalem to visit Peter, and finally back home to Tarsus (Gal. 1:11-24).

Barnabas went to Tarsus to ask Saul (Paul) to join him in the work at Antioch (Acts 11:25-26). The Antioch church then commissioned them to embark on a missionary journey to carry the Gospel to the Gentiles in Asia Minor (roughly modern Turkey) Acts 13:2-3.

Locate Tarsus on map.

Trace Paul's journeys on classroom maps.

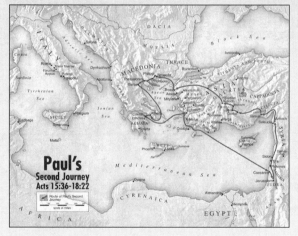

Paul's
Second Journey
Acts 15:36-18:22
Route of Paul's Second Journey
scale of miles

The student materials include maps and descriptions of each journey. Study them carefully so that you, together with the students, can trace each journey on its corresponding map and discuss the highlights of each trip. Note the letters Paul wrote during his journeys. These letters comprise most of the epistles of the New Testament.

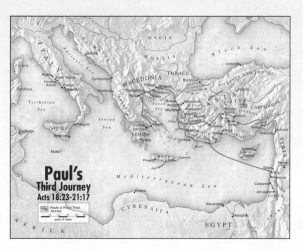

Paul's
Third Journey
Acts 18:23-21:17
Route of Paul's Third Journey
scale of miles

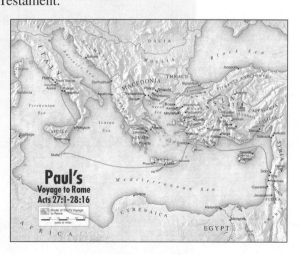

Paul's
Voyage to Rome
Acts 27:1-28:16
Route of Paul's Voyage to Rome
scale of miles

LESSON 6

Paul's Missionary Journeys

The story of the New Testament church begins with Pentecost, the event described in the second chapter of Acts. The presence of God through the Holy Spirit moved into His new "body," the people who belong to Christ and of whom He is the "head." This new body of people is to encompass every language, tribe, and nation. **Read Acts chapter 2** in preparation for discussion in class.

Because of increasing persecution of Jesus' followers in Jerusalem, many of them moved to other areas. The greatest concentration of believers was in Antioch of Syria, where they were first called "Christians." Barnabas came to Antioch to help with the work and was soon overwhelmed. In his search for help he remembered Saul who had persecuted Christians in Jerusalem but on a trip to Damascus had met the resurrected and glorified Lord and was soundly converted. Saul (renamed Paul) was now living in his hometown of Tarsus. Barnabas found him and requested that he come to Antioch to help with the work.

Prior to his conversion Saul was a devout, highly educated Jew. He described himself as "circumcised on the eighth day, of the people of Israel, of the tribe of Benjamin, a Hebrew of Hebrews; in regard to the law, a Pharisee; as for zeal, persecuting the church; as for legalistic righteousness, faultless." He had been proud of that heritage and based his salvation on his own righteousness. But when he met Christ, all of that changed. He later testified; "... whatever was to my profit I now consider loss for the sake of Christ. What is more, I consider everything a loss compared to the surpassing greatness of knowing Christ Jesus my Lord, for whose sake I have lost all things. I consider them rubbish, that I may gain Christ and be found in him, not having a righteousness of my own that comes from the law, but that which is through faith in Christ..." (Phil. 3:4-9).

The Antioch church, led by the Holy Spirit, commissioned Paul and Barnabas to go on a missionary journey to tell the good news of the resurrection and the open door to Gentiles of every nation. The following pages summarize each of his three journeys. Using the adjacent maps, try to find the places Paul visited and relate them to the events summarized in the outline. Notice especially the churches to which he wrote letters because these letters have become most of the "epistles" of our New Testament.

Throughout his ministry, Paul experienced harassment and persecution, most of which came from Jews who rejected his message. Some of these Jews professed to be Christians, but they insisted that new Christians must first become Jews (that is, accept Jewish ritual, law and practice) in order to become Christians. These teachers became known as "Judaizers." The apostles met in council at Jerusalem after Paul's first missionary journey to discuss this matter and concluded decisively that the Judaizers were in error, affirming that salvation in Christ is open to Gentiles as well as Jews on the basis of faith in the work of Christ, not in the works of the law. **Read about the deliberations of this council in Acts 15:1-35.** This issue occasioned Paul writing to the Christians in Galatia, who were disturbed by the Judaizer's teachings. This letter is "Galatians" in our New Testament.

Paul was martyred in the summer of A.D. 67 or 68. The Bible does not record his death, but universal tradition holds that he was beheaded. His final New Testament writing is 2 Timothy. You may want to read his last words in 2 Timothy 4.

First Journey—With Barnabas and John Mark

- Cyprus

  Governor Sergius Paulus interested in hearing the Gospel.

  False prophet, Elymas, rebuked by Paul and stricken with temporary blindness.

- Perga and Antioch

  John Mark deserted the missionary team and returned to Jerusalem.

  Hostility of the Jews increased.

- Iconium

  Many converts, both Jews and Greeks.

  Numerous miracles.

  A plan to instigate a riot and stone the missionaries is discovered, causing Paul and his companions to escape from the city.

- Lystra and Derbe

  Because of the miracles performed, the people attempted to worship the missionaries, thinking they were gods. The missionaries, however, refused worship and convinced the people that they were only human.

  Unbelieving Jews from Antioch and Iconium instigated a riot in which Paul was stoned, dragged out of the city, and left for dead. He revived and returned to Derbe the next day, where he and Barnabas saw many people converted as a result of their teaching.

- Return by sea to Antioch of Syria and report to the Antioch church.

- The Council at Jerusalem.   (Acts 15:1-35)

Second Journey — With Silas

- Overland through Tarsus and the Cilician Gates (a mountain pass).

- Revisited churches established during first journey in Derbe, Lystra, Iconium and Antioch. Timothy joined the team at Lystra.

- In a vision Paul hears the "Macedonian call," and changes his plans in order to travel to Macedonia.

- Troas. Here Luke, the "beloved physician," joins the team. He becomes the historian of Paul's journeys and the author of the Gospel of Luke and the book of Acts.

- Philippi. Lydia, a businesswoman in Philippi is converted, and her house becomes a center of worship. Paul and Silas are imprisoned and are rescued by an earthquake. Paul's testimony results in the jailer's conversion.

- Thessalonica. Many converts. A riot instigated by the Jews forces Paul and Silas to escape by night.

- Berea. Again, many converts. Jews from Thessalonica came and stirred up opposition. Paul then sailed for Athens, while Silas and Timothy remained at Berea.

- Athens. Paul (alone) began by holding discussions daily in the market place. He was invited by some of the Greek philosophers to come to the Areopagus to discuss the subject of the resurrection. It was here that Paul presented his famous "Areopagus speech" (Acts 17:22-31).

- Corinth. Paul met Aquila and Priscilla and lived in their home while earning a living by tent making. He remained in Corinth about eighteen months and was greatly encouraged by the arrival of Silas and Timothy. He admitted that when he first came to Corinth he was in "weakness and fear, and with much trembling" (1 Cor. 2:3), probably intensified by being alone. He was rejected by the Jews, so he moved his teaching ministry out of the synagogue and into the home of a convert named Justus. The Jews attacked him and brought him into court, where the proconsul Gallio threw out the case.

  An eloquent scholar named Apollos came to Corinth while Paul was there. Under the tutoring of Aquila and Priscilla, Apollos became a powerful defender of the faith throughout the region.

  While in Corinth, Paul sent two letters to the church in Thessalonica, which are preserved as **First and Second Thessalonians** in the New Testament.

- Ephesus. Paul returned home via Ephesus, with the intent of reaching Jerusalem in time for Pentecost (probably March 22, A.D. 53). Aquila and Priscilla accompanyied him to Ephesus, then remained there while Paul went to Caesarea, Jerusalem, and finally to Antioch.

Third Journey

- Traveling through the provinces of Galatia and Phrygia, Paul revisited the churches in Derbe, Lystra, Iconium, and Antioch.

- Ephesus. Paul taught in the synagogue for three months, but when opposition from the Jews became too strong, he moved to a lecture hall owned by Tyrannus. He taught there daily for two years with such awesome results that "all the Jews and Greeks who lived in the province of Asia heard the word of the Lord" (Acts 19:10). There were so many converts that the craftsmen making idols were losing money, prompting them to start a riot. The city clerk addressed the crowd in Paul's defense and restored order.

  While in Ephesus, Paul wrote a letter to Christians in Corinth, known to us as **1 Corinthians.**

- Troas. Paul preached in Troas with great success, but was much disturbed because Titus, who had been sent to Corinth, had not returned to meet him (2 Cor. 2:12-13).

- Philippi. Anxious to find Titus, Paul sailed to Neapolis and immediately proceeded overland to Philippi, where both Titus and Timothy joined him (2 Cor. 1:1; 7:6). Titus then carried a letter to Christians in Corinth, which we know as **2 Corinthians.**

  Hearing that some Jews were corrupting the churches in Galatia by teaching that Gentile Christians must be circumcised and keep the Jewish law in order to be saved, Paul wrote the letter of **Galatians** to them.

- Corinth. After traveling through several Macedonian cities and visiting their churches, Paul spent three months in Corinth. While there, he wrote the letter of **Romans** to Christians in Rome.

- Returning by the same route to Troas, Paul sailed to Ephesus where he met with the elders of the church in a deeply emotional farewell, recognizing they would probably never see him again (Acts 20:17-38).

- Paul proceeded to Jerusalem, against the advice of friends and associates who feared for his life. A prophet, Agabus, predicted that Paul would be taken prisoner in Jerusalem and turned over to the Gentiles. Paul declared that he was ready, not only to be bound, but to die for the name of Christ (Acts 21:10-14). Arriving in Jerusalem, he was falsely accused and dragged out of the temple to be killed.

Journey to Rome

- Roman military personnel intervened when the Jews attempted to kill Paul. They took him into protective custody. Paul requested and received opportunity to speak to the crowd. When the commander ordered that he be flogged and questioned, Paul declared his Roman citizenship and right of protection under Roman law, causing the commander to release him.

- Paul's nephew warned him of a conspiracy by the Jews to kill him. When this news was shared with the commander, he ordered Paul to be transferred to Caesarea that night under guard of 200 Roman soldiers, 70 horsemen, and 200 spearmen.

- Through a series of judicial delays, Paul was held in prison in Caesarea for two years before he exercised his right as a Roman citizen to have the emporor hear his case.

- The voyage to Rome involved immense hardship, including a shipwreck at Malta (Acts 27).

- Paul was imprisoned in Rome for two years, released, and then imprisoned a second time under much worse conditions. During the first imprisonment he wrote **Philemon, Colossians, Ephesians** and **Philippians.** During his release he wrote **1 Timothy** and **Titus.**

- During the second imprisonment and while awaiting execution, Paul wrote the deeply moving letter to Timothy, recorded in the New Testament as **2 Timothy.** In this letter he told of his being generally abandoned. "Only Luke is with me...no one came to my support, but everyone deserted me..." (2 Tim. 4:11, 16). He declared, "I am already being poured out like a drink offering, and the time has come for my departure. I have fought the good fight, I have finished the race, I have kept the faith. Now there is in store for me the crown of righteousness, which the Lord, the righteous Judge, will award to me on that day— and not only to me, but also to all who have longed for his appearing" (2 Tim. 4:6-8). Shortly after writing these words, he was beheaded.

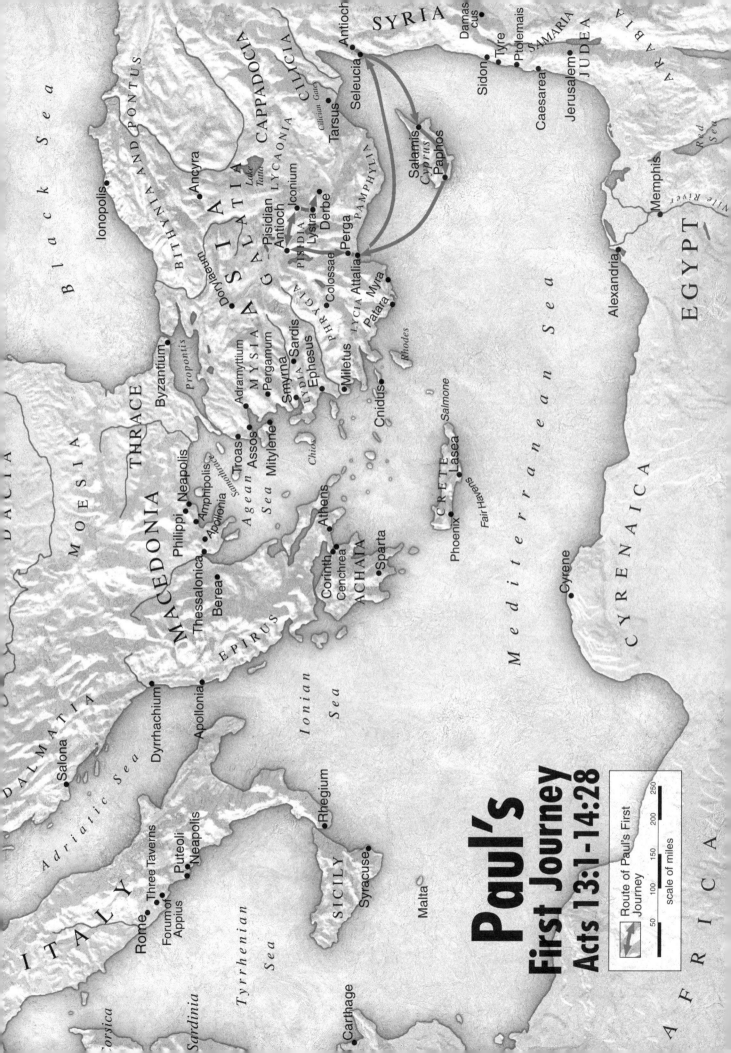

SYRIA

Damascus
Tyre
Ptolemais
SAMARIA
Sidon
Caesarea
Jerusalem JUDEA
Red Sea

Antioch
Seleucia
Tarsus
Cilician Gates
CILICIA
CAPPADOCIA

Salamis
Cyprus
Paphos

Memphis
Alexandria
Nile River
EGYPT

Ionopolis
BITHYNIA AND PONTUS
Ancyra
Dorylaeum
Lake Tatta
LYCAONIA
GALATIA
Pisidian Antioch
Iconium
PISIDIA
Lystra
Derbe
PHRYGIA
Colossae
Perga
Attalia
PAMPHYLIA
LYCIA
Myra
Patara

Black Sea

THRACE
Byzantium
Propontis
Adramyttium
MYSIA
Pergamum
Smyrna
Sardis
LYDIA
Ephesus
Miletus
Cnidus
Rhodes
Chios
Samothrace

MACEDONIA
Neapolis
Philippi
Amphipolis
Apollonia
Thessalonica
Berea
EPIRUS
Troas
Assos
Aegean Sea
Mitylene

Athens
Corinth
Cenchrea
ACHAIA
Sparta

CRETE
Salmone
Lasea
Fair Havens
Phoenix

Mediterranean Sea

CYRENAICA
Cyrene

AFRICA

DALMATIA
Salona
Dyrrhachium
Apollonia
Adriatic Sea

MOESIA
DACIA

ITALY
Rome
Three Taverns
Forum of Appius
Puteoli
Neapolis
Rhegium
Tyrrhenian Sea
SICILY
Syracuse
Carthage
Ionian Sea
Malta

Corsica
Sardinia

Paul's First Journey
Acts 13:1-14:28

Route of Paul's First Journey

scale of miles
50   100   150   200   250

SYRIA

Antioch

Damascus

Tyre
Ptolemais
SAMARIA

Sidon
Caesarea
Jerusalem
JUDEA

A R A B I A

Seleucia

Cilician Gates
Tarsus

CILICIA

CAPPADOCIA

Ancyra

BITHYNIA AND PONTUS

Ionopolis

B l a c k   S e a

Salamis
Cyprus
Paphos

Memphis

Dorylaeum

LYCAONIA

Iconium

Lake Tatta

GALATIA

Pisidian Antioch

Lystra
Derbe

PISIDIA

PHRYGIA

Colossae

PAMPHYLIA

Perga
Attalia

LYCIA

Myra
Patara

Rhodes

Alexandria

ASIA

Adramyttium

MYSIA

Pergamum

Smyrna
Sardis
LYDIA
Ephesus
Miletus

Cnidus

M e d i t e r r a n e a n   S e a

Byzantium

Propontis

THRACE

Neapolis

Troas
Assos
Mitylene

Chios

A e g e a n   S e a

Samothrace

Amphipolis

Apollonia

MACEDONIA

Philippi
Thessalonica
Berea

Athens
Corinth
Cenchrea
ACHAIA
Sparta

CRETE
Salmone
Lasea

Phoenix
Fair Havens

Cyrene

CYRENAICA

Carthage

MOESIA

DACIA

EPIRUS

I o n i a n   S e a

Dyrrhachium

Apollonia

DALMATIA

Salona

A d r i a t i c   S e a

ITALY

Rome
Three Taverns
Forum of Appius
Puteoli
Neapolis

Rhegium

SICILY

Syracuse

T y r r h e n i a n   S e a

Malta

Corsica

Sardinia

Paul's
Second Journey
Acts 15:36-18:22

Route of Paul's Second Journey

scale of miles

50   100   150   200   250

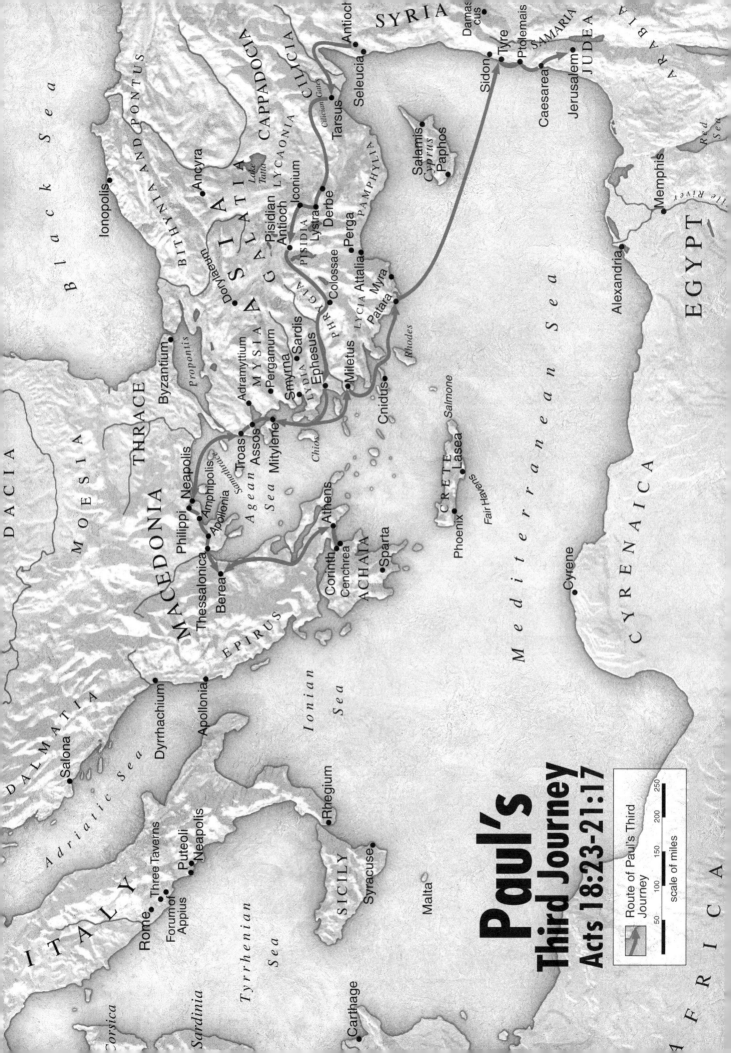

Paul's Third Journey
Acts 18:23–21:17

Route of Paul's Third Journey

scale of miles

50 100 150 200 250

SYRIA

Damascus

Antioch

Tyre

Ptolemais

SAMARIA

Sidon

Caesarea

Jerusalem JUDEA

ARABIA

Seleucia

Tarsus

Cilician Gates

CILICIA

CAPPADOCIA

Lake Tatta

Ancyra

GALATIA

ASIA

Dorylaeum

BITHYNIA AND PONTUS

Iconium

LYCAONIA

Pisidian Antioch

PISIDIA

Derbe

Lystra

Colossae

PHRYGIA

Perga

PAMPHYLIA

Attalia

LYCIA

Myra

Patara

Rhodes

Salamis

Cyprus

Paphos

Memphis

The River Nile

EGYPT

Alexandria

Ionopolis

Black Sea

DACIA

MOESIA

THRACE

Byzantium

Propontis

Adramyttium

MYSIA

Pergamum

Smyrna

Sardis

LYDIA

Ephesus

Miletus

Cnidus

Chios

Salmone

CRETE

Lasea

Fair Havens

Phoenix

Mediterranean Sea

Troas

Assos

Mitylene

Aegean Sea

Samothrace

Neapolis

Philippi

Amphipolis

Apollonia

Thessalonica

MACEDONIA

Berea

EPIRUS

Athens

Corinth

Cenchrea

ACHAIA

Sparta

Ionian Sea

DALMATIA

Salona

Dyrrhachium

Apollonia

Adriatic Sea

Rhegium

SICILY

Syracuse

Malta

Tyrrhenian Sea

Sardinia

Corsica

ITALY

Rome

Three Taverns

Forum of Appius

Puteoli

Neapolis

Carthage

Cyrene

CYRENAICA

AFRICA

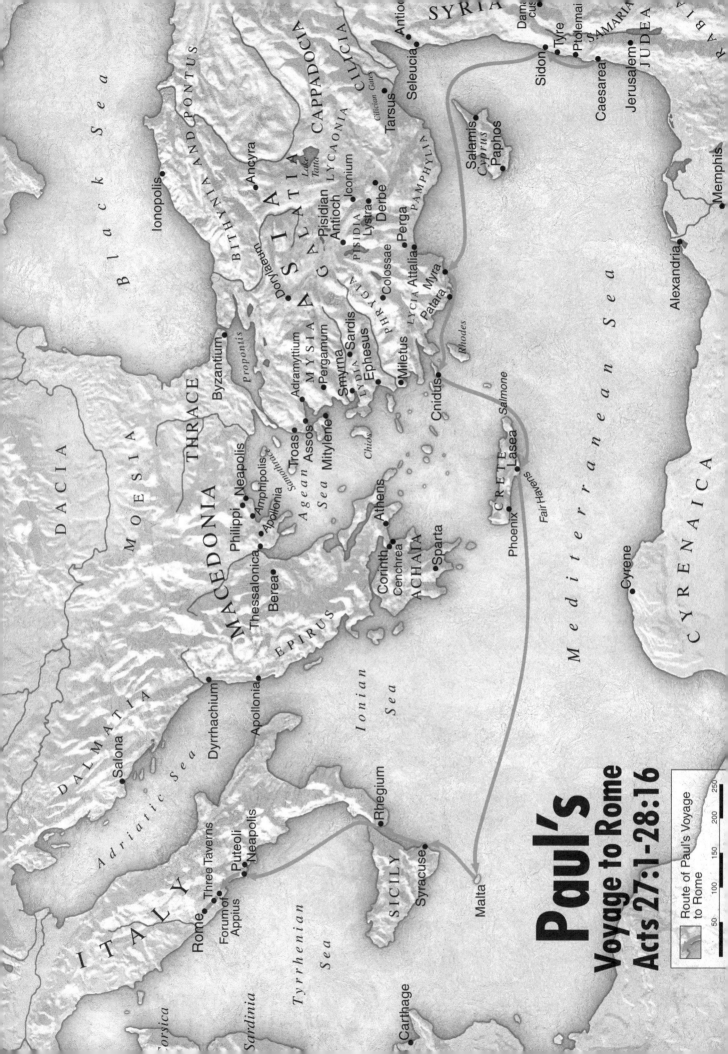

Paul's
Voyage to Rome
Acts 27:1-28:16

Route of Paul's Voyage to Rome

50   100   150   200   250

LESSON 7

The Revelation and Review of Bible Survey

Equipment Needed

1) Map showing location of Patmos

Teaching Supplies Needed

1) Copies of Bible Lands map (page 30) for students to practice telling the Bible story in three minutes.
2) Copies of student lesson 8 to distribute to the class.

Lecture

Students should become familiar with the various interpretations of Revelation given in the Student section. However, it is impossible in a survey course to get into the interpretation of the book in much detail. We simply want our students to become familiar with the content and some suggestions to help with interpretation. It may be well to inform students that the general subject of end-time prophecies will be touched upon again in Lesson 18.

Students have a one-page outline of the major themes of the book of Revelation. Have them turn to it and note the major divisions of the book. Start your discussion with these background facts:

1. The book was written by the apostle John, probably around A.D. 95 or 96, although some scholars contend it may have been as early as A.D. 89. John, the last surviving apostle, was exiled on the island of Patmos because of his faith.

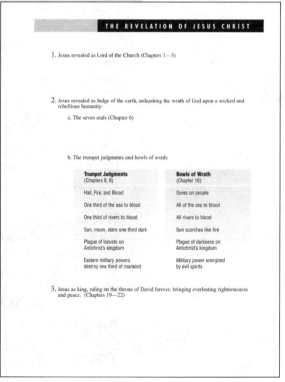

THE REVELATION OF JESUS CHRIST

1. Jesus revealed as Lord of the Church (Chapters 1—3)

2. Jesus revealed as Judge of the earth, unleashing the wrath of God upon a wicked and rebellious humanity:

    a. The seven seals (Chapter 6)

    b. The trumpet judgments and bowls of wrath:

Trumpet Judgments (Chapters 8, 9)	Bowls of Wrath (Chapter 16)
Hail, Fire, and Blood	Sores on people
One third of the sea to blood	All of the sea to blood
One third of rivers to blood	All rivers to blood
Sun, moon, stars one third dark	Sun scorches like fire
Plague of locusts on Antichrist's kingdom	Plague of darkness on Antichrist's kingdom
Eastern military powers destroy one third of mankind	Military power energized by evil spirits

3. Jesus as king, ruling on the throne of David forever, bringing everlasting righteousness and peace. (Chapters 19—22)

2. It had been a long time since Jesus' ascension and things were not "going well" for Christians. All the apostles, except John, had been martyred and persecution of Christians was intense under Emperor Domitian. Christians were wondering, "Where is Jesus?" "What is He doing?" "Why hasn't He returned?" The

Show the location of the Island of Patmos on map.

Revelation of Jesus Christ answers these questions.

3. The Revelation is the same kind of literature as, and really a continuation of, the book of Daniel. In fact, if the futurist interpretation is assumed, it is an elaboration of the last part of Daniel's visions of the future (Daniel 2 and 7). A study of Daniel prior to studying the Revelation will help you interpret the symbols in the Revelation.

As you review the simple outline of the book in the Student section, point out that the question of "Where is Jesus, and what is He doing?" receives a three-part answer in this prophecy:

1. Today, Jesus is Lord of the Church. He is the glorified, all-powerful, Son of God and Son of Man, majestic in the heavens. But as Lord of the church, He is also present in every congregation. Nothing escapes His watchful eye. He evaluates the work of every local church. Though the church does not see Him, He is present. John illustrates this by describing Jesus' evaluation of each of the seven first-century churches in Asia Minor (Chapters 2 and 3).

As time permits, explore some of the principles in these evaluations because they also apply to the Lord's evaluation of His church today. A chart is included in the Student section (pages 93 and 94). List the "good" things and the "bad" things in each church.

2. A significant change takes place at the beginning of chapter 4, where the scene shifts to Jesus as Judge of the earth. Justice will come. The enemies of God and His saints may be in control today, but they will receive their just punishment. The wrath of God will be unleashed upon a wicked and rebellious humanity. This judgment is described as seven seals, leading into seven trumpet judgments and culminating in seven bowls-of-wrath judgments. Note the similarity between the trumpet judgments and the bowls of wrath. It seems each of these categories becomes more intense as the judgments continue. They may not be chronological, however. Perhaps all these things take place simultaneously as depicted in a left to right order on the outline (Student section, page 92).

3. This lengthy passage ends with Jesus coming as King, ruling on the throne of David forever, and bringing in everlasting righteousness and peace (chapters 19—22).

This, in a nutshell, is the most commonly accepted understanding of the book among those who hold the futurist interpretation. Not everyone agrees. Commentators disagree about which descriptions are symbolic and which are literal. Others disagree about which events described in the book were fulfilled in the past. Wide divergence of opinion exists about the meaning of specific symbols and descriptions. However, the view given above is the majority opinion of evangelical interpreters.

Review of Bible Survey

Divide the class into pairs and have them practice telling "The Bible Story in Three Minutes" to each other. An example of telling the story is given on pages 90 and 91 of the Student section, but students should tell it from memory.

LESSON 7

The Revelation and Review of Bible Survey

The last book of the Bible is popularly called "Revelations" but the proper name for the book is "The Revelation of Jesus Christ." The title comes from the first five words of the book.

The purpose of the book is to reveal Jesus—His glorified state and His plans and purposes for this world. At the time of this writing (approximately A.D. 90) Jesus had ascended to heaven some sixty years earlier. The author, John the Apostle, was in exile on the island of Patmos. All the other apostles had faced martyrdom. Jesus had promised to return, but "Where was He?" "What was He doing?" "What about the future?" To answer these questions God revealed Jesus to His followers so they could know and understand His purposes.

Our word "revelation" is a translation of the Greek apokalypsis, meaning "to unveil." Similar to the way a new painting, statue, etc., might be unveiled to a waiting crowd at its dedication, this book unveils Jesus to those who otherwise cannot see Him. Because of this Greek word, Revelation is sometimes called "apocalyptic" literature. In modern usage the words "apocalypse" or "apocalyptic" often relate to end of the world scenarios, but the root meaning of the word is to reveal or unveil.

The Old Testament book of Daniel is also apocalyptic, and many of the symbols used in Daniel carry over to the Revelation. It is, therefore, advisable to study Daniel before attempting a study of the Revelation.

The Revelation is a perfect completion of the library that began with Genesis. Everything that was lost in Genesis because of sin is regained in the Revelation through the work of Christ. The writer and pastor, Archibald G. Brown, summarizes this perfectly: "In Genesis I see earth created; in Revelation I see it passing away. In Genesis sun and moon appear. In Revelation I read they have no need of the sun or moon. In Genesis there is a garden, which is the home for man; In Revelation there is a city; the home for the nations. In Genesis there is the marriage of the first Adam; in Revelation there is the marriage of the second Adam. In Genesis there is the first grim appearance of that great enemy Satan; in Revelation there is his final doom. In Genesis there is the inauguration of sorrow and suffering, you hear the first sob, you see the first tear; in Revelation there is no more sorrow and no more pain, and all tears are wiped away. In Genesis we hear the mutter of the curse, which falls because of sin; in Revelation we read 'there shall be no more curse.' In Genesis we see man driven out from the garden with the tree of life; in Revelation we see him welcomed back, with the tree of life at his disposal." [2]

Various scholars interpret the Revelation in several different ways. Among the various interpretations are:

1) The Preterist Interpretation. In this view, the book relates almost entirely to events surrounding the time of its writing or shortly thereafter. "Moderate," or "partial" preterists believe nearly everything except the return of Christ was fulfilled in the first few centuries of church history. "Extreme," or

"complete" preterists believe even the return of Christ has taken place already (at the destruction of Jerusalem in A.D. 70), and we are now in the Kingdom age.

2) The Historical Interpretation. Those who hold to this view believe the book forecasts the entire period of church history from the time of its writing to the present and beyond.

3) The Spiritual Interpretation, which holds that the symbolism of the book represents spiritual truth and has no identification with actual world events.

4) The Futurist Interpretation. This view considers most of the book (from chapter 4 on) to relate to actual world events still future to us. It divides the book according to the statement in 1:19, applying chapters 2 and 3 to "what is now," and the remainder of the book to "what will take place later." The Futurist Interpretation is most commonly accepted by evangelicals today, but all four of these methods of interpretation are "alive and well" in various branches of the church and among different scholars.

A brief outline of the book is provided, based on the Futurist Interpretation (page 92).

Review of Bible Survey

This completes the unit we call "Surfing the Bible." It is an overview of Bible history and chronology that will be of lifelong help in keeping the events of Bible history in order whenever you study or teach the Bible. To keep it from slipping away from your memory, we recommend three activities: 1) Review, 2) Review, and 3) Review!

One of the best forms of review is to use the Bible Lands map on page 30 of your manual and tell the Bible story. We suggest limiting yourself to three minutes as you tell the story. This helps keep you "on track." In the next class session you may have an opportunity to team up with a partner to practice this exercise.

Previous students have often asked for an example in print of how to tell the Bible story in three minutes, so we have complied. The example is printed below. However, it is just an example. We want you to be able to tell this story from memory and, as such, no two "stories" will be exactly alike. *Be sure to tell the story with map in hand and point out the locations where these major events take place.* Relating chronology and geography in this way aids retention. Wherever you see a location printed in italics in the story, point to the location on the map.

The Bible Story in Three Minutes or Less

The story starts with Adam and Eve in the Garden of Eden, located in *Mesopotamia.* Many generations passed until Noah, also in *Mesopotamia,* experienced the Flood. From here, people spread out in every direction; the descendants of Shem to the *East,* Ham to the *South,* and Japheth to the *West* and *North.*

God called Abraham from his home in *Ur* about 2000 B.C.. He traveled around the *Fertile Crescent* to *Canaan,* where his descendants, Isaac, Jacob, and Joseph were born. God changed Jacob's name to "Israel."

Joseph was taken prisoner to *Egypt,* where the children of Israel were at first highly favored, but following a change in rulers, they became slaves and endured severe persecution. Finally, after they had been in Egypt some 400 years, God called Moses to lead them out of Egypt, through the *Sinai Desert* to *Mt. Sinai* (use your own preference for the Exodus route and location of Mt. Sinai), where they received the law. From Mt. Sinai they wandered around in the desert and finally arrived at the summit of *Mt. Nebo,* where Moses died.

Joshua followed Moses and led the nation into *Canaan,* where they captured the territory and divided the land among the twelve tribes. The period of the Judges followed, when for approximately 400 years there was no central government and "everyone did as he saw fit." During this time the nation endured seven cycles of slavery and oppression because of their sin.

The twelve tribes came together under one government during the United Kingdom period. The three kings of this period were Saul, David, and Solomon. David lived about 1,000 B.C.. His son, Solomon, built the first temple.

After Solomon's death, civil war divided the nation into the *Northern Kingdom (Israel)* and the *Southern Kingdom (Judah)*. The Assyrians ultimately took Israel into captivity and populated the land of Israel with Assyrians. The resulting racial mixture became known as Samaritans, much despised by the "pure" Jews to the south.

The *Southern Kingdom (Judah)*, was taken captive by the *Babylonians*. They remained in captivity in Babylon for seventy years, then returned and rebuilt the temple and the city of *Jerusalem* under the leadership of Ezra and Nehemiah.

After "400 years of silence" in the Bible record, Jesus appeared on the scene at exactly the right time. His ministry consisted of four major periods: The Early Judean, Great Galilean, Later Judean, and Perean ministries, leading to the Passion Week in *Jerusalem* and the resurrection.

Paul carried the Gospel to the Gentile world of Asia Minor, Greece, and Rome in three missionary journeys and a final journey to Rome, where tradition says he was eventually martyred by beheading. His letters to the various churches of Asia Minor and Rome are a major part of the New Testament.

The Bible story concludes with the Revelation of Jesus Christ, written by John while he was a prisoner on the island of *Patmos*.

1. Jesus revealed as Lord of the Church (Chapters 1—3)

2. Jesus revealed as Judge of the earth, unleashing the wrath of God upon a wicked and rebellious humanity:

   a. The seven seals (Chapter 6)

   b. The trumpet judgments and bowls of wrath:

Trumpet Judgments (Chapters 8, 9)	Bowls of Wrath (Chapter 16)
Hail, Fire, and Blood	Sores on people
One third of the sea to blood	All of the sea to blood
One third of rivers to blood	All rivers to blood
Sun, moon, stars one third dark	Sun scorches like fire
Plague of locusts on Antichrist's kingdom	Plague of darkness on Antichrist's kingdom
Eastern military powers destroy one third of mankind	Military power energized by evil spirits

3. Jesus as king, ruling on the throne of David forever, bringing everlasting righteousness and peace. (Chapters 19—22)

	Good	Bad
Ephesus Revelation 2:1-7		
Smyrna Revelation 2:8-11		
Pergamum Revelation 2:12-17		

	Good	Bad
Thyatira Revelation 2:18-29		
Sardis Revelation 3:1-6		
Philadelphia Revelation 3:7-13		
Laodicea Revelation 3:14-22		

UNIT

II

The Story of the Church

LESSON 8

From the Apostles to Constantine

A.D. 70-313

Equipment Needed

1) Chalkboard or whiteboard

Teaching Supplies Needed

1) Copies of student lesson 9 to distribute to class.

The topic of church history includes such an immense amount of information that it is helpful for you to have some background resources available. Any number of church history books could be used for this purpose. Perhaps you already have one or more in your library.

Depending on how serious you are about studying church history, you may want to consider contacting the Christian History Institute, which has a wide variety of church history resource materials, including a monthly magazine. Their address is Christian History Institute, P.O Box 540, Worcester, PA 19490. Their phone number is 1-800-523-0226, website http://chi.gospelcom.net/. At this site you can also order pamphlets and articles on specific subjects of church history.

It is not required that you purchase extra materials to be qualified to teach this unit. This Leader section provides sufficient information for your lectures.

This week's lesson covers seven major topics: The Fall of Jerusalem, Characteristics of Early Christians, Persecutions, Heresies, Early Church Leaders, the Canon of Scripture, and Emperor Constantine.

Lecture
The Fall of Jerusalem

Josephus is our primary source of information about the fall of Jerusalem (A.D. 70). He was the official historian for the Romans, and he traveled with the Roman legions that invaded Judea and conquered Jerusalem. He was also a Jew who defected to the Romans. As such, he was despised by many Jews because they considered him a traitor. Historians debate his motives in switching his allegiance to the Romans. Whatever those motives were, his knowledge of Scripture and the history of the Jews, together with his on-the-scene observation from the Roman side, qualified him in an unusual way to report these events.

The Student section includes a couple of brief quotes from Josephus related to the siege of Jerusalem, but here is another quote you may wish to share with the class:

> "Thus did the miseries of Jerusalem grow worse and worse every day, and the seditious were still more irritated by the calamities they were under, even while the famine preyed upon themselves, after it had preyed upon the people. And indeed the multitude of carcases that lay in heaps one upon another was a horrible sight, and produced a pestilential stench, which was a hindrance to those that would make sallies out of the city and fight the enemy; but as those were to go in battle array, who had been already used to ten thousand murders, and must tread upon those dead bodies as they marched along, so were not they terrified, nor did they pity men as they marched over them; nor did they deem this affront offered to the deceased to be any ill omen to themselves...and now the Romans, although they were greatly distressed in getting together their materials, raised their banks in one-and-twenty days, after they had cut down all the trees that were in the country that adjoined to the city, and that for ninety furlongs round about, as I have already related. And truly the very view itself of the country was a melancholy thing; for those places which were before adorned with trees and pleasant gardens were now become a desolate country every way, and its trees were all cut down; nor could any foreigner that had formerly seen Judea, and the most beautiful suburbs of the city, and now saw it as a desert, but lament and mourn sadly at so great a change; for the war had laid all signs of beauty quite waste; nor if any-one that had known the place before had come on a sudden to it now, would he have known it again; but though he were at the city itself, yet would he have inquired for it notwithstanding." [1]

After the destruction of Jerusalem, the Roman legions advanced on the last hold-out of the Jews at the top of Masada, a high rock promontory built earlier by Herod for his own defense. The battle for Masada, in which it is thought the defenders finally committed mass suicide rather than suffer defeat at the hands of the Romans, was the final death of the Jewish nation. It was not restored until 1948.

Both unbelieving and Christian Jews were scattered throughout the empire. Like sparks from a robust fire, Christians from Jerusalem spread the Gospel everywhere. Within 200 years Christians comprised the majority in many cities and provinces.

Characteristics of Early Christians

Note the summary of five major characteristics of early Christians on page 104 of the Student section. Ask for discussion about these characteristics. How are they similar to the way contemporary culture perceives Christians? How are they different?

Ask for student responses from their assignment (page 108 of the Student section).

An anonymous ancient "Letter to Diognetus," dated from the second century, gives interesting insight into how Christians were perceived at that time. This is part of a letter written by an unknown author, apparently answering a question from a "Diognetus" about Christians. You may wish to share all or part of it with the class:

"Christians are not distinguished from the rest of mankind either in locality or in speech or in customs. For they dwell not somewhere in cities of their own, neither do they use some different language, nor practice an extraordinary kind of life. Nor again do they possess any invention discovered by any intelligence or study of ingenious men, nor are they masters of any human dogma as some are.

"But while they dwell in cities of Greeks and barbarians as the lot of each is cast, and follow the native customs in dress and food and the other arrangements of life, yet the constitution of their own citizenship, which they set forth, is marvelous, and confessedly contradicts expectation.

"They dwell in their own countries, but only sojourners; they bear their share in all things as citizens, and they endure all hardships as strangers. Every foreign country is a fatherland to them, and every fatherland is foreign.

"They marry like all other men and they beget children; but they do not cast away their offspring. They have their meals in common, but not their wives. They find themselves in the flesh, and yet they live not after the flesh.

"Their existence is on earth, but their citizenship is in heaven. They obey the established laws, and they surpass the laws in their own lives.

"They love all men, and they are persecuted by all. They are ignored, and yet they are condemned. They are put to death, and yet they are endued with life.

"They are in beggary, and yet they make many rich. They are in want of all things, and yet they abound in all things. They are dishonoured, and yet they are glorified in their dishonour. They are evil spoken of, and yet they are vindicated.

"They are reviled, and they bless; they are insulted, and they respect. Doing good they are punished as evil-doers; being pushed they rejoice, as if they were thereby quickened by life.

"War is waged against them as aliens by the Jews, and persecution is carried on against them by the Greeks, and yet those that hate them cannot tell the reason of their hostility.

"In a word, what the soul is in a body, this the Christians are in the world. The soul is spread through all members of the body, and Christians through the diverse cities of the world. The soul hath its abode in the body, and yet it is not of the body. So Christians have their abode in the world, and yet they are not of the world." (2)

Early church organization was simple. Elders had the oversight of the synagogues, and the same concept carried over into the church. They were also called "bishops," which means "overseer." Deacons (from the Greek word meaning "servant") assisted elders in their work. "Pastors" (the word means "shepherd") cared for the spiritual needs of the flock. Teachers taught the doctrines of the apostles. The whole church made decisions under the direction and guidance of the Holy Spirit. Note the phrase, "It seemed good to the Holy Spirit and to us…" (Acts 15:28). Everyone in the church carried out the work of the ministry. Pastors and teachers helped equip the saints for their work of ministry (see Eph. 4:11-13).

Justin Martyr gives us a glimpse into what a worship service was like in the second century. He says:

> "On the day called the Day of the Sun all who live in cities or in the country gather together to one place, and the memoirs of the apostles or the writings of the prophets are read, as long as time permits; then, when the reader has ceased, the president verbally instructs, and exhorts to the imitation of these good things. Then we all rise together and pray." [3]

Persecutions

A list and description of the more severe persecutions during this time are cited in the Student section, pages 104 & 105. Review these briefly with the class.

Heresies

Early Christians often found it necessary to "draw a straight line" between truth and error, especially as it related to who Jesus is. The word "orthodox" refers to true belief ("Ortho" means to draw a straight line, and "doxa" means "opinion"). Christians had to clearly define their beliefs because of the proliferation of "heresies," which were schools of thought or sects opposed to orthodoxy. The struggle between orthodoxy and heresy has continually plagued the church to this present day.

The major heresy of the day was a system of belief called "Gnosticism." The word comes from the Greek "gnosis," meaning "to know." Gnostics thought they had everything figured out, and claimed a person could be saved only by being an "insider" to their secret knowledge. Gnostic belief was foundational to a variety of different cults by various names.

Gnosticism was complex and came in many forms. An inherent principle was the belief that spirit is good and matter is evil. Therefore, God, if He is "good," could not be the creator of the universe. He could not be connected with matter. The Gnostics proposed a series of "aeons," or emanations that started with the true god and descended to the material universe. These aeons provided a "buffer" between god and matter. Gnostics worshiped these aeons, which is probably the reason for Paul's warning in Colossians 2:18-19.

Some Gnostic concepts were rooted in ancient Greek philosophy. Heraclitus, Zeno, Philo, and others spoke of a guiding divine mind or principle they called the "Logos" (Greek for "word"). The Logos revealed the deep divine secrets known only to the initiated. This concept, together with a "dualism" taught by Plato, combined with Christian ideas to produce a bizarre belief system. Plato taught that the physical universe was a shadow of the real spiritual world, which he called the world of "ideas." Human souls are from the world of ideas trapped in physical bodies. Death releases us from this material "prison" and allows us to return to the true spiritual world. Gnostics expanded this teaching to mean matter got here by some mistake or the work of an evil being. To become good, you needed to deny the body and everything material.

A diagram may help understand the system better. As time permits, you may wish to share the following diagram with the class:

This is how they told the story:

The "Pleroma" is the fullness of the divine being, represented by the circle. The "Unknown Father" is the true god, who lives with Silence in the Pleroma. He is also known as "The Abyss" and "The Unbegotten." He is pure spirit and is totally unknowable.

This god, together with Silence, produced the aeons "Mind" and "Truth." These aeons, in turn, produced "World-Life" and "Man-Church." Ten more aeons were produced by World-Life and twelve more by Man-Church.

The last aeon to be born from Man-Church was Wisdom. Wisdom desperately wanted to know the Unknown Father, who is unknowable. In her great distress she, without the aid of a male counterpart, gave birth to Achamoth. Because of

The "Pleroma" (Fullness of the divine being)

The "Unknown Father"
The Abyss,
The Unbegotten
(with Silence)

Mind (male) — Truth (female)

World-Life — Man-Church

Ten more "aeons" — Twelve aeons

Wisdom

Achamoth

Demiurge ("Workman")

Achamoth's unnatural birth, she could not remain in the Pleroma and, therefore, fell out of it. Achamoth gave birth to Demiurge, the "Jehovah" of Jews and Christians and the creator of matter.

When Wisdom realized what she had done, she grieved to the point where she was absolutely comfortless, and all the other aeons grieved with her. They appealed to Mind-Truth for help. Mind-Truth, in mercy, created two more aeons: Christ and the Holy Spirit. Then harmony was restored to the Pleroma.

Christ is the Logos, who reveals this knowledge to the world. Those who receive it are the elect, who, when they are released from their material bodies, will return to the Pleroma. Everything material will ultimately be destroyed.

This is a greatly simplified explanation of Gnosticism. It is important for you to know some of this because so many of the early cults were spin-offs of Gnosticism. Docetists, for example, believed Jesus' body was not real. It just "seemed" to be material ("Doce" is Greek for "seem"), somewhat like a ghost. Manichianites, Ebionites, and other cults had their roots in Gnosticism. As you study early heresies (and even modern ones), you will repeatedly discover Gnostic backgrounds. Even some monastic movements, with their emphasis on denying the body, carry shadows of Gnostic teaching.

Scripture clearly refutes these Gnostic ideas. John 1:1 declares that the "Word" (Greek "Logos") is eternal, that He is God, and He is the Creator of the material universe. 1 John 1:1 testifies that He is not a ghost, but one whom "we have seen with our eyes" and "our hands have touched." Notice especially 1 John 4:2, possibly a direct reference to Gnosticism, particularly the cult of Docetism. Moreover, our bodies are not evil, but rather are a "temple of the Holy Spirit" (1 Cor. 6:19).

The church put its belief about who Jesus is into words in the Apostle's Creed, which became a normative statement of Orthodoxy. "I believe in God Almighty, Maker of heaven and earth; And in Christ Jesus, his only Son, our Lord; Who was born of the Holy Spirit and the Virgin Mary…" etc. No doubt about the humanity and deity of Jesus, or of God being the creator of the universe. In the Nicene Creed, the church affirms belief in "…God the Father, Almighty; Maker of heaven and earth, and of all things visible and invisible." Much of the early theology of the church was a direct refutation of Gnostic error.

Early Christian Leaders

As time permits, review the brief descriptions of some of the early Christian leaders given in the Student section. Encourage comments about the contributions these people made to the history of the church and their examples for us. Ask for response to question 3 of the assignment, "Which of the early Christian leaders…would you like to learn more about? Why?"

The Canon of Scripture

The word "canon" is a Latin term meaning "measuring rod" or "index." Used in reference to Scripture, it means the list of books included in the Bible. During this period the New Testament was forming, and certain books were recognized as inspired Scripture while others were not.

In the beginning, not all Christians agreed about which books should be included in the canon. However, as time went on, consensus developed as certain books had a self-authenticating quality about them, were apostolic in origin, and were used in worship. Eventually the Orthodox Church accepted the New Testament as we know it and used it. Today we can go back to several "canons" used by church leaders in the early church and see how this acceptance grew.

The issue of the "apocryphal" books, which still divides the church, arose later. These are the books included in Catholic Bibles today but not in most Protestant Bibles. We will deal with this question in the next lesson.

Emperor Constantine

The conversion of Constantine and his Edict of Milan in A.D. 313 completely turned the issue of religious freedom and the position of Christianity in the empire upside down. Now this despised sect of Christians— persecuted, tortured, and abused, became the favored religion of the empire, financed and courted by politicians and kings. Was this turn of events good or bad for the church? Find out what class members think. We will come back to this question in the next lesson.

LESSON 8

From the Apostles to Constantine

A.D. 70-313

The story of the church begins with Pentecost. Filled with the Holy Spirit, the members of the early church carried the good news of the resurrection across their part of the world. The response was phenomenal. People by the thousands turned to Christ and accepted Him as Lord and Savior.

A tremendously significant event for Judaism and Christianity at this time was the destruction of Jerusalem in A.D. 70. The Jews had been consistently rebellious against their Roman conquerors. Many of them had hoped Jesus would be another Judas Maccabaeus and deliver them from Roman rule. Disappointed that He was not, they continued intermittent rebellion. Finally, the Roman Legions, led by Titus (who later became emperor), invaded Palestine in A.D. 69 with the intent of putting down Jewish rebellion once for all. They surrounded Jerusalem at Passover when a large number of people from the countryside of Judea were in the city. After a long and cruel siege, Jerusalem fell on September 8, A.D. 70.

Josephus, a Jewish scholar and historian who defected to the Romans, provides the most complete record of the unbelievable misery of the Jewish defenders. He traveled with Titus as official historian for the Romans and gives us an eyewitness account of the fall of Jerusalem. He describes mass starvation, with no way to dispose of the bodies except throwing them over the wall or disposing of them through the gates. He claims that "no fewer than six hundred thousand were thrown out at the gates" and he quotes one gatekeeper as claiming that "there had been carried out through that one gate which was entrusted to his care no fewer than a hundred and fifteen thousand, eight hundred and eighty dead bodies."[3]

The siege of Jerusalem ended with the temple's complete destruction. The Romans even tore the stones apart to extract the gold that lay among them. This act fulfilled Jesus' prophecy in Matthew 24:1-2. Only the Western foundation wall was left standing—today's "wailing wall."

The dispersion of Christians from Jerusalem, which had begun earlier, was now complete. Jerusalem was completely destroyed, and the temple site was abandoned. Christians, as well as Jews, dispersed throughout the civilized world. As Christians migrated, they carried the news of the resurrection with them. By the middle of the second century churches flourished in nearly every province of the empire.

Christianity in its early days was definitely a grass roots movement. The common people, not political or religious leaders, were at the heart of the work and carried the Gospel across the empire. (The word "Gospel," means "good news"). One early critic of Christianity, the philosopher Celsus, described Christianity as being composed of "only worthless and contemptible people, idiots, slaves, poor women and children." His criticism reminds us of Paul's words to the Christians in Corinth: "Brothers, think of what you were when you were called. Not many of you were wise by human standards; not many were influential; not many were of noble birth. But God chose the foolish things of the world to shame the wise; God chose the weak things of the world to shame the strong. He chose the lowly things of this world and the despised things— and the things that are not— to nullify the things that are, so that no one may boast before him" (1 Cor. 1:26-29). However, by the end of the second century many of the keenest minds of the day and some of the greatest scholars were Christians.

Much study has gone into trying to understand how Christianity became such a forceful and com-

UNIT II

pelling movement. Many Christians today want to get back to the power and influence of the early church. Of course, the power was spiritual. But it is interesting and informative to study the characteristics of those early Christians. Scholars tell us five important traits describe them and their style of worship:

1) **Simplicity.** Unlike modern denominational and church organization, early church structure seems to be simple. They apparently met in homes, in an environment where "common people" would feel welcome. Their teaching was understandable, even to those without formal education, and there were no complex or secret rituals.

2) **Emphasis on teaching, fellowship, and prayer**. They met together regularly for worship, and an important part of that time was spent instructing people about "the apostles' teaching." (Acts 2:42). They consistently carried out Jesus' final instruction of making disciples and "teaching them..." (Matt. 28:20).

3) **A fellowship of love.** Unlike nearly every other group in their society, the early Christians recognized no class or racial distinctions. Men and women, peasants, slaves, rich and free—all were equally welcome. Outcasts found identity and a sense of belonging in the Christian community. Christians were known for their unusual and friendly hospitality. Their ministry was financed entirely by personal giving, most of which went to help support the needy.

4) **Enthusiastically persuading others to believe.** In contrast to the Jewish attitude of "live and let live," the Christians couldn't stop talking about their faith in the risen Christ and persuading others to join them. They were confident in the truth of their message and the reality of the resurrection.

5) **High moral standards.** In a pagan culture steeped in immorality and injustice, Christians stood out like lights in a dark room. Their insistence on living on a high moral plane and teaching others to do so set them apart as definitely different.

However, the early Christians were not without enemies. Some of their enemies accused them of grossly false things. For example, they were accused of being cannibals (they ate flesh and drank blood), and of immorality (because in their "love feasts" they greeted each other with a "holy kiss."). Many people just couldn't understand them and thought they were some kind of "third race" because they were neither Jewish nor pagan.

The most serious charge of all, however, was the accusation that they were "atheists" and guilty of "treason," because they refused to worship the emperor as god. The Romans, you see, didn't care how many or what gods a person worshiped, as long as the emperor was one of them. Christians refused to worship anyone but the true God. This resulted in severe persecution.

We sometimes have mental images of all early Christians being continually persecuted and fed to the lions. This is not entirely accurate. There were very severe persecutions and many believers died for their faith, but the persecutions were sporadic. It depended on when and where they lived. The major persecutions were:

1) Under Emperor Nero in Rome from A.D. 54 to 68. Christians were crucified, burned at the stake in Nero's garden, dragged to death, or torn to pieces by wild animals, and otherwise killed by the most gruesome and horrible means without distinction of gender or age. It is thought that Nero did this to draw attention away from rumors that he, himself, had set fire to Rome. Nero, in turn, accused the Christians of setting the fire that burned for six days and totally destroyed a large part of Rome. It is probable that Peter and Paul were martyred during this persecution.

2) Under Emperor Domitian around A.D. 95. This persecution began because Domitian instituted a tax to pay for the worship of Jupiter, and both Christians and Jews refused to pay it. Also, Domitian took the title "Master and god," which didn't set well with either Christians or Jews. It was during this persecution that John was exiled to Patmos and wrote the Revelation.

3) In the province of Bithynia when Pliny the Younger was governor, about A.D. 112. Copies of some of the letters Pliny sent to the emperor at the time (Trajan) and the emperor's response still survive. Pliny informed the emperor that he did not seek out Christians to persecute, but if they would openly declare themselves to be Christians, he gave them an opportunity to deny the faith. If they do not, he executed them. The emperor commended Pliny for this policy. Pliny's letters give us some insight as to how Christians worshiped at that time. He wrote that they met before sunrise on Sundays, sang hymns responsively in worship of Christ, pledged themselves to moral conduct, and shared a "holy meal."

4) Under Emperor Marcus Aurelius (A.D. 161-180). He disliked Christians and brought many Christian leaders to Rome for public execution. Executions were also held in the provinces of Gaul and North Africa.

5) Under the Emperor Decius (A.D. 249-251). He required sacrifice to the Roman gods. Those who obeyed were given a certificate of compliance. Those caught without a certificate were subject to imprisonment or execution. Systematic persecution took place throughout the empire. Many church leaders died, including the bishops of Rome, Antioch, and Jerusalem.

6) Under Emperor Valerian (A.D. 253-260). Valerian confiscated the property of church leaders and required them to offer sacrifice to the "old gods." Many refused and were imprisoned or exiled. Some were executed. Christians were forbidden to hold meetings or visit Christian cemeteries on pain of death. He was about to unleash a more extensive persecution of Christians when his plan was interrupted by war with Persia.

7) The "mother of all persecutions" occurred under Emperor Diocletian (A.D. 284-305). Diocletian ordered the cessation of all Christian meetings, the destruction of any buildings where Christian services were held, the deposing of any Christian leaders, burning the Scriptures, confiscation of all property of professing Christians, and imprisonment, slavery, or death of Christians. A historian at the time, Eusebius of Caesarea, reported that the prisons were so overcrowded with Christians there was no room for criminals. The persecution of Christians was so severe that it turned the stomach of even the pagans, many of whom became sympathetic to Christians. Ironically, this most severe persecution in the Roman empire was also the last.

The church faced not only problems from the outside (persecution), but also problems from within in the form of heresy and false teaching. Some of the major heresies to plague the church at the time were:

1) Gnosticism, a belief in the "dualism" between spirit, which was considered good, and matter, which was considered evil. This complex belief system included many sub-divisions. Gnostics believed Jesus was not God because they thought He couldn't be God and physical at the same time. "Gnostic" comes from the Greek word, gnosis, which means "to know." Gnostics felt they possessed superior knowledge.

2) Ebionites, who denied the deity of Jesus. They said Jesus was merely a man who received the fullness of the Spirit at His baptism and became the Messiah.

3) Docetism, which was the opposite of Ebionism. Docetists believed Jesus was God but denied His humanity. Doce is the Greek word for "to seem." They claimed Jesus just seemed human—sort of a ghost. Docetism was a form of Gnosticism.

4) Marcionism, named after its founder, Marcion. He taught that the God of the Old Testament was a different God from the New Testament God. He developed his own bible by rejecting all of the Old Testament and retaining only part of Luke and ten New Testament epistles. This bible is called the "Marcionite Canon."

5) Manicheanism, again named after its founder, Mani of Mesopotamia. He taught a strange doctrine of light and darkness, claiming primitive man was pure light from the Mother of Life in the Kingdom of Light. But he was tricked into darkness by the King of Darkness. Consequently, people have bodies that are darkness. Christ can help the believer get out of the darkness into the light, which included diets of "light" foods and ascetic living. You can see how Mani was influenced by Gnostic teaching.

6) Montanism, which was an extreme reaction to the formalism creeping into the church. Montanus claimed direct inspiration from God for his teachings. He insisted the age of Jesus and the apostles was past, and he was the spokesman for the new age of the Spirit. His teaching caused many churches to split. Montanist meetings were wild—even fanatical.

7) Monarchianism, which was the first Unitarianism. Monarchianism denied that Jesus was a separate person of the Godhead. Two proponents of Monarchianism were Paul of Samasota (bishop of Antioch) and Sabellius. Sabellius taught that God is one person who reveals Himself sometimes as Father, other times as Son, and occasionally as Spirit, similar to an actor wearing different masks and performing different roles. Many people today are Sabellian without knowing it. This view, along with all the others above, was declared heretical in later church councils.

These early centuries of the church are sometimes called "The Age of Catholic Christianity." The term has nothing to do with the Catholic church, as opposed to the Protestant church. This is obvious, since there was no Protestant church at the time. The word "Catholic" simply means "universal." When we use the term in reference to this period it means there was one universal body of believers. There were no organizational divisions in the Christian church. The religious choices of the day were to be in the universal church, in a cult like one of those described above, or in one of the pagan religions.

With persecution from the outside and heresy from within, Christians looked to their leaders to help sort out truth from error and protect them from persecution. This was especially necessary because many ordinary citizens could not read. They depended on their leaders to read and interpret Scripture for them.

In each locality, bishops were recognized as such leaders. Often the bishops would concur with each other. The major centers of Christianity, such as Rome, Caesarea, Antioch, and Alexandria, became prominent in leadership, and so did their bishops. Rome, being the largest church and the capital of the empire, gave the bishops of Rome considerable influence.

Some outstanding Christian leaders lived during this time. Below is a list of a few of them. You are encouraged to read more about them as you have opportunity. You will be blessed!

1) Ignatius, Bishop of Antioch, who was executed in A.D. 110, during Governor Pliny's persecution, wrote seven letters on his way to Rome for his execution. In them he begged Christians in Rome not to try to block his execution because he considered it an honor to die for Christ.

2) Polycarp, Bishop of Smyrna. He had been a disciple of the Apostle John. Polycarp was martyred at the age of 86 in a public stabbing and burning in A.D. 155. The historian, Eusebius, gives a full description of the event. When the Proconsul in charge of the "trial" demanded that Polycarp renounce his faith and curse Christ, Polycarp replied with the immortal statement: "Six and eighty years have I served him, and he has done me nothing but good, and how could I curse him, my Lord and Saviour? If you would know what I am, I tell you frankly, I am a Christian."[4]

3) Justin Martyr, converted from paganism to Judaism and from Judaism to Christ. He became a defender of Christians before the emperor and repeatedly wrote letters to the emperor pointing out the illegality of the persecutions. Justin was martyred in Rome in A.D. 165.

4) Tertullian, a North African lawyer. He was a prolific writer whose major topics were the defense of the faith against both the Roman government and heresy. One of Tertullian's primary concerns was that Christians exemplify high moral character. He was the first to write in Latin, so many of the

terms he used became part of church literature later. He stated: "The blood of the martyrs is the seed of the church."

5) Irenaus, Bishop of Lyon (appointed in A.D. 177). He studied under Polycarp and wrote extensively against Gnosticism. A major theme of his writing was the person of Christ as fully man and fully God.

6) Clement of Alexandria. Clement organized a major center of learning in Alexandria where he invited Gnostics and others with heretical ideas to discuss philosophy. Through these discussions, he led many to Christ. Clement believed the study of philosophy was preparation for Christianity. He had the skill of engaging scholars and people of culture in serious discussion and brought intellectual respectability to Christian belief.

7) Origen, born in Alexandria in A.D. 185, was probably the greatest scholar and most prolific writer of the period. He also taught at the school in Alexandria following Clement and contributed much to biblical scholarship. He later moved to Caesarea, then traveled as sort of a "conflict resolution consultant." Origen added much to the scholarship of the time, but was criticized for two strange doctrines he held: the pre-existence of the soul and universal salvation and an allegorical interpretation of Scripture.

During this time the "canon" of Scripture was being established. "Canon" relates to a Latin term meaning "measuring rod" or "index." In church history we use the word to refer to the list of books Christians accept as genuine Scripture. During these early years of the church, not everyone's list was the same. Gradually, however, the church came to consensus on this issue. Although later church councils put their approval on the books considered by the church to be Scripture, there was never any council or other group that actually made that decision. There was simply a growing acceptance of certain books—the ones that comprise our New Testament today. The issue of the "apocrypahl books" came up later (the additional books in Catholic bibles).

This period of church history comes to a dramatic climax October 28, A.D. 312, when Constantine advanced on Rome, achieved victory over his rival at the Milvian Bridge outside of Rome, became a convert to Christianity and emperor of the Roman Empire. The occasion of his conversion was a dream in which he allegedly saw a cross in the sky with the inscription, "In this sign conquer." Encouraged by the vision to proceed in battle, he was convinced Christ was the true God who gave him victory. Suddenly, the *emperor* was a "Christian"!

Constantine issued the "Edict of Milan" in A.D. 313, establishing freedom of religion and recognizing the Christian day of worship (Sunday) as a legal holiday. He granted innumerable benefits to the church, including money from the imperial treasury and tax exemption for ministers. He built magnificent church buildings at public expense. Also at public expense, he brought bishops from all over the empire together for the first of the major church councils, over which he personally presided. The historian, Eusebius, attended and describes in moving detail the emotions of bishops and other church leaders, some maimed, blinded, or missing limbs because of persecutions they had endured. Now they reclined at a table with the emperor, protected by the Roman legions outside, and they discussed theology. It was an incredible reversal that changed the course of history forever in the Western world!

The debate still rages as to whether this turn of events was good or bad for the church. Think about it. The issue will come up again in the next lesson. The subsequent period of church history was definitely different.

Assignment

It is sometimes said "history repeats itself" and that the state of the church today is increasingly similar to what it was in the early days of church history under the Roman Empire.

From your impressions in reading the above material, write a paragraph or two in response to each of the following questions:

1) How do you think the church of the first three centuries was similar to the church today?

2) In what ways do you think the state of the church today is different from what it was in the days of the Roman Empire?

3) Which of the early Christian leaders mentioned on pages 106 and 107 would you like to learn more about? Why?

Be prepared to share your answers with the class.

LESSON 9

The Early Medieval Church

A.D. 313 - 800

Equipment Needed

1) Chalkboard or whiteboard
2) Map showing locations of Byzantium (Istanbul), Rome, Kiev, and Moscow

Teaching Supplies Needed

1) Copies of Student lesson 10 to distribute to the class.

Lecture

Review Constantine's rise to power and the Edict of Milan from last week's lesson. Then invite the class to suggest benefits to the church of imperial favor by Constantine and succeeding emperors and possible liabilities to the church that came with these benefits. (Refer to the assigned question on page 118 of the Student section). Write the responses on the board as students give them.

Some possible benefits may include:
- Freedom from persecution
- Financial favors
- Prestige
- Positions of influence in government
- Unhindered evangelism

Some liabilities may include:
- Many joining the church who were not truly converted.
- Unconverted "Christians" bringing pagan ideas, holidays, and practices into the church.
- A power struggle between church and state.
- The church, growing in power, prestige and riches, also growing in corruption and serious abuses. Instead of focusing on internal change in people (change of the heart), the church focused on enforcing its mission externally through political power.

Ask the class: Is there any lesson in this scenario for us?

Write responses to discussion question.

Christology

The Student section (pages 115 and 116) gives a brief synopsis of the errant beliefs of the major cults of the time with regard to Christology. Review each of these briefly.

Point out that these teachers, now considered heretical, were struggling to define the person of Christ without the benefit of twenty centuries of study, as we have. They were hammering out definitions for the first time. However, be prepared to explain why the church councils rejected each heresy. Some of the reasons were:

Arianism—The apostles clearly believed Jesus is God. Passages such as John 1:1; 20:28; and many others leave no doubt about this issue. (Mention that this subject will be discussed further in Lesson 15). If Jesus were not divine, He would not be sinless, and therefore could not have died for our sins (Heb. 7:26-28). Arianism was considered directly contrary to the apostles' doctrine and, therefore, heretical.

Apollinarianism—The human personality cannot be dissected so easily into three "parts," because we humans are an organic and spiritual whole. If someone were not human in spirit he would not be human at all. Therefore, claiming Jesus was human in soul and body but divine in spirit makes Him God in the body of some kind of animal. The Council of Constantinople couldn't accept that kind of description and declared Apollinarianism heretical.

Nestorianism—This description of Jesus sounded too much like schizophrenia! The Council of Ephesus declared Jesus to be one person, not two.

Eutychianism—Eutychias' explanation seemed to minimize Jesus' humanity into insignificance. He said Jesus' humanity was absorbed into His deity "like a drop of wine in the sea." The Council of Chalcedon didn't buy that idea because it robbed Jesus of true humanity.

Church councils and subsequent discussions continued to confirm the Nicene Creed, the standard of orthodoxy in both the Eastern and Western churches. They affirmed that Jesus is one person with two natures. He was fully man and fully God.

Call attention to the chart of the four major church councils in the Student section, page 119. Note how each successive church council focused on one of the major heresies described above. In reviewing the Nicene Creed, note how much emphasis is placed on God being the Creator of matter and the humanity as well as the deity of Christ. It was a direct refutation of Gnosticism.

Chart of Church Councils

THE FIRST FOUR ECUMENICAL COUNCILS

Date	Council	Problem Addressed	Conclusion
325	Nicea	Arianism	Christ is fully God
381	Constantinople	Apollinarianism	Christ is fully human
431	Ephesus	Nestorianism	Christ is one person
451	Chalcedon	Eutychianism	Christ has two natures

The Decree of Chalcedon

We all with one voice confess our Lord Jesus Christ one and the same Son, at once complete in Godhead and complete in manhood, truly God and truly man... acknowledged in two natures, without confusion, without change, without division, or without separation; the distinction of natures being in no way abolished because of the union, but rather the characteristic property of each nature being preserved, and coming together to form one person.

The Apocrypha

Christians are naturally curious about why some books are included in Catholic Bibles and not in Protestant Bibles. It is an important question and its roots go deeply into ancient history.

The original Hebrew Bible, the one Jesus and the apostles used, had the same thirty-nine Old Testament books the modern Protestant Bible has. But another Old Testament was in use at the time called the Septuagint. It was a Greek version translated by seventy scholars ("Septuagint" means "seventy"). This translation was completed somewhere around 270-250 B.C. for the benefit of Jews and others who were more fluent in Greek than Hebrew.

Disagreement arises over how and when additional books were added to the Septuagint. These additional books were writings people felt had spiritual benefit and should be included in devotional reading. Some scholars think some or all of them were translated at the same time as the Septuagint. Others think some or all of them were added later. Whatever the case, the Septuagint at the time Jerome translated the Bible into Latin (around A.D. 400) included these "Apocryphal" books. The word "Apocrypha" means "hidden," probably referring to their obscure origin or lesser authority.

Jerome worked on his translation for twenty-three years using both the Septuagint and ancient Hebrew texts as his sources. He did not consider the apocryphal books inspired or having the same level of authority as the original thirty-nine books, but he included them for the benefit of readers who found them spiritually beneficial.

Augustine, the great scholar who was a contemporary of Jerome, felt the apocryphal books should be included in the canon of Scripture. Augustine's influence was great, so during medieval times the apocryphal books were considered part of Scripture.

> **Note:** The word "canon," when used with Scripture, is Latin for "index," meaning the list of books that should be considered Scripture.

Later, during the Reformation, the reformers did not think the apocryphal books should be on the same level of authority as the rest of Scripture and insisted the church should consider only the books of the original Hebrew Old Testament and the New Testament books accepted by the early church as canonical. In reaction, the Roman Catholic Church at the Council of Trent (1546) declared the Vulgate version (Jerome's translation), including the apocryphal books, to be the official and only true version. Since that time we have had Catholic versions and Protestant versions. The Catholic Church no longer uses the term "apocryphal" when referring to these books. They are now called "Deuterocanonical," which means "the second canon."

The number of these apocryphal books changed through history. Some were added; some deleted as the centuries passed. Today there are nine books in the Roman Catholic edition that are not in the Protestant version. They are: Tobit, Judith, an additional section of Esther, 1 and 2 Maccabees, the Book of Wisdom, Ecclesiasticus, Baruch, and an additional portion of Daniel.

The Imperial Move East

Show locations of Rome and Byzantium on map.

Constantine decided to move the capital of the empire from Rome to the city of Byzantium, the seat of the Byzantine Empire, rich in culture and distinctive architecture. The imperial presence in the city made it even more magnificent.

Constantine and successive emperors enriched the city with lavishly beautiful public and religious buildings, including the incredible Church of St. Sophia. Encourage students to find literature, pictures, etc., of ancient Byzantium and share them with the class. Constantine renamed the city Constantinople (no vanity there!), and in recent times it was renamed again as Istanbul.

As a result of the move East, residents and bishops in Rome often felt abandoned by their emperor. Therefore, Roman bishops became more and more influential as political, as well as religious, leaders.

Another result was a growing cleavage between the church in the West, centered in Rome, and the church in the East, centered in Constantinople. The Eastern Church, known as the Eastern Orthodox, eventually divided from the West. The major conflict between the two concerned the issue of "icons," which are images of Christ, the Virgin Mary, a saint, or other representation. To Eastern Orthodox believers, icons are much more than mere symbols. They are actual "gateways to heaven," necessary for true worship and prayer. The use of icons stirred a major controversy. Many people who objected to their use became violent and destroyed icons. They became known as "iconoclasts' (literally, "image breakers").

Locate Constantinople, Kiev, and Moscow on the map.

The Eastern Church also rejected the primacy of the papacy. The two branches of the church are divided on other issues, as well. There are differences in organization and structure, with the Eastern Church governed by regional patriarchs rather than a pope who oversees the entire church. The ecclesiastical center of the Eastern Church gradually moved from Constantinople to Kiev, and finally to Moscow.

The Rise of the Papacy

Ask for student response to question two on page 118 of the Student section. This question should promote some lively discussion. Weave the information below into this discussion.

The development of the papacy in the West grew out of the need for bishops in Rome to provide political as well as spiritual leadership. Protestants generally contend that the concept of the papacy, as we know it, began with Leo I. He succeeded in saving Rome from Attila the Hun and the Vandals. After that event, the bishops in Rome quite naturally assumed power.

Everyone agrees on the list of popes from Leo to the present time. Roman Catholic observers, however, have a list of popes beginning with Peter. They refer to Matthew 16:18-19 for biblical support of Peter as the first pope. Protestants (and Eastern Orthodox) argue that this passage has nothing to do with inaugurating anything like a papacy and the list of names from Peter to Leo is simply a list of Roman bishops, more or less accurate. They insist these early bishops cannot rightfully be called popes because there was no such office recognized at the time. This disagreement will probably never be settled in our lifetime and to engage in the argument with Protestant and Catholic believers is futile. In this class, our purpose is simply to explain the difference of opinion and the reasons for it.

Assist the class in briefly tracing the rise of the papacy. Review the information in the Student section and discuss it with the class.

The Empire of the Franks

Some knowledge of the Empire of the Franks is essential to understand the development of the church in medieval Europe. A brief reference to the Franks appears in the Student section (page 117). If time permits, you may wish to elaborate.

The Franks were a fierce warrior tribe in west Germany and France. Their warriors looked intimidating, with long blond or red hair that fell across their foreheads. Their weapon of choice was a single-edged ax, which they threw like a tomahawk.

The first significant king of the Franks, from the Merovingian family, was Clovis. He became a Christian through the influence of his wife, Clothilda. As was the custom of the day, the entire tribe became Christian, following the decision (and coercion) of the king. As one might expect, these "semi-Christians" brought many pagan practices into the church. There is no reason to doubt the sincerity of Clovis' conversion, but he remained a fierce warrior in the style of the Franks. The Franks' favorite saint was Peter, because Peter knew how to use a sword (John 18:10).

Clovis united the Frankish tribes into a political unit growing in power and influence (France owes its name to the Franks). He supported the church and the church, in turn, gave its approval and support to Clovis.

After Clovis' death, his pleasure-loving sons gave little attention to administration of the government. They left that to the "Mayors of the Palace," a succession of political leaders from the Carolingian family.

The succession of these Carolingian rulers and their significance in church history appears below:

Pepin of Heristal (687-714)

Pepin fought successfully against the Germans and other tribes and established dictatorial rule over a large territory. He gave support to Christian missionaries in his territory. He held absolute rule over the kingdom but allowed the "do nothing" Merovingian kings to retain their titles.

Charles Martel (714-741)

Charles was the son of Pepin of Heristal. During his reign, Muslim armies swept across north Africa and Spain. Martel ("martel" means "the hammer") engaged and defeated the Muslim army at Tours, a city in France. The Battle of Tours (732) stopped the Muslim advance and saved Europe for Christianity.

Pepin the Short (741-768)

Pepin co-ruled with his brother until 747, when his brother entered a monastery. Pepin appealed to the pope, suggesting the true rulers (the Carolingians) should be recognized as kings, rather than the Merovingians, who still held the title but did nothing. The pope agreed, and commissioned the missionary, Boniface, to crown Pepin "King of the Franks" in 751. Three years later the pope awarded

List the Kings of the Merovingian and Carolingian families on the board, with their dates, as you describe them.

Locate the city of Tours, France on the map.

Pepin an even higher title, "Chosen of the Lord." Pepin reciprocated by sending an army to drive the Lombards out of Italy. Pepin then gave the church a large strip of territory across central Italy known as "The Donation of Pepin." This was the beginning of the papal states, accepted as an actual nation, ruled by the Vatican. The papal states today, however, are much smaller than Pepin's original donation.

Charlemagne (Charles the Great; 768-814)

Charlemagne was the greatest (and the last significant) king of the Franks—possibly the greatest king ever in medieval Europe. His innovations in administration, advancements in culture, and development of education, are known as the "Carolingian Renaissance." He was learned in music, astronomy, and the arts, and he established universities, some of which still exist as national universities in Europe. He required the clergy to be educated, and his favorite book was Augustine's City of God. He, for the first time, ruled on the basis of written law, and set up a system of governors over provinces with inspectors insuring conformity to the law and holding semi-annual conferences for communication and control. His territory included Germany, northern Spain, Austria, Italy and France.

Charlemagne enjoyed the full support of the church. He insisted the state and the church were two arms of the same body. He also used the analogy of the church as the soul and the state as the body of humanity. The papacy was thrilled with his view. On Christmas day, 800 A.D., Pope Leo III crowned Charlemagne "Emperor of the Romans." The centuries-old dream of the revival of the Roman Empire was now realized. But it was no longer just the Roman Empire; it was the "Holy Roman Empire."

After Charlemagne's death, the Holy Roman Empire continued to exist but began to fragment and decline. The relatively good will between church and state during Charlemagne's reign also began to decline and finally degenerated into continual conflict. In the 1700s the cynical French philosopher, Voltaire, ridiculed the Holy Roman Empire as being "neither holy, Roman, nor an empire."

Inform the class that the next lesson will include discussion of the great cathedrals of Europe. Suggest that if anyone has visited any European cathedrals, she should come prepared to tell about it and bring pictures, if possible.

LESSON 9

The Early Medieval Church

A.D. 313 - 800

The word "medieval" derives from a Latin term meaning "middle." In reference to church history, it refers to the Middle Ages, the period of church history from the early church to the modern church. It has a character all its own.

Historians differ about when the Middle Ages started and ended. Some say it didn't start until A.D. 600 and ended around A.D. 1500. There is justification for claiming any of these dates because significant events occurred at all of these times, and they changed the course of church history. For our purposes, we are bracketing the time from the Edict of Milan (A.D. 313) to the first glimmers of Reformation (the 14th century) and calling it the Medieval Church period. This lesson covers the first half of the Medieval Period.

The usual study of church history in our part of the world (and this course follows the "usual") is quite limited to the Western Church. Paul's missionary journeys led to the development of the church in Asia Minor and Europe. The American church descends from this heritage. Other branches of the church exist on other continents, as well, so we should be aware that this study of church history is really only part of the total story, but it is the part that most affects us in our time and place.

As you read through the sordid story of events in the palaces and high places, don't forget that hundreds of thousands of common people were serving the Lord quietly and faithfully in the villages and countryside. Many of them did not make headlines or find their way into history books, but the faithful members of God's people have always been there.

We will approach this period of history by breaking it down into four sections: 1) The early period, 2) The Imperial move East, 3) The Rise of the Papacy, and 4) the Holy Roman Empire.

The Early Period

Falling into Imperial favor, the church benefited by elaborate church buildings provided by the emperor. Suddenly it was "fashionable" to be a Christian, and many people came into the fellowship of Christians to gain respect and prestige. Slowly, the official policy of Rome evolved from religious liberty to Christianity becoming the official religion of the empire, with pagans finding themselves the persecuted.

During this period, the church wrestled with a definition of who Jesus is. The study of the person of Jesus is called "Christology." Several views on Christology emerged that differed from the teaching of the apostles. These included:

Arianism, a persistent cult that plagued the church for hundreds of years, and still exists under different names. Arius taught that Jesus was not God, but was the highest of created beings. Jesus, Arius insisted, ranked lower than God but higher than man. Arius was very influential because he was an excellent communicator and made up jingles that sailors and others sang as they rowed their boats or worked on the docks. The jingles, of course, promoted his beliefs, much like modern commercials.

Apollinarianism, named after Appollinarius, pastor at Laodicea. Apollinarius believed man is made up of three parts; body, soul, and spirit. Jesus, he taught, was human in His body and soul, but divine only in His spirit.

Nestorianism, named for Nestorius, Bishop of Constantinople. Nestorius taught that Jesus was two persons in one body—a divine and a human personality.

Eutychianism, named after the leader of a monastery near Constantinople, who insisted Jesus was one nature, not two, but that the human nature was simply absorbed by the divine.

You would be hard pressed to remember all these strange names, of course, but it is good to have some idea of the struggle these early Christians went through in trying to define the person of Christ. Because of the disagreements, Constantine thought it wise to bring church leaders together from around the empire so they could come to a consensus. He was probably much more interested in the empire's unity than in doctrine. At a council in the city of Nicea in A.D. 325, Arianism was rejected as heretical because it denied the deity of Christ. To this day, the declaration of Jesus' deity is remembered in churches with the recitation of the Nicene Creed.

Subsequent emperors convened other councils. The second was held in Constantinople in A.D. 381, where Apollinarianism was rejected; the third at Ephesus in 431, where Nestorianism was rejected; and the fourth major one was in Chalcedon in 451, where Eutychianism was rejected. Orthodox doctrine has always held that Jesus is one person with two natures, both fully man and fully God.

Two outstanding individuals in this early period need to be mentioned. One is Jerome (340-420), who translated the Old and New Testaments into Latin. This became the Vulgate version, the authorized translation of the Roman Catholic Church until Vatican II (1962-65). The other is Augustine, a very influential scholar and church leader.

About 600 years before Jerome and Augustine's time, (around 250 B.C.) a translation of the Hebrew Bible was completed for the benefit of Jews in Egypt and North Africa who were more literate in Greek than Hebrew. This translation was called the Septuagint, meaning "seventy," because according to legend seventy scholars completed the translation in seventy days. The Septuagint became a standard text for Greek speaking people for centuries.

Jerome used not just the Septuagint but also original Hebrew texts in translating the Old Testament. As a result, he produced an excellent translation for its time.

The original Hebrew Old Testament had thirty-nine books, the same number as found in Protestant Bibles today. Gradually, other books were added to the canon of the Septuagint because they were considered to have spiritual value. These became known as the "Apocrypha, or "hidden" books. Jerome translated some of these, but considered them to be of less value than the original and not inspired. Augustine, however, felt they should be included in the Canon. The argument never died. During the Reformation, the Protestant church did not include these Apocryphal books in the Bible. The Roman Catholic Church, however, declared in the Council of Trent (A.D. 1546) that they should be included. It is worthy to note that Jesus and the apostles never quoted from the apocryphal books.

Augustine was one of the greatest scholars in the history of the church. He was Bishop at Hippo in North Africa during the latter part of the fourth century. Struggling with the unbelievable destruction of Rome, the eternal city, Augustine wrote the monumental classic, The City of God. His teachings were foundational to the growing doctrine of the church, both Protestant and Catholic.

The Imperial Move East

Emperor Constantine felt it best to move the seat of the empire from Rome to Byzantium, a strategically located city at the narrow southwest entrance to the Black Sea, an area in which the richest culture of the world flourished. Byzantine culture and architecture are still much admired. Constantine changed the name of the city to Constantinople (for obvious reasons) and embellished it with beautiful buildings and churches. It held the name Constantinople until 1930, when the name officially changed to Istanbul (Turkey).

The move east caused division in the church between the Western Church (Roman Catholicism and what became European/American Protestantism) and the Eastern Church (Eastern Orthodox). Differences in doctrine, practice, and church structure became more pronounced. Also, the bishops of Rome and other major cities in the West often felt abandoned by the emperors, who were hundreds of miles away to the East.

The Rise of the Papacy

In the West, the bishops of the major cities, especially Rome, assumed constantly greater powers of leadership. This was often by necessity, as these bishops guided the church and became involved in political issues.

Leo I, Bishop of Rome from 440 to 461, found himself catapulted into the political spotlight by his brave defense of the city. In 451 Attila the Hun threatened Rome. Largely abandoned by the emperor and the imperial army in faraway Constantinople, Leo single-handedly took on Attila. In face-to-face negotiation he persuaded Attila to spare the city and leave Italy, which Attila agreed to do. Suddenly Leo was not only bishop, but the political savior and undisputed leader of the church in the West.

Only three years later, the Vandals from Scandinavia approached Rome. Again, Leo came to the rescue. He met Gaiseric, the leader of the Vandals at the city gate and begged for mercy. Listening quietly, Gaiseric finally called out "Fourteen days' looting!" After the two weeks of looting, the residents of Rome breathed a sigh of relief. The city had been spared, although churches, homes, the palace, and other treasures had been hauled away on Vandal ships.

Leo had come to power as the Pontifex Maximus, the old title for high priest of religion throughout the empire. Protestants trace the beginning of the papacy to Leo. Roman Catholics disagree, tracing the succession of bishops of Rome back to Peter.

In A.D. 590 Gregory I was appointed Pope. He assumed the position at a very difficult time of floods, wars, and plagues, and did not want to accept the office. He was an excellent administrator, great preacher, prolific writer, humble, with an honest and deep spiritual concern for the faithful. But he was often given to depression. He called himself "the servant of the servants of God."

Gregory influenced the practices in the Western Church more than any other pope. He was a defender of orthodoxy, a Latin scholar, but not learned in theology or the original languages of the Bible (Greek and Hebrew). He had great skill in training bishops and others in pastoral care and wrote a book to guide pastors in such ministries.

However, many of the practices of the Roman Catholic Church that Protestants object to can be traced to Gregory. He taught that baptism gives forgiveness of sins to that point in time, but penance is necessary for subsequent sins. He believed in the help of saints in prayer, relics as aids to devotion, and purgatory as an intermediate state to prepare for heaven. He also believed the Eucharist (Communion) has power in itself to make one holy, and man must cooperate with God's grace to earn merit by good works.

From the late fifth to the beginning of the ninth centuries, the Empire of the Franks was developing in Western Europe. The Franks were sympathetic to and cooperative with the church. They even provided military assistance to the Papacy. The Papacy, in turn, gave support and prestige to the kings of the Franks. This fit well with a widespread popular longing for revival of the old Roman Empire. The "marriage" of Frankish political power and the church came to a climax with Charlemagne (Charles the Great) who reigned from 768 to 814. On Christmas day, A.D. 800, Pope Leo III crowned Charlemagne "Emperor of the Romans."

Charlemagne's empire and his rule were magnificent and became known as the "Carolingian Renaissance," because Charlemagne was from the family of the Carolingians. Charlemagne governed by law rather than an absolute dictatorship. He developed an efficient system of administration, started schools, encouraged the clergy to receive an education, and generally led the empire and the culture toward one of the highest and most respectable governments in the world's history. Church and government were united in a cooperative effort. It marked the height of the Holy Roman Empire.

Sadly, after Charlemagne's death the empire began to disintegrate and never did develop into anything comparable to ancient empires. Centuries later the French philosopher, Voltaire (1694-1778), derided it as being "neither holy, Roman, nor an empire." In the next lesson we will trace this decline, the reasons for it, and see how the stage was set for the Protestant Reformation.

Assignment

Write a paragraph or two as you respond to each of the following questions. Be prepared to share your answers with the class:

1) Do you think Constantine's imperial favor to the church was a good or a bad event? Why?

2) Why do you think the Papacy grew to such a powerful office in the Western Church during the early medieval period? The Eastern (Orthodox) Church rejected the concept of a Papacy. Which do you think was right? Why?

Date	Council	Problem Addressed	Conclusion
325	Nicea	Arianism	Christ is fully God
381	Constantinople	Apollinarianism	Christ is fully human
431	Ephesus	Nestorianism	Christ is one person
451	Chalcedon	Eutychianism	Christ has two natures

The Decree of Chalcedon

We all with one voice confess our Lord Jesus Christ one and the same Son, at once complete in Godhead and complete in manhood, truly God and truly man... acknowledged in two natures, without confusion, without change, without division, or without separation; the distinction of natures being in no way abolished because of the union, but rather the characteristic property of each nature being preserved, and coming together to form one person.

LESSON
10
The Late Medieval Church
A.D. 800-1350

Equipment Needed

None

Teaching Supplies Needed

1) Copies of student lesson 11 to distribute to the class.

This lesson is structured around four topics:
1. The Great Cathedrals
2. Late Medieval Church Leadership
3. The Crusades
4. The Inquisition

Lecture
The Great Cathedrals

During the Middle Ages every city in France and Germany worthy of its name built a church or cathedral and competed with its neighbors for having the highest spire. Mention the literal meaning of the word "cathedral" is "the church where the bishop is in residence." However, the word is commonly used loosely to refer to any large and impressive church building.

Pictures of great European cathedrals may be helpful.

Point out the difference between Romanesque and Gothic styles. Romanesque features large, heavy, internal pillars, not very tall, and smaller internal rooms. The flying buttresses of Gothic style allowed slender pillars, great heights, huge wall space for windows, and wide, open internal space.

Ask anyone who has visited a cathedral to share their experience.

Invite discussion about the "Point to Ponder" on page 126 of the Student section. The application to current times is obvious. Is it justifiable to build elaborate and highly decorated church buildings in our day? There may be no "right" or "wrong" answer to the question, but the discussion should reflect common sense and balance.

Late Medieval Church Leadership

Discuss the development of the sacraments and the intellectual pursuits of scholars like Thomas Aquinas, who attempted to reconcile faith with logic. Because the issue of "Sacramental Theology" will be addressed again in Lesson 17, don't go into great lengths about it now.

The papacy of Innocent III (in office from 1198 to 1216) reflected, without doubt, the height of papal power. Claiming primacy on the basis of being the successor of Peter and the "Vicar of Christ," Innocent III exercised unbelievable (to us!) rule over kings and authorities. He considered himself the authority over the state as well as the church and even voided an election in Germany when his favorite candidate lost. When he was at odds with the King of England in 1212, he declared the English throne vacant and invited the French to invade.

Innocent called for the Fourth Lateran Council (1215), which put the stamp of approval on his autocratic rule. This Council is also known for its anti-Semitism. Jews were largely ostracized from society and required to wear a special badge.

Draw a contrast between the arrogance of papal authority and the gentle ministry of monks like Francis of Assisi.

The fourteenth century "Great Schism" of the church is described on page 127 of the Student section. Draw attention to it. All of these events and the corresponding corruption in the church contributed greatly to the reaction demonstrated in the Reformation.

The Crusades

A list of the crusades is provided on pages 127 & 128 of the Student section. Simply make a few statements about the overall results of the crusades (page 128), and give opportunity for student response. You may want to offer time to briefly discuss the statement on page 127 about the Crusades coming in response to 400 years of Islamic invasions. Thanks to Islamic terrorism in our day, the motivation for the Crusades is better understood. Of course, that doesn't justify them.

The Inquisition

In the twelfth and thirteenth centuries, the papacy was alarmed by what it perceived to be growing heresy within Europe. From a Protestant evangelical point of view, some of these movements were, indeed, heretical, but others were simply efforts to return to the simple Gospel and a rejection of what they considered to be unbiblical practices in the church and the authoritarianism and corruption common in church leadership at that time.

To counter the perceived heretical movements, Pope Alexander III in 1162 called on secular rulers to help combat heresy. In 1179 he announced a new crusade—this one against heretics in France.

From this beginning, the Inquisition took a dire turn. Subsequent popes enlarged and intensified the Inquisition, and the fear of the inquisitor spread across Europe.

Many convicted heretics were punished, imprisoned, or burned at the stake. Legal defenses against charges by the inquisitor were minimal or non-existent.

The Inquisition, added to the "Great Schism," the sale of indulgences to support papal wars, the "dispensing of grace" for money, the arrogance of the popes, and rampant abuse and exploitation, finally led to reformation. Point out, however, that the faults of the church evident in human leadership were not necessarily typical of the church at large, if we think of the church as the entire body of God's people. Faithful, concerned, and spiritually oriented people have always been at the heart of the church. They were the ones who finally called a halt to the abuse.

The next lesson is about the Reformation. The various reformers would not have had any success if there was not a universal groundswell of discontent already present among the common people of Europe.

LESSON 10
The Late Medieval Church
A.D. 800-1350

Under the Holy Roman Empire, Europe became a "Christian community." The church was not only the religious center, but also the center of political and economic life. The spires of the local cathedral stood tall above all other village buildings and served as a gathering place for everyone from kings to peasants.

This period witnessed great expansion of commerce, massive building projects, advances in scholarship, and an exploding population. Overall, the population tripled. In some of the wealthiest areas it multiplied tenfold.

The Cathedrals of Europe

This was the age of great cathedral building. The cathedrals, many of them still in use today, demonstrated the attempt by Christians to create a place of worship that would lift the spirit into the presence of God and open the windows of heaven to the worshiper. It was as though a cathedral was suspended between heaven and earth—a mystical place where the drudgery of ordinary life could be set aside and the soul brought into communion with God.

Technically, the term "cathedral" means the church where the bishop was resident, regardless how humble. However, in common usage, the term is often applied to large and impressive churches.

The early cathedrals' style was Romanesque. Built using Roman architectural style with large, heavy internal pillars, they were strong and stable, but not very tall. Further, they were quite dark inside with many internal divisions of space. In the 12th century a new style, called "Gothic," evolved, which transferred the weight of the roof and upper arches to flying buttresses outside the building. This change allowed for much taller structures with huge window spaces, slender internal pillars, and large open spaces, because now the support of the building no longer rested entirely on the walls and pillars.

The Gothic style triggered aggressive building projects in the next two centuries. It is claimed more stone was quarried for churches in France alone than all the stone quarried in ancient Egypt. Rivalries erupted among cities, with each town and village seeking to outdo its neighbors with a larger, more spectacular cathedral. The structures commonly exceeded 100 feet in height. The tower of the Cologne Cathedral in Germany (begun in A.D.1248) soars 512 feet into the sky. The Cathedral at Chartres in France boasts 300,000 square feet (about 7 acres!) of stained glass windows. Some of the cathedrals exceeded medieval engineering capabilities and collapsed during or shortly after construction.

The cathedrals were adorned with awesome works of art that were more than just decoration. Through the artistry of statues, images, stained glass, and other media, the clergy attempted to relate spiritual truths and Bible stories to illiterate people.

A Point to Ponder

The cathedrals of Europe are considered by some to be examples of deep spiritual commitment to the Lord, offering beautiful places of worship for everyone, regardless of social status. Perhaps they demonstrate the kind of art and architecture we should have more of in our plain and practical age.

On the other hand, critics say the cathedrals exhibited worldly pride and carnal rivalry, and were built at a horrible waste of money and resources that could have been better used to help the many peasants and other poor people in medieval Europe.

What do you think? Ponder this a bit and be prepared to share your thoughts with the class.

Church Leadership

Europe at this time was seeking to recover from the "Dark Ages," so called because it was a time of intellectual stagnation, poverty, and cultural decline. However, universities were established and scholars like Peter Abelard and Thomas Aquinas were struggling with the great issues of the relationship of logic and faith. Aquinas (A.D.1225-74) was a prolific writer. His famous *Summa Theologiae* attempted to summarize all theology and used human logic to support Christian faith. This massive and comprehensive work became the standard for Catholic theology and a source of much theological discussion, both Catholic and Protestant, and continues as such to the present day. In 1879 the pope declared Aquinas' theology "eternally valid."

This was also the time when the theology of the sacraments was refined and developed. The concept that the wine and bread actually become the body and blood of Christ when consecrated by the priest had been growing in acceptance since around A.D. 1000. Finally, at the Fourth Lateran Council (A.D. 1215) this doctrine of Transubstantiation was declared to be the official position of the church. Along with this belief, the understanding of baptism as the means of salvation coupled with the doctrine of original sin caused enormous pressure for baptism to be applied to infants soon after birth.

The Fourth Lateran Council and the writings of Aquinas organized and summarized the sacraments. As late as the twelfth century, theologians listed as many as thirty sacraments. Eventually, they reduced them to seven: baptism, confirmation, the Eucharist, penance, extreme unction, ordination, and matrimony.

On the more practical side, monks and others in the countryside were applying the principles of poverty and simplicity to work out their faith. This was the time of Francis of Assisi (A.D. 1182-1226) who obtained approval from Pope Innocent III to begin a group called the "Friars Minor" (Lesser Brothers). These friars went about preaching and caring for the poor and sick. It is said that even the animals enjoyed Francis's preaching. He is often depicted in works of art with animals at his side. Francis's prayer is often repeated:

Lord, make me an instrument of thy peace.
Where there is hatred, let me sow love;
Where there is injury, pardon;
Where there is doubt, faith;
Where there is despair, hope;
Where there is sadness, joy.
O Divine Master, grant that I may not so much seek to be consoled as to console;
Not so much to be understood as to understand;
Not so much to be loved as to love;
For it is in giving that we receive;
It is in pardoning that we are pardoned;
It is in dying that we awaken to eternal life.

In contrast to the simple and humble ministry of Francis of Assisi and many like him, papal authority grew in power and riches. The height of papal power (and arrogance) came under the rule of Innocent III

(A.D. 1198-1216). Intelligent and highly educated, Innocent III studied philosophy and theology in Paris and canon and civil law in Italy.

Innocent III had an exalted view of his office. He saw himself as a mediator between God and man, even above civil authority. He considered himself to be as the sun, the source of light. The emperor was compared to the moon that reigns only by reflected light. Innocent did not consider himself accountable to anyone but God.

Innocent's weapons to keep the political rulers and others in line were excommunication and the interdict. Excommunication was applied to individuals who would then be deprived of the means of salvation. The interdict was similar, but applied to cities or nations. The arrogant power of the papacy at this time caused seeds of rebellion that later tore the Western Church apart.

The papacy reached the height of absurdity when in 1305 Clement V, a Frenchman, was elected pope. He chose to move the papacy to Avignon, France, as did his six French successors for 70 years. This angered many of the faithful in the empire, who were determined to move the papacy back to Rome, calling the French papacy "The Babylonian Captivity of the Papacy." In 1377 Pope Gregory XI moved back to Rome but died within the year. A political power play followed between French and Italian cardinals resulting in two popes—one in Italy and the other in France. This is called "the Great Schism" in Roman Catholic church history.

Finally, the political leaders called an empire-wide council to depose both popes and elect a new one. Neither of the two former popes would abdicate, so now there were three popes. Lacking support, the two original ones finally lost power and the church was back to a single pope.

During this time abuses abounded. Popes sold indulgences to finance armies to fight each other. Church and State competed for power and influence. Many faithful Christians abandoned the traditional church and called for a return to poverty and simplicity. Some of these formed brotherhoods within the church. Others formed groups outside the church, sometimes at great cost of personal safety.

The Crusades

The attempt of popes and some lay Christians during the 12th and 13th centuries to wrest control of the Holy Land from Muslim invaders has been a source of embarrassment to the church ever since. A series of Crusades scarred the history of Europe, the story of the church, and the lives of those who participated.

It must be remembered, however, that the Papacy was responding to appeals from the Eastern emperor to halt the persecution of Christians by Muslims and Seljuk Turks. It was intolerable to think that the Holy Land should fall victim to these invaders. Consequently, Christians in the West responded in good faith.

A short summary of the crusades includes:

First Crusade
This crusade was the most successful, actually conquering Jerusalem and a long strip of coastal land along the Mediterranean. Crusaders established the "Feudal Latin Kingdom of Jerusalem."

Second Crusade
Accomplished nothing.

Third Crusade
Fredrick of Germany, Richard the Lion Hearted of England, and Philip Augustus of France combined to lead this crusade. Frederick drowned, and Richard and Philip fought each other. Finally, Richard and the Muslim leader, Saladin, agreed to a three-year truce with free access to Jerusalem.

Fourth Crusade
Diverted to attack Constantinople instead of conquering Jerusalem. The crusaders ravaged the city that was supposed to be their ally.

UNIT II

The Children's Crusade

The saddest of all crusades came about when church leaders determined their inability to defeat the Muslims was due to their personal sinfulness. Children, it was decided, are innocent, and therefore would have a greater spiritual power. So 50,000 children were mobilized for this crusade, most of whom died on their way to the East or were sold into slavery.

The 5th, 6th, and 7th Crusades all ended in defeat.

The results of the Crusades can be summarized in five statements:

1) They led to bloody atrocities, sometimes to their own people.
2) They caused a permanent animosity between East and West and between Christians and Muslims.
3) Returning crusaders brought Eastern ideas and philosophies into Europe, much to the dismay of the church.
4) They caused a backlash of reform within the church by people sick of the violence and politics.
5) They led to the decline of the Papacy.

The Inquisition

Seeking to stem the tide of reform and rebellion within the Western Church, Pope Lucius III ordered bishops to "inquire" into the beliefs of members of their parishes. They would hold an inquest, seeking out heresy or disloyalty. In 1220, this court of inquiry was assigned to the Dominicans to carry out.

The inquisitor was given absolute power to pass judgment, responsible only to the pope. The inquisition would be held in secret and the subject was required to prove his innocence. Finally, in 1252, Pope Innocent IV authorized torture of the accused to gain information.

The abuses of the inquisition are legendary and the horrors unimaginable. The irony at the close of this age is that when the church was at its height of political power, the spiritual sensitivity of its leaders was at its lowest point. The winds of reform were beginning to move. Next week's study discusses the Reformation and the brave men and women who changed the course of church history in the West.

Assignment

What can we learn from medieval church history that might apply to the government and practice of the church today? Write a few sentences below to summarize your thoughts and be prepared to share your answers with the class.

LESSON

The Reformation

A.D. 1350-1550

Equipment Needed	Teaching Supplies Needed
1) Chalkboard or whiteboard 2) Classroom map of Europe	1) Copies of student lesson 12 to distribute in class.

This lesson and those that follow cover a relatively short period of time, compared to Lessons 9 and 10. However, they cover very important periods because they set the stage for understanding how we "got to where we are" in the present state of the church. One of our teaching objectives in this section of the series is for students to be able to look through the Yellow Pages of their telephone directory under "Churches," and trace the background of each major denomination represented.

It will be helpful to relate developments during the Reformation by both individual reformers and by their locations in Europe. As you discuss this material with the class, repeatedly show the geographical "big circle," starting in England, moving through Bohemia, Germany, Switzerland, Holland, Scotland, and back to England. Some of your students may have visited sites in Europe related to the Reformation. If so, invite them to share their experience.

Lecture

Each of the reformers in this lesson made a major contribution toward purifying the doctrines and practices of the medieval church. There is so much information available about each reformer that whatever background reading you do in church history or general history books will be helpful. Before your lecture begins, ask each student to name the reformer they thought was most significant (from their assignment). When you talk about that reformer, ask the students who chose him to explain briefly why they selected him.
In a sentence, the major contributions of each were:

Wycliffe (England)
Making the Scriptures available for everyone, and calling for a return to the simplicity of early church doctrine and practice.

Hus (Bohemia)
Similar to Wycliffe's emphasis, but Hus' martyrdom gave new energy to the Reformation movement.

Luther (Germany)

The biblical principle of justification by faith rather than works, without the intermediary of church, priests, pope, and sacraments.

Zwingli (Switzerland)

Communion as a symbol and commemoration only, rather than having sacramental value in dispensing grace to the recipient. His *Sixty-seven Articles* emphasized salvation by faith, the headship of Christ in the church, the authority of the Bible, and the right of clergy to marry.

Calvin (Switzerland) –

His monumental writing, *Institutes of the Christian Religion*, a comprehensive summary of Reformed doctrine guided much of the development of Protestant theology in the West. In his writings, Calvin placed heavy emphasis on the sovereignty of God.

Knox (Scotland)

Carried Calvinism to Scotland, with the subsequent development of the Presbyterian Church.

The Anabaptists (Switzerland and Holland)

Emphasis on "believer's baptism," meaning only those old enough to make a personal profession of faith are proper candidates for baptism.

Diagram Henry VIII's family relationships on the whiteboard and list his wives.

King Henry VIII (England)

Henry ruled from 1509 to 1547. His involvement in the Reformation was more political and personal than theological. The court and personal life of Henry VIII and those of related monarchs of the time were quite complex, and students are usually curious about how it all fits together. If you have resources, such as history books covering this period, some background reading would be helpful before trying to explain this to the class. In brief, it goes something like this:

1. Henry VIII's father, Henry VII, tried to build good relations with his neighbors through marriages. His daughter, Margaret, married James, King of Scotland. (Margaret's great-grandson, James VI of Scotland, became James I of England in 1603. He authorized the King James translation of the Bible). Henry VII's other son, Arthur, married a Spanish princess, Catherine of Aragon. When Arthur died, his father insisted that his son, Henry VIII, marry Catherine. He and Catherine had one child, a daughter, Mary, who later reigned as Queen Mary I (1553-1558). She is also known as Mary Tudor. Because of her intense persecution of Protestants during her reign, she is often referred to as Bloody Mary.

2. Henry VIII was frustrated because he did not have a male child. He claimed this was because he had violated the commandment in Leviticus 20:21 by marrying his brother's widow. He asked Pope Clement VII to approve a divorce from Catherine. Clement refused, probably influenced in part by the fact that Clement was under the political control of Catherine's nephew, the powerful Charles V, ruler of Spain and emperor of Germany.

3. Henry VIII's desire for a divorce was no doubt motivated by more than concerns of succession and commandments of Scripture. It turns out he was desperately in love with Anne Boleyn, a lady of his court.

4. After long and protracted legal and political maneuverings, Henry finally broke the Church of England away from papal control and put it under his own control. This cleared the way for his divorce and legal marriage to Anne Boleyn. They had one daughter who later became Queen Elizabeth I (1558-1603).

5. After three years, Henry accused Anne of adultery and had her beheaded. He then married Jane Seymour. With Jane, Henry finally had a son, who later became King Edward VI (1547-1553). Jane died in childbirth. Edward became king at age ten and died at age sixteen.

6. Henry then married Ann of Cleves, a German princess, whom he divorced after a few months.

7. His next marriage was to Catherine Howard, an English girl only nineteen years old. She, too, was beheaded less than two years after the marriage.

8. His final marriage was to Catherine Parr, the widow of an English nobleman. She survived Henry!

All of this just to point out that Henry VIII's involvement in the Reformation, unlike the other reformers, was not motivated by doctrinal, ethical, or moral concerns. It was primarily political and personal. Henry, though claiming to be Protestant, held to the doctrines and practices of the medieval church. In fact, before all this mess happened, a grateful pope gave Henry the title, "Defender of the Faith," because of his attacks on Luther.

The final result of Henry's actions was the formation of the Church of England, known to us in America as the "Anglican," or "Protestant Episcopal" Church. It is similar to the Roman Catholic Church in practice, but without allegiance to the Pope. In England, the church is under the control of the British monarchy through the Archbishop of Canterbury. The "Anglican Communion" in various countries today is united around their common acceptance of *The Thirty-Nine Articles*. This doctrinal statement dates from the time of Henry VIII, and has been developed and modified over time, reflecting Catholic, Lutheran, and Calvinist influence.

Review the lives and contributions of each of these reformers, allowing ample time for discussion and questions. These early years of Reformation set the stage for the American Protestant church today.

Use the chalkboard to list the four major branches of the Protestant church that have come down to us from the Reformation. All four have their beginnings in this period. They are:

1. Lutheran (Martin Luther)
2. Reformed (Calvin, Zwingli, Knox)
3. Anglican (Henry VIII)
4. Anabaptist (Grebel, Manz, Menno Simons)

Write the four branches of the Reformation on the whiteboard.

Students must be familiar with these four branches in order to understand the remaining portion of church history.

The hallmarks of the Reformation (with the possible exception of early Anglican) were:

Write on whiteboard:
1) Salvation by faith
2) Scripture as authority
3) Definition of church
4) Priesthood of believer

1. Salvation is based on the work of Christ, made effective in the believer by faith.

2. Scripture is the supreme authority in faith and practice.

3. The "church" is defined as the body of believers who belong to Christ, not as the Papacy or other ecclesiastical authority.

4. Every individual believer may come to Christ directly, without priest, church, or sacramental intermediary. Luther called this the "priesthood of the believer," based on 1 Peter 2:4-10.

If students ask where the term "Protestant" came from, inform them that it dates from the Diet (assembly) of Spier in Germany in 1529, which declared Roman Catholicism to be the only official church in Germany. Some German princes, followers of Luther, entered a *Protestation* (a dissenting opinion) into the proceedings. Thereafter, they were called "Protestants."

LESSON 11

The Reformation
A.D. 1350-1550

The dates we include with the lesson titles are arbitrary. Reformation occurred throughout the history of the church, and continues today. The Holy Spirit constantly works through His people to cleanse and purify the church. However, during the 200 years covered in this week's lesson, there was so much anger and dismay about the abuses in and by the church, that "everything not nailed down was coming loose." A general uprising of Christian people demanded the church return to the principles of Scripture, and the Bible be made available to common people. We call this period the Reformation, and the people who led the charge are known in church history as the reformers.

The first winds of reform began in England, moved to Bohemia, then descended on Western Europe like a storm.

John Wyclif (Wycliffe) - 1328-1384

Wycliffe, a professor of philosophy at Oxford University in England, found himself in trouble with the pope early in his career because he defended the government's right to seize the property of corrupt clergymen. He survived because his friends, people of considerable influence, protected him.

Wycliffe went on to criticize other doctrines and practices of the church at that time. He believed people can go directly to Christ and receive forgiveness of sins without the need of a priest to mediate for them. He objected to the doctrine of "transubstantiation," the belief that the wine and bread actually become the body and blood of Christ when blessed by the priest in the mass. He wrote and lectured widely, and assailed the corrupt practices in the church, calling for a return to the simplicity and purity of the early church. He was especially critical of the pope because the pope lived in splendor and luxury. Wycliffe believed the servant of the church should practice apostolic poverty and be primarily concerned about bringing people to Christ, not seeking power, prestige, and wealth. At that time the country was poor, but the church was rich. The pope was receiving five times as much in taxes as the king! Wycliffe wrote, "Christ is truth, the pope is the principle of falsehood. Christ lived in poverty, the pope labors for worldly magnificence. Christ refused temporal dominion, the pope seeks it."[5]

Wycliffe's greatest emphasis, however, was to hold up the Bible as the final authority in faith and practice, and to give common people access to it. Consistent with that, he translated the Bible into English and determined to make it available to anyone who could read. The "official" church regarded this translation as a terrible sacrilege because they felt English was a vulgar language and the Bible should only be written in Latin. Moreover, they insisted it should be available only to clergy, who alone were qualified to properly interpret it.

Wycliffe's position and prestige at the University of Oxford helped him gain an audience, and his ideas spread quickly. He appointed poor preachers to go out into the countryside with the simple message of the Gospel. Their enemies called them "Lollards," meaning "mumblers." They would carry a few pages of Wycliffe's English Bible and preach wherever they went. Their numbers grew enormously, as did their influence.

The pope condemned Wycliffe in 1377 and forced him out of his position at Oxford in 1382. This bold reformer died in 1384 and had a peaceful burial. Later, however, when the Reformation grew in intensity, church leaders dug up his bones and burned them.

John Hus - 1374-1415

The Lollards' message and Wycliffe's influence spread all the way to Bohemia and came to the attention of Jan (John) Hus. Hus was a professor at the University of Prague and a preacher in Bethlehem Chapel, near the university.

When Hus heard about Wycliffe's teachings in England, he identified with the cause. He, too, was upset over papal abuses and had paintings on his walls contrasting the behavior of Christ and the popes. Hus said the pope rode a horse, but Christ walked barefoot. Jesus washed His disciples' feet, but the pope wants others to kiss his feet. His fiery sermons fanned the flames of reformation across Bohemia and attracted a large following.

Hus complained about many other practices of the church, including the pope's sale of indulgences to finance his wars. The pope's anger led to an interdict against the entire city of Prague, forcing Hus to leave town. An interdict is similar to excommunication, but applies to an entire city or country rather than an individual. In a city under an interdict, funerals, weddings, the sacraments, and most Christian rituals are prohibited.

Hus continued writing, however, and his influence grew. In 1415 he received an invitation to the Council of Constance, then in session, to explain his views. Even though he was under the protection of safe passage guaranteed by the emperor, he was placed under inquisition, condemned, and burned at the stake July 6, 1415 without an opportunity to make his presentation to the council.

Martin Luther - 1483-1546

If popes and church leaders thought their troubles were over with the deaths of Hus and Wycliffe, they had no idea of what lay ahead. Probably the best known of the reformers is Martin Luther.

Luther, the son of a German coal miner, intended to become a lawyer. His plans changed one day at the age of twenty-two when he was caught in a thunderstorm and knocked to the ground by lightning. Afraid he would die, he called out to the patroness saint of miners, "St. Anne, save me! And I'll become a monk." He kept his promise and entered the Augustinian monastery at Erfurt.

At the monastery, Luther sought in vain to find relief from his heavy sense of guilt and sin. He did everything required by the monastery rules and much more but found no relief. In a desperate attempt to "crucify the flesh," he turned his small room into a literal prison and went for days without food. He wrote later: "I was indeed a pious monk and followed the rules of my order more strictly than I can express. If ever a monk could obtain heaven by his monkish works, I should certainly have been entitled to it. Of this all the friars who have known me can testify. If it had continued much longer, I should have carried my mortifications even to death, by means of my watchings, prayers, reading, and other labors." [6]

Luther had access to the Bible and could read it in Latin. After months of searching, he came upon Romans 1:17, "the righteous will live by faith." Suddenly he realized salvation does not come from works, but by faith in the work and sacrifice of Christ. It was a revolutionary realization that transformed not only Luther, but Western Christianity. Later, he wrote: "Night and day I pondered, until I saw the connection between the justice of God and the statement that 'the just shall live by his faith.' Then I grasped that the justice of God is that righteousness by which through grace and sheer mercy God justifies us through faith. Thereupon I felt myself to be reborn and to have gone through open doors into paradise." [7]

Luther's new understanding totally changed his view of church doctrine. If justification comes by faith and not works, then buying indulgencies was not necessary and the sale of them was a distortion of truth. In addition, the intercession of priests and the sacraments were not necessary for salvation, and the Word of God, not the pronouncements of popes and councils, was the final word of authority.

Armed with this new understanding, Luther denounced the unbiblical practices in the church. He wrote and preached tirelessly and translated the Bible into German. His teachings were widely received, and in town after town priests removed statues from churches and discontinued the Mass.

In 1512 Luther became a doctor of theology and professor of biblical studies at the University of Wittenberg. It was common practice in those days if someone wanted to debate an issue, to nail an announcement on the church door. Luther did so by nailing a copy of his *95 theses,*" in which he challenged the sale of indulgences and other practices of the church.

In subsequent debates the battle lines were drawn. Pope Leo X ordered Luther's works burned, and in June, 1520, condemned Luther and gave him sixty days to recant from his "heresy." Luther responded by burning the pope's pronouncement, and in 1521 he was officially excommunicated.

The emperor, Charles V, took over the case and declared Luther an outlaw, "Satan himself under the form of a man and dressed in a monk's frock." [8] Luther was summoned to trial at the "Diet" (meaning "assembly") at a place called Worms. There he declared again that Scripture was the only authority he would submit to in spiritual matters. "Unless therefore I am convinced by the testimony of Scripture...I cannot and I will not recant, for it is unsafe for a Christian to speak against his conscience...Here I stand, I can do no other; May God help me! Amen!" [9]

Fredrick the Wise, Duke of Saxony, spared Luther's life by whisking him away to a lonely castle at Wartburg. There, Luther continued his work of translation and writing for nearly a year. He revised the Latin liturgy of the church and translated it into German. He changed the worship service from the mass to preaching, teaching, and singing.

When people talk about the Reformation, Luther's name is usually the one connected with it. The heritage of his work comes down to us through the Lutheran church, but his influence persists throughout Western Christianity.

Huldreich Zwingli - 1484-1531

From Germany the Reformation spread to Switzerland where Zwingli (in Zurich) became one of the prominent leaders. Zwingli basically agreed with Luther but split with him about the doctrine of the communion or the Lord's Supper. Luther taught what he called "consubstantiation," by which he meant that the wine and bread do not actually transform into the body and blood of Christ, but that the presence of Christ in a mystical way goes along with these sacraments to the benefit of the believer. Zwingli taught that the communion is simply a symbol and remembrance of Christ's work on the cross and has no sacramental significance. The two men differed on some other points, as well. In teaching about moral conduct and individual lifestyles, Luther felt anything the Bible did not prohibit was acceptable. Zwingli, on the other hand, permitted only what the Bible specifically allowed.

John Calvin - 1509-1564

Meanwhile, in Geneva, a scholar and lawyer who shared the beliefs of the other reformers worked on putting it all together in writing. He was John Calvin, and his major writing, *The Institutes of the Christian Religion,* influenced much of Western Christianity.

While Luther's major thesis was salvation by faith, Calvin's was the sovereignty of God. God has a plan, Calvin believed, and this plan is being worked out according to His sovereign will. Calvin left little room for individual freedom of choice. He was deeply impressed with the majesty and holiness of God.

Calvin taught that no one, pope or emperor, had the right to absolute power. That power belonged to God alone and was manifested through His people. Calvin's influence extended beyond the spiritual, and his teaching became the basis for much of the political movement toward representative government in northern Europe.

Calvin's teachings about salvation are sometimes summarized by the acronym, "Tulip." Every seminary and Bible school student knows about the "Tulip," or the "Five points of Calvinism." They are:

T - *Total depravity:* By this Calvin meant our entire being is affected by sin and no one is able to save himself. Only the grace of God can do that. No one is even able to make the choice for Christ without first being enabled to do so by the grace of God.

U - *Unconditional election:* If you are chosen by God to be among the elect, that choice is made without any conditions in yourself. No one can boast, said Calvin, that they are or did something to influence God's choice. It is entirely without human merit.

L - *Limited atonement*: Christ died only for the elect, not for everyone.

I - *Irresistible Grace*: If God chose you for salvation, you will be saved. You cannot refuse salvation indefinitely.

P - *Perseverance of the Saints*: Once you are among the elect by God's choice, you will never lose your position in Christ. You are assured of eternal salvation.

Calvin's teachings spread throughout central and northern Europe and came to America primarily through Reformed and Presbyterian churches. His influence extended to both churches and governments, and he felt the government had the responsibility of enforcing true belief. Consistent with that, he was a major factor in the government of his city. It was sometimes called "Calvin's Geneva."

Later, Calvin's five points were modified by James Arminius in Holland. We will discuss that in the next lesson.

John Knox - 1513-1572

Knox carried Calvinism to Scotland, where he ran into a raging conflict with Mary, Queen of Scots. The struggle between Calvinist Protestantism and Catholicism in Scotland and England became legendary. Persecutions and atrocities abounded.

Knox was influential in developing what we know today as the Presbyterian Church. Presbyterianism is a middle ground between "Episcopal" church government, which follows a hierarchy of authority, and "Congregational" government. In Presbyterianism, church officers are elected into a hierarchy, but from "the bottom up." These representatives direct and administer the work of the church. Presbyterian church government became a model for the representative governments later established in the West. It no doubt had an influence on the kind of government we have in the United States, although in recent time the U.S. government has moved from a representative government to more of a democracy. The same trend has been apparent in western churches, as well.

The Anabaptists

Lesser known men such as Conrad Grebel and Felix Manz supported Zwingli's reforms in Switzerland. However, they felt that 1) Christians should not be involved in government, and 2) baptism should be reserved for those old enough to make a free choice for Christ and should be administered by immersion. For this reason, many people who had been baptized as infants were "rebaptized." Their critics called them "Anabaptists" meaning rebaptism. The Anabaptists met persecution at the hands of both Catholics and fellow Protestants who disagreed with them. Some Anabaptists were chained to posts on the shore and drowned as the tide rose.

Many Anabaptists fled to Amsterdam which offered a refuge for persecuted people. In Amsterdam they joined a teacher named Menno Simons who shared their beliefs but also taught pacifism. The followers of Menno Simons became known as "Mennonites." The Anabaptist tradition comes down to us through Mennonite, Baptist, and other related groups.

The Church of England

The Reformation in England took an entirely different turn from the rest of Europe and relates primarily to the infamous monarch, Henry VIII.

King Henry VIII is remembered both for his successive wives, some of whom he killed, and also for his affair with Anne Boleyn. He found himself in a dispute with Pope Clement VII about his marriage, and finally the pope excommunicated him. Henry countered by declaring the papacy invalid in England and placed the church directly under the crown. The result was a Catholic church without a pope, or more accurately, with the king as pope. This church is known in history as The Church of England. We know it today in the United States as the Episcopal Church, or as it is sometimes called, the Anglican Church.

The story of all that transpired in England in those days in the courts of King Henry and its effect on the church is interesting, but too detailed to deal with in this course. You may wish to research it further.

The Reformers brought much of the Western Church back to the recognition of Scripture as the authority in faith and practice. They also made the Bible available to the common person in his own language; established the truth that salvation comes by faith in Christ's work rather than through sacraments, indulgences, and good works; and brought people into a direct personal relationship with Christ.

We need to appreciate the fact that the worldwide task of Bible translation in our time has its roots in the Reformation. The fact that we have so many translations of the Bible available to us today is due, in part, to the concern of the reformers.

Bible translation is a fascinating subject. Usually, each translator will study the original Hebrew (for the Old Testament) or Greek (for the New Testament) and translate Scripture into the contemporary language of the culture in which he lives. Not only do translators need to translate into different languages, but those languages, themselves, change. For example, when we read the story of the workers in the vineyard in the NIV translation, Matthew 20:5-6 reads: "He went out again about the sixth hour and the ninth hour and did the same thing. About the eleventh hour he went out and found still others standing around. He asked them, 'Why have you been standing here all day long doing nothing?'"

In Wycliffe's 1380 version the same verses read: "For so the eftsoone he wente out about the sixte hour, and the nynethe, and dide on liche manere. But aboute the elleuenthe houre he went out, and food other stondynge; and he seide to hem, what stonden ye her ydil al day?" That's why we continually need new translations!

Assignment

Among all the reformers mentioned in this week's lesson, if you had to choose the one you think was the *most* important in bringing change to the church, who would it be? Write a paragraph explaining *why* you chose this person. Be prepared to share your opinion and reasons with the class.

LESSON 12

Religious Wars and the Counter-Reformation

A.D. 1550-1700

Equipment Needed

None

Teaching Supplies Needed

1) Copies of student lesson 13 to distribute to the class.

This lesson divides into four parts:
1) The response of the Catholic Church to the Reformation
2) The development of theology within the Reformation movement
3) The Puritan and Separatist movement within Anglicanism
4) The renewal of personal piety

Some lecture ideas are presented below for each section, including some "thought questions" you may wish to use in class.

Lecture
The Response of the Catholic Church to the Reformation

By the middle of the 16th century the Reformation movement was "unstoppable." The Catholic Church could neither control nor reverse it, leaving her to wonder how to deal with these "new and dangerous ideas."

A few of the leaders within the Catholic Church felt many of the Reformers' concerns were justified and the church should take action to deal with abuse and corruption. Some even felt the church should seek reconciliation with Protestants and include them in efforts toward renewal.

One such group was "The Oratory of Divine Love," a small, but spiritually oriented, group, whose primary concern was individual conversion and personal piety. Pope Paul III appointed one of its members, Gasparo Contarini, to head up a reform commission.

The commission's report, issued in 1537, called for the church to be less worldly and political, to look into abuses related to indulgences and immoral behavior, and return to the simple life and teaching of the apostles and the early church. It is interesting to speculate about how church history might have been different if the commission's recommendations had been followed.

Pope Paul III did respond to these recommendations by calling for a general church council to discuss reform. However, political issues delayed the council from opening until 1545. Meanwhile, Pope Paul issued the "Index," a listing of prohibited books. It included all the Reformers' books and all Protestant translations of the Bible. The mere possession of one of these books was punishable by death. He also intensified the Roman Inquisition.

About this time, Ignatius Loyola came to prominence. Ignatius experienced a deep personal encounter with God and became a flaming evangelist of the spiritual life. His spiritual fervor was so great that he came under suspicion by the Inquisitor more than once. Ignatius pursued more education and developed a program for sainthood called *Spiritual Exercises*. His followers became known as the Society of Jesus, or "Jesuits."

The Jesuits were intensely loyal to the Catholic Church and determined to serve the pope in bringing dissidents back into the fold. They promised the pope they would go wherever he sent them, anywhere in the world, to reclaim dissidents to the church and win converts.

One of the original Jesuits was Francis Xavier, who carried out missionary work throughout India, Japan, and Southeast Asia. In fact, the aggressive work of the Jesuits extended to four continents and was effective in reclaiming much of France and Central Europe for the Catholic Church.

When the general council of the church to discuss reform was finally held in the city of Trent, in northern Italy (1545-1563), the Jesuits held firm control of the leadership. Their intense loyalty to the Catholic Church and the papacy was strongly apparent in the decisions of the council. What could have been a council of reconciliation and healing turned into one of repudiation of almost everything the reformers stood for. The council affirmed salvation comes by grace and works. "Good works" included the sacraments, etc., of the church. The council also declared that the church (meaning the popes, bishops, and councils) was the sole interpreter of the Bible and church tradition was equal in authority with the Bible. The council upheld the seven sacraments, the sale of indulgences, the sacrifice of the mass, prayers to the saints, and basically everything medieval. The Council of Trent set the stage for what the Catholic Church would be for the next 400 years, and virtually wiped out any opportunity still remaining for reconciliation with Protestantism. It also led to unbelievable bloodshed, including the "St. Bartholomew's Day Massacre" (August 24, 1572) and the "Thirty Years' War," (1618 to 1648).

Suggested discussion question:

How do you think the last 450 years of church history might have been different if the Council of Trent had followed the suggestions of The Oratory of Divine Love, rather than the Jesuits? What lesson, if any, does this situation hold for us?

The Development of Theology within the Reformation Movement

John Calvin was undoubtedly the leading theologian of the Reformation, with Martin Luther the greatest activist. Perhaps Calvin holds this distinction partly because of his writings, primarily his *Institutes of the Christian Religion*.

Parts of Calvin's theology, however, were challenged by other reformers. The most significant challenge came from James Arminius (1560-1609), a professor of theology at Leyden University, near Amsterdam, Holland. Most Protestant Christians today have heard about "Calvinism" and "Arminianism," as conflicting doctrines. Few, however, understand the differences and similarities. Most people are surprised to learn that Arminius was a Calvinist, and he agreed with Calvin on more issues than he disagreed. The two agreed on the doctrines of original sin, the nature and work of Christ, justification by faith, the supremacy of Scripture over church councils and popes, and the rejection of indulgences, purgatory and sacraments as a means of salvation, etc.

So, if they agreed on so much, how could they be considered adversaries? The fact is, their major disagreement was on only one issue, but an important one. It was the issue of free will versus the sovereignty of God. In lesson 11 we presented Calvin's views by using the acronym "TULIP." Arminius disagreed with each of these "five points of Calvinism." Arminius taught that man is able to choose salvation, that God's determination of who will be saved and who will be lost is based on His foreknowledge of man's choice (1 Pet. 1:2), that Jesus' atonement was for all people, though effective only for the elect, that God's grace was not irresistible, and that it is possible to lose one's salvation. These "five points" are not really five issues, they are five aspects of a single issue. The single issue is the absolute sovereignty of God versus the free will of man. It could be said, then, that Calvin and Arminius agreed on much, but disagreed on one issue. That disagreement still divides Christians, and will probably not be resolved until we're all in eternity.

There were other issues reformers disagreed about, such as the meaning and significance of communion, church structure and organization, and relationships between the church and the state, etc. However, all the reformers agreed on the essentials, which included:

1. Justification through faith in the work of Christ
2. The authority of Scripture in faith and practice
3. The definition of the church as being all the people who belong to Christ (in contrast to only popes, bishops and priests), and
4. The ability of each individual believer to come to Christ directly without the necessity of priest, church, or sacramental intermediary.

The disagreements among the reformers were minor, compared to the vast body of belief they held in common. The same is still true among the denominations that have come down to us from the Reformation.

Suggested discussion question:

Why do you think the Calvinist/Arminian controversy is so difficult to resolve? How important is it to your faith? How does it compare in importance to the four issues listed above on which all the Reformers agreed?

The Puritan and Separatist Movement within Anglicanism

The Puritan and Separatist movement within the Anglican church is briefly sketched on page 144 of the Student section. Review this with the class, emphasizing the importance of Amsterdam as a refuge for religious dissidents experiencing persecution in their own countries. Because of that, Anabaptists from Switzerland, Puritans and Separatists from England, and others, mixed together in Amsterdam.

Some of the Separatists returned to England with the conviction that their church needed to be entirely separate from any state church, be congregational in government with each church self-governing, baptize only believers (as the Anabaptists taught), but still be loyal citizens of their country, including military service (unlike some of the Anabaptists). The leader of this group, John Smythe, baptized himself in 1608. This is usually considered the beginning of the Baptist denomination. Other Anabaptists followed the lead of Menno Simons, and are known to us as Mennonites.

The mainstream of Separatists did not join with Anabaptists, but broke away from the Anglican Church and established Congregational churches in America. The Pilgrims were of this group. It was their intent to establish a Christian commonwealth in America. Many of the Anabaptists who came to America shortly after the Pilgrims resisted the idea of a Christian commonwealth and advocated a complete separation of church and state.

Suggested discussion question:

What advantages/disadvantages do you see in the concept of separation of church and state? How do you think the history of America might be different if the Puritan intent of a Christian commonwealth had been our federal policy?

The Renewal of Personal Piety

The Student section includes a brief review of Blaise Pascal, Philip Spener, and George Fox, as representative examples of a growing emphasis during this time on the importance of personal piety. Point out to the class that the three examples given come from three different traditions; Catholic, Lutheran, and Anglican.

Suggested discussion questions:

1. Why do you think the personal piety movement became prominent in different places, among totally unrelated individuals, at this particular time?
2. Is there any relationship between this phenomenon in the 17th century, and earlier "retreats" from the "official" church? For example, the monasticism of earlier centuries.
3. If there is such a connection, what elements did Protestant churches of the 17th century have in common with the Catholic Church of earlier times to cause this rejection of the formal church and emphasis on personal piety?
4. Do we see any evidence of a withdrawal from the organized Church today? If so, who...where...why???

LESSON

Religious Wars and the Counter-Reformation

A.D. 1550-1700

Reaction to the Reformation

The Roman Catholic Church's reaction to the Reformation in the sixteenth and seventeenth centuries is called the Counter-Reformation. It included genuine reform within the church, such as correcting certain moral and other abuses among the clergy and incorporating new ways of doing ministry. However, it also included intensified political pressure and persecution against those considered to be heretics.

The Oratory of Divine Love, a brotherhood of significant individuals within the Catholic Church believed in the necessity of individual spiritual conversion and personal piety as the key to reform. Pope Paul III (1534-1549) appointed several of these leaders, along with others, to form a commission to look into reform in the church. The head of the commission, Gasparo Contarini, called for reconciliation with the Protestants, a return to the faith of the apostles, and the practices of the early church. The commission report stated that the church needed to focus on spiritual matters and be less worldly, and identified severe problems, including prostitution in Rome, abuses of indulgences, bribery, and other internal problems.

Pope Paul III, himself guilty of having three illegitimate sons and a daughter, took favorable action on the report and called for a general council of the church to deal with the problems. He also approved the "Society of Jesus" (Jesuits), under the leadership of Ignatius Loyola, to reconvert Protestants in Europe back to Rome and to evangelize the heathen. One of the Jesuits, Francis Xavier, carried on extensive missionary work throughout India and the Orient. Others were effective in slowing down and even reversing the Reformation movement in France, Holland, and Central Europe.

The Jesuits were very influential in the general council called by Pope Paul III, known as "The Council of Trent" (1545-1563). In spite of earlier feelings of reconciliation with Protestants, the Council of Trent evolved into a strong repudiation of almost everything Protestants stood for. The Council determined that salvation comes by faith *and* works, that authority rests not in Scripture alone or even primarily, but in the traditions and teachings of popes and bishops as well. It affirmed the sale of indulgences, the Mass, the seven sacraments, prayers to saints, the authority of the pope, and the canonicity of the Apocrypha. The division in the church was now permanent and entrenched.

Political leaders took sides in the conflict. This division led to bloody and prolonged warfare throughout Europe. Countries became Protestant or Catholic, following the lead of their kings and rulers. Sometimes the same country switched back and forth as their leaders changed, with those in power persecuting those who were not. From 1618 to 1648 the Thirty Years' War raged across Europe, leaving Germany and other areas in shambles.

Reaction to Calvinism

While the Jesuits were leading the Roman Catholic charge, Calvinism was the widely accepted cause on the Protestant side. Calvinism itself, however, had its Protestant critics. Among them was James Arminius (1560-1609), a professor of theology at Leyden University near Amsterdam, Holland. Arminius objected to certain aspects of Calvinism, because he thought Calvin made God responsible for sin and perceived man as a mere automaton in the hands of God. Arminius pointed to what he considered to be evidence in Scripture for human free will, and he sought to modify Calvinism to take free will into account. Like Calvin, Arminius taught that man inherited Adam's sin and was under the wrath of God. But he believed that man could exercise his free will to choose salvation. He taught that God's predestination of certain ones to salvation and others to damnation was based on his foreknowledge of a person's choice. Therefore, election was not unconditional.

Arminius also believed that Christ died for all people, but His sacrifice was effective only for believers. Unlike Calvin, he believed a person may choose salvation or reject it. It was even possible, he taught, for a believer to lose his salvation. Arminius, then, rejected or modified all five points of Calvinism.

Arminius did not reject Calvinism outright but sought to modify it to fit his understanding of Scripture. Arminianism and Calvinism both became acceptable forms of Protestantism. To this day, Protestants tend to align themselves with one or the other of these positions.

A second reaction to Calvinism was called the Anabaptist view and this was previously discussed in Lesson 11.

Reaction to Anglicanism

The Church of England, itself claiming to be Protestant, experienced even further division. Many devout believers in the Anglican church thought their church still retained too many of the abuses characteristic of Catholicism at the time, and they sought to purify it from within. These people became known as Puritans. Their efforts initiated some change but not as much as they longed for. Some of the Puritans gave up trying to promote change from within the church, and left it entirely. They were still Puritans, but they were called Separatists. The Separatists started their own congregations that were governed by the will of the congregation, rather than an ecclesiastical hierarchy. For this reason they became known as Congregational churches.

Some of the Separatists migrated to Amsterdam because of the severe persecution in England. In Amsterdam, they fellowshipped with the Anabaptists. A group of these Separatists returned to England later and finally decided to start a new life in the new world. They arrived to America in 1620, and we know them as the Pilgrims. Along with a much larger group of Puritans that arrived a few years later, they established Congregational churches in Massachusetts.

It was the intention of these Protestant immigrants fleeing England to establish a righteous commonwealth in Massachusetts. Sadly, some of them became nearly as intolerant of other groups as the Anglicans had been of them. This gave rise to still more separation.

Roger Williams, a young preacher, arrived in Boston in 1631. He was a graduate of Cambridge, an ordained minister of the Church of England, and an excellent communicator. The Congregationalists in Boston were delighted and offered him the pastorate of the First Church in Boston. But he refused, much to the indignation of the authorities. When questioned about his refusal, Williams condemned the Congregationalists for their confiscation of Indian lands and their intolerance of other faiths. He claimed the state must never be the judge of men's souls or interfere with religious beliefs. He pointed out the absurdity of a nation changing its religious beliefs every time a new ruler came to power. "It has been England's sinful shame," he said, "to fashion and change garments and religions with wondrous ease, as a higher power or stronger sword has prevailed." [10]

Because of his outspoken criticism, Williams was brought to trial and convicted of "diverse new and dangerous opinions." He was banished from Boston in January 1636. Leaving his wife and child behind, he walked through a cold and desolate wilderness for fourteen weeks, finally arriving at a friendly Indian settlement where he was given refuge. He named the place Providence, and the territory, Rhode Island.

Williams is often credited for establishing the first Baptist church in America, and his ideas were later incorporated into the principle of the separation of church and state.

Renewal of Personal Piety

Meanwhile, back in Europe, both Catholics and Protestants reacted to the bloodshed, politics, and worldliness in the church. Some of the significant leaders in this movement were:

Blaise Pascal (1623-1662). Pascal, a Roman Catholic, objected to many of the Jesuit practices, including their emphasis on works. He called for the church to return to the teachings of Augustine. He, himself, had a deep spiritual experience with Christ, which he described in his writings. Eight years after his death, some of his works were published as the *Pensees* (thoughts) of Pascal. Pascal's *Pensees* are still being published and are of spiritual benefit to many people.

Philip Spener (1635-1705) Spener, a Lutheran, reacted to the intellectualizing and formalizing of Lutheranism. He called for repentance and genuine discipleship, and formed cell groups of the born again in each church. They became known as the "pious," and the movement was named "Pietism." Pietism became a very forceful movement, first in the Lutheran church, and later in other groups.

George Fox (1624-1691) Fox, in the shadow of the Anglican church in England, reacted to formal religion. He felt the church had become worldly—even apostate—a system of liturgy controlled by the state that had lost its spirituality.

For a long time Fox sought personal spiritual fulfillment and was frustrated and dissatisfied by the advice he received from clergy. Finally, he experienced a meaningful mystical encounter with Christ. Deeply moved, he began to preach about the reality of coming directly into communion with Christ apart from ceremony or ritual. A number of individuals began to respond to his teaching, whom he called "Friends." He taught that slavery and participation in war were both wrong. He preached that the Holy Spirit revealed God through an "inner light." Frustrated with formal religion, he taught the importance of a simple, personal relationship with Christ.

The movement grew quickly. By 1660 there were about 60,000 Friends in England. Persecution against them was intense. In 1650 Fox was arrested. At his trial, the judge, who knew about the emotional meetings the Friends sometimes experienced, said in derision, "You folk are the tremblers, you are the quakers." The name stuck, and they are still known as Quakers.

Probably because of their criticism of the formal church, Quakers were persecuted everywhere. Even in Boston they were jailed or expelled, and several were hanged before King Charles II stopped executions in the colonies. Some found refuge in Rhode Island, where Roger Williams offered them safety even though he disagreed with their theology. Finally, the Quaker, William Penn, received a territory in the colonies, where Quakers could live safely. He called it Pennsylvania, meaning "Penn's Woods."

This entire period was marked by upheaval and instability for Christian people. Traditions were falling everywhere, persecution was rampant, and new concepts were constantly appearing. One of the new concepts finally brought an end to the religious wars.

Assignment

Write a sentence or two in response to each of the following questions. Be prepared to share your answers with the class:

1) What do you think the Roman Catholic Church could have done differently during this period to prevent the continued "fracturing" of the church?

2) What mistakes do you think the Protestant made?

3) Why do you think there was such broad-based support in both Roman Catholic and Protestant circles for the "personal piety" movements?

LESSON 13

The Rise of Denominationalism

A.D. 1700 - 1900

Equipment Needed

1) Chalkboard or whiteboard

Teaching Supplies Needed

1) Copies of student lesson 14 to distribute to the class.

The lecture portion of this lesson follows a five-part outline:
1. The concept of denominationalism
2. The culture of the eighteenth and nineteenth centuries
3. Protestant missions in the eighteenth and nineteenth centuries
4. John Wesley
5. The Methodist church

Lecture

The Concept of Denominationalism

Help students realize the significance of denominationalism within Christianity. Usually, Christians are reminded of only the negative aspects. They are aware of the fact that many different denominations means the church is divided and broken, contrary to the will of God.

However, there are positive aspects as well. It has permitted various denominations with differing beliefs to coexist peacefully in the same country. When the government does not take sides, as in America, it greatly reduces the bloodshed that was the scourge of Western European Christianity in previous centuries.

Suggested discussion questions

1. Why do you think the concept of denominationalism came to be accepted during the last two centuries? (Discussion may center on changes in the culture, weariness of conflict, and religious wars, etc.)
2. How seriously does denominationalism fracture the church? Is it really unbiblical? Why or why not?
3. Encourage discussion about what constitutes true unity in Christ. Would organizational unity *really* make the church more unified? Is doctrinal disagreement among denominations worse than doctrinal disagreement among members of

the same church? If so, why? Can there be Christian unity even between denominations that *don't* merge? How? Were there ever divisions of opinion that separated Christians in the New Testament? When? How did they handle it? (Note Acts 15:36-41 and Gal. 2:11). This discussion can be very transforming for class members. It could also become contentious. Pray for the wisdom and guidance of the Holy Spirit before your class lesson.

The Culture of the Eighteenth and Nineteenth Centuries

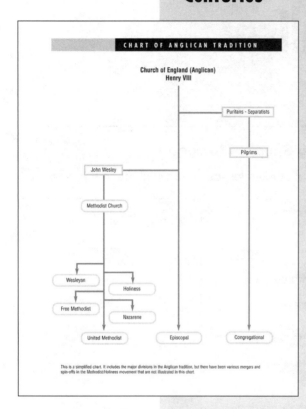

CHART OF ANGLICAN TRADITION

Church of England (Anglican)
Henry VIII

Puritans - Separatists

Pilgrims

John Wesley

Methodist Church

Wesleyan

Holiness

Free Methodist

Nazarene

United Methodist · Episcopal · Congregational

This is a simplified chart. It includes the major divisions in the Anglican tradition, but there have been various mergers and spin-offs in the Methodist/Holiness movement that are not illustrated in this chart.

Tremendous changes in the culture affected the church and the way people thought about religion in general. One reason people didn't kill each other over religious issues any longer was they no longer cared that much about religion. The culture was growing secular. The idea of God as creator and ruler of the universe began to dim. The Bible was no longer the "sole authority for faith and practice." In place of the Bible as authority, human reason and science were deified. The spectacular benefits coming from science caused people to think science and human reason would eventually bring the utopia philosophers had sought for centuries.

Add to this the philosophy of individual liberty popularized by John Locke and others, and you have a culture that rejects the old notions of authority. The "old authorities" included superstition and magic, along with popes and kings. Unfortunately, the authority of Scripture was also included in the package being rejected. Critics of Scripture found every possible reason, both real and imagined, to reject the claim Christians made for the authority of Scripture. We still reap the damage from their efforts today.

Scripture and church authority were not the only citadels being attacked in the West. The old capitalist economic system also became a target. Karl Marx and Friedrich Engels claimed capitalism was the cause of all the world's miseries. Their "solution" was the Communist revolution.

Revolution was the order of the day. The success of the American Revolution inspired the French to revolt. Political revolution shook the culture like an earthquake, and the industrial revolution dramatically changed day-to-day living. The rise of factories and new methods of distribution of goods caused people to move from the countryside into large cities and changed the way they earned a living. Craftsmanship rooted in the family gave way to employment in the factories. Family roots disappeared, and new problems of poverty, disease, ghettos, unemployment, and child labor arose. These conditions fueled revolutionaries like Marx and Engels.

The change and unrest in society also changed the church's ministry. In answer to the need, many Christians and Christian groups responded with ministries targeted at human suffering, especially in England. William and Catherine Booth launched the Salvation Army in 1865 to reach out to needy people with both the Gospel and practical physical help, such as food, clothing, and housing. Robert Raikes, a wealthy London publisher, popularized the Sunday School movement in 1780 to give children an opportunity for a Christian education. By 1831, 1,250,000 children were enrolled in Sunday Schools in England. In 1844 George Williams founded the Young Men's Christian Association to provide exercise, social life, and lodging in a Christian environment. In 1836 George Müller began establishing orphanages that eventually housed, fed, and clothed thousands of children. The most intense area of concern was the slavery issue. The champion of abolition was William Wilberforce, a Christian in the British Parliament. He succeeded in bringing slavery to an end in England. The benefits to society and relief of human suffering accomplished through these various ministries and others are literally incalculable.

Ask students to share their answers to the assignment on page 156 of their section. Emphasize how well the church responded to the social needs of its time. The church has always been in the forefront of bringing relief and help to needy people. Ask for some recent examples.

List the names of Christianleaders founding relief organizations as you discuss them:
- William and Catherine Booth
- Robert Raikes
- George Williams
- George Müller
- William Wilberforce

UNIT II

Protestant Missions in the Eighteenth and Nineteenth Centuries

The eighteenth and nineteenth centuries witnessed an unparalleled expansion of Protestant missionary effort. Some of the most notable missionaries in church history come from this period. Many sacrificed home, health, family, and fortune to carry the Gospel to foreign lands. Their efforts and the generosity of those who supported them have seldom been equaled by any religious movement in history.

Students should become familiar with at least the following three missionary enterprises: the Moravians, William Carey, and David Livingstone.

List on whiteboard as you discuss them:
- Nikolaus Ludwig von Zinzendorf and the Moravians
- William Carey
- David Livingstone

The Moravians

A paragraph description of the origin of the Moravian Church is given in the Student section, page 154. The Moravian Church was possibly the most missionary minded church in history. It maintained an "around-the-clock" prayer meeting for 100 years. Moravians longed to take the Gospel to every land that touches the shores of the Atlantic Ocean. They went into foreign lands, sometimes under immense hardship and sacrifice, to share the Gospel. Some even became slaves in order to take the Gospel to slaves. During the 100-year period of their prayer meeting, they were quite successful in accomplishing their goal. One of their greatest "successes" was to reach John Wesley with the Gospel. He in turn preached the Gospel on two continents.

William Carey (1761-1834)

Carey was a shoe repairman in a humble shop in Northamptonshire, England. His earnest faith drove him to a study of the Scriptures. He mastered Latin, Hebrew, and Greek. In addition to his work as a cobbler, he pastored a small Baptist church. His vision, however, was

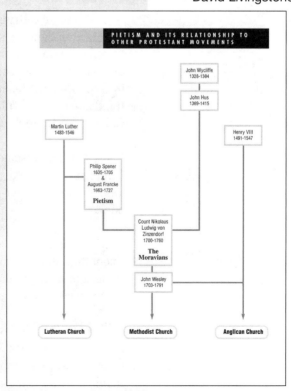

PIETISM AND ITS RELATIONSHIP TO OTHER PROTESTANT MOVEMENTS

John Wycliffe 1328-1384
John Hus 1369-1415
Martin Luther 1483-1546
Henry VIII 1491-1547
Philip Spener 1635-1705 & August Francke 1663-1727 — Pietism
Count Nikolaus Ludwig von Zinzendorf 1700-1760 — The Moravians
John Wesley 1703-1791
Lutheran Church   Methodist Church   Anglican Church

large. He kept a map of the world over his workbench, where he traced the voyages of Captain James Cook, Columbus, and others. His prayer was to carry the Gospel to the people of these remote areas.

Carey faced two immense hurdles. The first was financial. He could barely provide for himself and his wife, who was a victim of mental illness. The second obstacle was the attitude of fellow-believers in England.

Steeped in the prevailing ultra-Calvinism of their time, Christians in England thought it was foolish to seek to convince people to come to Christ. If they were among the elect, God would call them. He didn't need someone, they contended, to try to convince them. Preachers of the time avoided making personal application of the salvation message to individuals because they thought it was interfering with God's election. They felt it was wrong to use "means," that they defined as human agencies or methods, to convince someone to receive Christ.

With neither personal finances nor support, Carey launched into the immense task of taking the Gospel to India. Andrew Fuller, a fellow pastor who taught that the ultra-Calvinistic ideas of English Protestants were wrong, encouraged Carey. He wrote; "We have sunk into such a compromising way of dealing with the unconverted, as to have well nigh lost the spirit of the primitive preachers, and hence it is that sinners of every description can sit so quietly as they do, year after year, in our places of worship." [4]

In 1792 Carey published his own book, *An Enquiry into the Obligation of Christians to Use Means for the Conversion of the Heathen*. A few others shared his belief, and in the same year, he and eleven colleagues formed the Baptist Missionary Society. The formation of such a society outside the church was a new concept. Others caught the vision, and a year later Carey and his family departed for India.

At that time, the British East India Company virtually controlled India. The company was unhappy about a Baptist missionary in their territory and characterized "the sending out of missionaries into our Eastern possessions...the maddest, most extravagant, most costly, most indefensible project which has ever been suggested by a moonstruck fanatic. Such a scheme is pernicious, imprudent, useless, harmful, dangerous, profitless, fantastic." [5] The company refused to let Carey live in Calcutta, so he took up residence in Serampore in Danish territory.

Carey was an outstanding student of Hindu culture. He felt learning about Hinduism was a necessity to effectively witness to Hindus. He also completed six total and twenty-four partial translations of the Bible in addition to writing other books.

The life and ministry of Carey is a thrilling, heart-wrenching, exemplary, story. Encourage students to read more about him. His pioneer work opened the gates of Protestant foreign missions, through which a stream of missionaries flowed to nearly every country on the globe.

David Livingstone (1813-1873)

Livingstone is probably the best known pioneer missionary to Africa, although his father-in-law, Dr. Robert Moffat, preceded him to South Africa. Moffat's work is rich in exciting experiences of God's providential protection and care. Again, encourage students to read anything they can find about Moffat.

Livingstone's vision was both spiritual and humanitarian. He worked desperately to bring an end to slave trade and to open central Africa to commerce and industry, but his consuming passion was to bring the Gospel to Africa. Africans loved him, and therefore a close bond of friendship and fellowship developed between them and Livingstone. A scientist and a keen observer, Livingstone maintained journals that are of great value to this very day.

What most people today know best about Livingstone is that there was no communication with him for three years, with great fears for his safety. A correspondent for the New York *Herald*, Henry Stanley, left England in search of him. The two met at Lake Tanganyika in 1871. Stanley greeted the missionary with the casual, "Dr. Livingstone, I presume." Livingstone died in Africa, but his body lies at Westminster Abbey.

The Voluntary Societies

Many of these early missionaries did not find support for their efforts in traditional churches. Consequently, a new method of support surfaced and was known as "voluntary societies." These organizations arose so individuals could support specific missionaries apart from their own church. Consequently, a given missionary society might realize financial and prayer support from individuals in various denominations and churches. It was a new concept, and the forerunner of the many "parachurch" Christian organizations today.

Call attention to the Pietism and its Relationship to Other Protestant Movements chart (page 158 in the Student section). Discuss this chart, tracing the influence of Lutheranism through Pietism through the Moravians, combined with the followers of Wycliffe and Hus, on to John Wesley. Wesley, in turn, influenced all of subsequent evangelical theology and practice. Note this chart does not imply any organizational connection between these various movements, only *influence*.

John Wesley (1703-1791)

John Wesley was perhaps the most influential spiritual leader in England in this entire period. The Student section devotes considerable space to a description of his work. A few highlights about Wesley as a person are briefly itemized below:

- He grew up in a minister's family, his father being an Anglican minister and his mother the daughter of a "Nonconformist" minister.
- He had eighteen brothers and sisters, three younger and fifteen older.
- When he was age six, the parsonage burned down, and John was rescued from a second-story window by neighbors. Throughout his life he called himself "a brand plucked from the burning." Of course, his statement had both spiritual and physical meaning.
- He read widely, focusing on classic devotional books and the church fathers. He always sought to be *fully* committed to God.
- He, and his brother, Charles, formed small groups at Oxford University. These groups were for the purpose of growing in holiness and Christian service. They developed methods to grow in their spiritual life and commitment. From this, their enemies called them "Methodists."
- John's missionary trip to America was a dismal failure. Consult the Student section for details of his encounter with Moravians, subsequent conversion,

and incredible ministry.
- Wesley was so committed to his ministry that he was difficult to live with. He married in 1751. His wife, Mary, tried to travel with him but finally gave up from exhaustion and nervous breakdown. She died in 1781.

Wesley's teaching on holiness is the source of the "holiness tradition." He taught that it is not only possible, but necessary, for a Christian to experience complete sanctification (spiritual purity). Some of his followers interpreted this as "sinless perfection," but that was not Wesley's intention. His belief was that one can be made perfect in love. It is a perfection of intent and purpose, a purity of motive, which results from the love of God filling one's heart. He saw it as a progressive work that begins by an initial act of faith after a person's salvation. Wesley's teaching on holiness has come down to us through the Methodist Church and various Holiness and Wesleyan denominations. It is also in the background of the "two stage salvation" teaching in Pentecostal and Charismatic groups, where the necessity of a "second blessing" or "baptism of the Spirit" is taught.

Guide students in tracing the development of the Methodist Church. Refer to the Chart of Anglican Tradition on page 157 of the Student section. Wesley never intended to leave the Anglican Church; he wanted only to form a society of individuals within the church who would experience personal salvation, commit themselves to a life of holiness, and be active in Christian service and evangelism. He always encouraged people to support the Anglican Church and participate in it.

The Methodist Church

The Methodist Society, however, after a matter of time, distanced itself from its mother church. When Methodism came to America, Methodists held a conference in Baltimore in 1784 and selected Francis Asbury and Thomas Coke as superintendents of the Methodist Society in America. At that point it became, in reality, a separate denomination.

Refer to the Student section for information about the ministry of George Whitefield in America. Whitefield was part of the Methodist revival, but disagreed with Wesley on the issue of election and eternal security. Wesley was Arminian, but Whitefield was Calvinist. In the course of time, the Arminian position prevailed in the Methodist Church.

The "Great Awakening" was one of the most important events in American history. To a degree never experienced before or after on a national scale, the Spirit of God moved across the young nation of America and impacted every facet of society. Any background reading you can do about this event will help you in the presentation of this lesson. If you have access to *Eerdmans' Handbook to Christianity in America*, pages 96 through 130, you will discover abundant information.

LESSON 13

The Rise of Denominationalism

A.D. 1700 - 1900

The concept of denominations is such an accepted part of our culture that we seldom think about its benefits or how it came into being. It is largely an American invention. Weary of violence within the church, there eventually developed a tolerance for difference of opinion and separate church structure within the same country. The idea of church and state being separate, with the government endorsing or promoting no specific religion, found its way into the United States Constitution and ultimately into the world. We know it as "denominationalism," the coexistence of different factions of the church, even different religions, within the same country without government interference. In America, at least, this arrangement has reduced the bloodshed.

The culture in general helped make tolerance more acceptable, because people in the West were becoming less concerned about the details of doctrine and religious beliefs. The early part of this period witnessed a move away from faith toward secularism and the worship of reason. It saw the birth of modern science, with scientists such as Isaac Newton and others helping people see there were natural causes to explain some of the phenomena in the world. Unfortunately, many now began to think that God and creation were no longer necessary factors in understanding the universe. At the same time, John Locke and other philosophers were promoting ideas of individual liberty and religious toleration. Deism, the belief that God created the world and then left it to run on its own, was becoming popular. Deists reject the idea of a God who is personally concerned about individuals or the affairs of this world. They also deny the possibility of miracles or special revelation from God. They regard the Bible as a purely human product.

With this kind of cultural background, the Reformation movement spilled unto American shores. The four major branches of the Reformation were Anglican, Lutheran, Anabaptist, and Reformed. During the eighteenth century, the greatest activity was taking place in the Anglican branch—not within the Anglican Church itself, but among the dissidents who were eventually forced out and started their own "denominations."

The story of the Anglican Church, its splits, and the formation of the Methodist as well as Congregational churches is probably best represented by a simple diagram in the Chart of Anglican Tradition page 157.

John Wesley, a "PK" (preacher's kid), was one of nineteen children born to Samuel and Susanna Wesley. His father was an Anglican minister and his mother was the daughter of a "nonconformist" minister. Nonconformists was the name given to ministers in the Anglican Church who objected to its practices and distanced themselves from it. Puritans and Separatists were among the nonconformists.

Wesley entered Oxford University at age seventeen. His brother Charles was also a student at Oxford. Charles became alarmed at the spread of deism at the university and started a small group for prayer and Bible study. Those who attended were accountable to each other for their Christian walk. Sharing his brother's concern, John joined the group and soon became its leader.

Other students at the university ridiculed the little group and called those who belonged to it names such as "The Holy Club," "Bible moths," and "Methodists." The Methodist name came about because the group talked about and practiced a method to grow in personal holiness. This name stuck.

The group didn't just read the Bible and pray. The members were active in Christian service as well. They visited jails, gave to the poor, and sought other ways to share their faith. They were encouraged when one of the undergraduates from Pembroke College, George Whitefield, joined their group.

John Wesley was constantly restless and unable to find inward peace. He was invited to go on a missionary trip to Georgia in the American colonies. The trip was a disaster. He described Native Americans as "gluttons, thieves, liars and murderers." He didn't even get along well with the white colonists. They resented his criticism of their fancy clothes and gold jewelry in church, and they objected to his rigid ways. John was cultured and "high church," and just didn't fit into the frontier. After an unfortunate love affair fell apart, he returned to England totally discouraged. He wrote: "I went to America to convert the Indians, but, oh, who shall convert me?"

A great benefit of his trip to America, however, was the opportunity to meet some Moravian missionaries. The Moravians were highly dedicated and missionary minded Christians who established a colony in Moravia. They were under the leadership of a wealthy Lutheran nobleman, Count Nikolaus Ludwig von Zinzendorf. Zinzendorf, a deeply committed Christian, invited Christian refugees to the safety of his estate, then led them into his vision of uniting all Christians in the task of worldwide evangelism. While in the colonies, Wesley was impressed with the Moravians' complete confidence in Christ and bold witness.

Back in London, Wesley met Peter Bohler, a Moravian preacher who talked with Wesley about being born again and having a personal faith in Christ by which he could attain true holiness. On May 24, 1738, Wesley had a spiritual experience that he describes in his own words: "In the evening, I went very unwillingly to a society in Aldersgate Street, where one was reading Luther's preface to the *Epistle to the Romans*. About a quarter to nine, while he was describing the change which God works in the heart through faith in Christ, I felt my heart strangely warmed. I felt that I did trust in Christ, Christ alone, for salvation; and an assurance was given me that He had taken away *my* sins, even *mine*, and saved me from the law of sin and death." [11]

Following this conversion experience, Wesley preached the Gospel with an enthusiasm seldom equaled in the history of the church. It is estimated that, during his lifetime he traveled some 250,000 miles by horseback preaching the Gospel. Though Anglican, he was repeatedly barred from preaching in the church because of the opposition of some Anglican clergy. Undaunted, he preached in the open air to as many as 30,000 people at once. He preached in inns, in jails, on ships, at coalmines and industrial plants, in courtyards—wherever people would listen. Once, refused entrance to his family's church, he stood on his father's tombstone and preached. He said he saw "the world as his parish," and considered it his duty to preach the "glad tidings of salvation" to anyone who would hear.

John Wesley was joined by his brother, Charles, the famous hymn writer. Charles wrote over 7,000 sacred songs and poems. John was the organizer and administrator, while Charles touched the hearts of people with his awesome music. Later, their college friend, George Whitefield (1714-1770), joined the movement and experienced extraordinary results in open air evangelism. Whitefield was one of the greatest preachers of all time. David Garrick, a famous actor, once said he would give a hundred guineas if he could say "Oh" like Mr. Whitefield.

The Methodist revival was on, and it shook England and America to its foundations. Whitefield toured the colonies on a very successful preaching mission. His ministry, however, was separate from the Wesleys', because Whitefield was a thoroughgoing Calvinist; whereas, Wesley was committed to the Arminian position. The breach was never healed.

The ministry of Whitefield joined with others in the colonies in what is known in history as the "Great Awakening." The Great Awakening was a spiritual revival in America that remains unprecedented. People everywhere were turning to God. When and where it started is still open to dispute, but Jonathan Edwards' sermon, *Sinners in the Hands of an Angry God,* was certainly one of the major influences used by the Holy Spirit to sweep across the young nation. In December, 1734, Edwards wrote: "The Spirit of God began extraordinarily to set in...there was scarcely a single person in the town, old or young, left unconcerned about the great things of the eternal world." [12] It was only the beginning of America's greatest period of revival.

The Great Awakening saw Methodist, Baptist, Congregational, and Presbyterian evangelists join in an awesome spiritual harvest. The revivals lasted throughout the 1730s and 1740s. Most church historians claim the Great Awakening affected all of American life, including social organization and politics, and changed church life in America dramatically.

This was also a time of revolution in society and culture. There was economic revolution, with the writings of Karl Marx and Friedrich Engels, and the publication of the *Communist Manifesto* in 1848. There was political revolution, including the French and American revolutions. There was scientific revolution, with Charles Darwin and Charles Lyell promoting theories that seemed to negate the necessity of a creator. There was theological revolution, with the onset of theological liberalism that discounted the theories of biblical inerrancy and the necessity of the new birth. There was the industrial revolution that left hundreds of thousands of people in desperate conditions in large cities and led to serious abuses of child labor. In addition to all this, the slavery issue was fanning the flames of controversy in churches and the halls of government.

The church responded with massive social movements. Among theological liberals, the "Social Gospel" had its beginnings. The Social Gospel purported that the healing of culture and society, rather than personal conversion, should be the church's main concern. Conservative and traditional Christians on the other hand, adhered to the necessity of personal salvation and linked it to massive relief efforts. God raised up specific individuals to bring healing to England and America. Among them were William and Catherine Booth, founders of the Salvation Army; Robert Raikes, founder of the Sunday school movement; George Müller, organizer and director of orphanages, and William Wilberforce, the untiring defender of liberty in the English parliament. Wilberforce was also the leading individual in the formation of "Clapham Village," a neighborhood of influential leaders near London who addressed a variety of social concerns, the most important being slavery. Wilberforce was the major influence behind the abolition of slavery in England. His stirring speeches in Parliament are legendary!

Around this time, the term "evangelical" emerged in reference to people like Wilberforce and others involved in Christian social causes. Evangelicals were Christians who believed in the inspiration and authority of Scripture, the importance of being born again, and the return of Jesus Christ. The term is still in use today.

The latter part of this period saw a "Second Awakening" in America. Evangelists such as Charles G. Finney (1792-1875) and Dwight L. Moody (1837-1899) were experiencing remarkable success. The work of D.L. Moody led to the formation of the Moody Bible Institute (Chicago) and its various publishing and educational ministries.

A significant individual during this time was Alexander Campbell (1788-1866). A Presbyterian minister who left the Presbyterian church because he rejected the idea of "denomination" and what he considered to be repressive church government, Campbell preached "no creed but Christ, no law but love," and wanted his group to be known only as "Disciples." He joined with Barton W. Stone, who had similar ideas. Stone simply called his group "Christians." Both had Presbyterian backgrounds, but attracted many former Baptists to their group. But they did not fully identify with either Baptists or Presbyterians. They practiced immersion, which separated them from Presbyterians, and believed in "baptismal regeneration," which separated them from Baptists. Baptismal regeneration is the belief that baptism is an essential part of salvation. They were often called "Campbellites," because they were identified with the teachings of Alexander Campbell and his father, Thomas Campbell. From this group the Disciples of Christ/Christian church of our day evolved.

In Europe during this time, impressive missionary activity emerged from the "rank and file" of Protestant Christians. In addition to the Moravian missionary movement already described, this was the time William Carey went to India, David Livingstone to Africa, and many other missionaries risked (and often lost) their lives to carry the Gospel to other continents.

So many things happened during this period that we suggest you read these six pages over two or three times before we meet in class. Much of twentieth century church history in America is rooted in this 200 year period of 1700-1900.

Assignment

Ponder the question, "Do you see any relationship between what was happening in European and American society and culture during this time and what was happening during the same period in the church?" If so, what is the connection? Write your answer in a few sentences and be prepared to share it with the class.

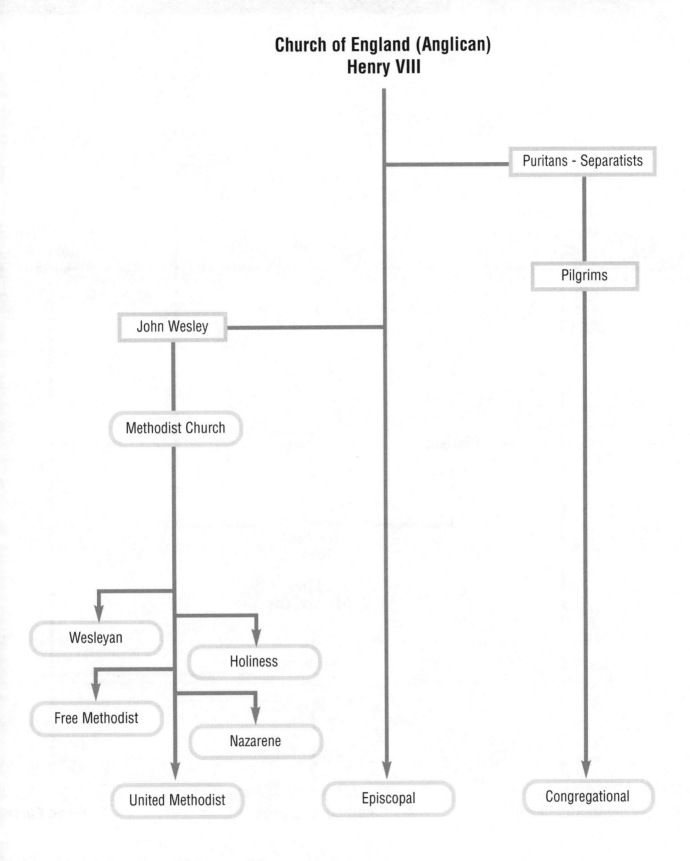

Church of England (Anglican)
Henry VIII

Puritans - Separatists

Pilgrims

John Wesley

Methodist Church

Wesleyan

Holiness

Free Methodist

Nazarene

United Methodist

Episcopal

Congregational

This is a simplified chart. It includes the major divisions in the Anglican tradition, but there have been various mergers and spin-offs in the Methodist/Holiness movement that are not illustrated in this chart.

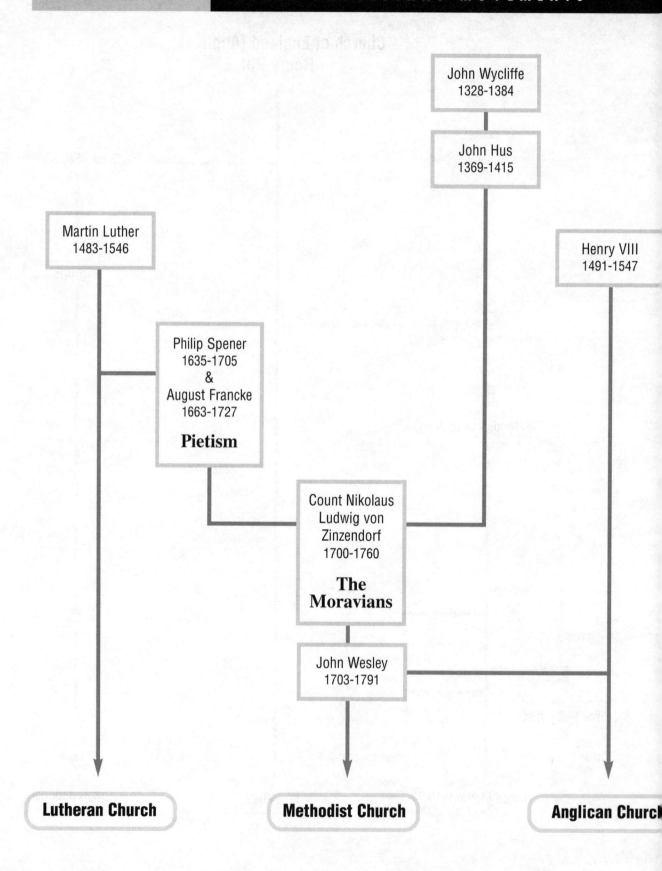

John Wycliffe
1328-1384

John Hus
1369-1415

Henry VIII
1491-1547

Martin Luther
1483-1546

Philip Spener
1635-1705
&
August Francke
1663-1727

Pietism

Count Nikolaus
Ludwig von
Zinzendorf
1700-1760

**The
Moravians**

John Wesley
1703-1791

Lutheran Church

Methodist Church

Anglican Church

LESSON 14

The Twentieth Century Church

Equipment Needed

1) Map of Europe

Teaching Supplies Needed

1) Copies of student lesson 15 to distribute to the class.

This Lesson Plan is in outline form to facilitate the ease by which you present the lecture. Please read the student materials carefully for details. Some students will have enough familiarity with the events of the twentieth century that they can provide important and interesting information. So for this class, your students will be one of your greatest resources. Encourage their participation.

Lecture

I. Twentieth Century Culture
    A. Secularism reigns
    B. Biblical ignorance
    C. The worship of science

II. The Rise of Pentecostalism
    A. Five background teachings
        1. The Holiness movement and the second work of grace." (Wesley)
        2. Higher Christian life teachings (Finney, Hannah Whitall Smith, The Christian's Secret of a Happy Life, Keswick Movement, etc.)
        3. Faith healing (A.B. Simpson and the Christian and Missionary Alliance)
        4. Dispensational Premillennialism
        5. Restorationism

    B. The Azusa St. Revival
        1. Charles Fox Parham, Topeka, KS (1901)
        2. William J. Seymour—The Evening Light Saints
        3. Azusa Street Revival, Los Angeles (1906-1909)
        4. Denominations rising out of the Azusa St. Revival: Assemblies of God, Church of the Foursquare Gospel, Church of God, Church of God in Christ, Pentecostal Holiness

III. The Charismatic Renewal

A. Beginnings
    1. Fr. Bennett, St. Mark's Episcopal, Van Nuys, CA (1960)
    2. Duquesne University (1967)
B. Differences from Pentecostal movement:
    1. Not a separate denomination; permeates all denominations
    2. Diversity of gifts, not just tongues
    3. All social levels
C. Controversial: Unifying or divisive?

IV. Evangelicalism

A. Background: Rise of Liberalism and Fundamentalism
    1. Liberalism—Biblical criticism, denial of basic doctrines (virgin birth, miracles, authority of Scripture, deity of Christ, need for personal conversion, etc. emphasis on "social Gospel")
    2. Reaction:
        a) Fundamentalism
          • Publication of The Fundamentals (1910-1915)
        b) The Independent Fundamental Churches of America (1923/1930)
        c) The American Council of Christian Churches (1941)
B. "Evangelicalism" a centrist position
    1. Hold to historic belief in authority of Scripture, need for individual personal relationship with Christ, vigorous evangelism, etc.
    2. Social concerns
    3. Broader in fellowship than Fundamentalism, narrower than Liberalism
    4. Billy Graham and Billy Graham Association
    5. The National Association of Evangelicals (1942). In contrast to the National Council of Churches (considered too liberal and inclusive) and the Independent Fundamental Churches of America and the American Council of Christian Churches (considered too separatist).

V. Renewal in the Roman Catholic Church

A. Vatican II (1962-1965) and Pope John XXIII
    1. Changes:
        a) Style of worship
        b) Mass in the vernacular
        c) Bible reading and study encouraged
        d) Relaxing of animosity toward Protestants—now considered to be "separated brethren" rather than heretics

VI. Attempts at Unity

A. The Ecumenical Movement
B. Denominational mergers
C. Fundamentalist and Evangelical concerns and reactions.

VII. The Challenge of Eastern Mysticism

A. The influence of Eastern religious ideas in American culture

B. Note: This subject will be explored further in Unit VI, "Postmodern Culture"

VIII. Review of denominational origins.

A. The four branches of the Reformation

1. Lutheran: Lutheran churches are easy to identify because they nearly always include "Lutheran" in their names, and all trace back eventually to Martin Luther. The two most prominent branches in the United States are the Lutheran Church in America (LCA) and the Missouri Synod.

> **Note:** Spend considerable time on this section to develop students' skill in identifying the origins of each denomination and something about their distinctive beliefs.

2. Reformed / Presbyterian: Reformed and Presbyterian Churches descended from the Calvinist movement in Europe and are similar in theology and practice. Presbyterian churches have their origin in the work of John Knox in Scotland.

> Note the charts of Anabaptist tradition and Anglican tradition on pages 168 and 157 of the Student section when discussing these traditions. Emphasize that these charts include only a few of the many denominations that descended from these origins.

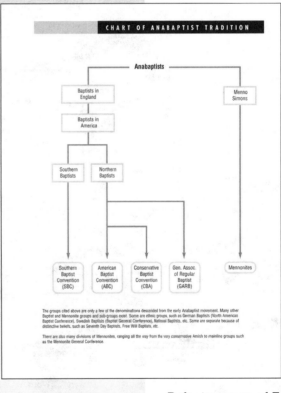

3. Anabaptist: The Anabaptist movement began in Switzerland and moved to Holland, where it mixed with Menno Simons' teachings and with Separatists from England. The spin-off from this resulted in the formation of various groups and denominations, the most significant of which were Baptist and Mennonite.

Baptist distinctives usually include: Believer's baptism by immersion, separation of church and state, congregational form of government, and autonomy of the local church.

Mennonite distinctives usually include the above, plus pacifism. Some Mennonite groups practice baptism by sprinkling.

Refer to a map of Europe, showing Switzerland, Holland, and England.

4. Anglican: The Anglican Church began with Henry VIII in England breaking away from the papacy and bringing the church under the crown through the Archbishop of Canterbury. Methodists and various Holiness groups descended from the Anglican church through John Wesley, and Congregational churches through the Puritans and Separatists.

Review the development of major Protestant denominations by selecting several and tracing them back to their origin. Student assignments were to trace their own origins back and serve as "experts" about their own tradition. Ask them to share the results of their study with the class.

LESSON 14
The Twentieth Century Church

The twentieth century saw an explosion of technology and knowledge. Is this phenomenon the fulfillment of Daniel's prophecy about the "time of the end"? He predicted "many will go here and there to increase knowledge" (Dan. 12:4).

Unfortunately, this increase in knowledge did not include the knowledge of God. Secularism pervaded society in the twentieth century. Human accomplishments in science seemed to promise the "good life" by natural means, and the worship of God dimmed. Finally, ravaged by two world wars, endless regional conflicts, and unbelievable atrocities between political factions and ethnic groups, the end of the twentieth century saw a return to spirituality. But the "spirituality" was not Christianity. Today, many worship something, but the "something" is not the God of the Bible.

Unlike the previous sixteen centuries, the twentieth century church in the West found itself in a defensive posture in the culture. Six characteristics defined the experience of the church in this century:

1) The rise of Pentecostalism
2) The Charismatic renewal
3) The revival of Evangelicalism
4) Renewal within the Roman Catholic Church
5) Attempts at unity
6) The challenge of Eastern Mysticism

This week's lesson provides a synopsis of each of these movements.

The Rise of Pentecostalism

To understand Pentecostalism, it is necessary to look at five major Christian influences prevalent at the turn of the century that blended into the Pentecostal movement.

The first influence was the Holiness movement that grew from the teachings of John Wesley, the Methodist Church, and related groups. Wesley believed Jesus' command to "be perfect" (Matt. 5:48) should be taken literally. Therefore, he taught that Christians need to go beyond merely "being converted"; they need to seek perfection. To Wesley, this was not "sinless perfection," but it was absolute purity of intent. He taught that even after conversion, a Christian needs to rid himself of "inbred sin." This, he believed, is accomplished in an instantaneous perfection of the will and brings about "entire sanctification." A Christian becomes sanctified in this "second work of grace" in a way similar to being converted in the initial act of repentance. The belief in a "second work of grace" among Holiness groups is often referred to in theological literature as "two stage salvation" or "entire sanctification."

A second influence at this time was the concept of "a higher Christian life," from the teachings of the evangelist Charles G. Finney and other Presbyterian and Congregationalist leaders. This also promoted a "second experience" for Christians. It was different from the Holiness understanding, however. This second experience was not as much for purification as for the Holy Spirit to endow the believer with a special power to witness and serve God.

The third influence was a new emphasis on faith healing, popularized by A.B. Simpson, the founder of the Christian and Missionary Alliance. Simpson taught that the atonement of Christ provides physical healing in the same way it provides spiritual healing, and that this power is available to all true believers.

The fourth influence was a growing acceptance of "dispensational premillennialism." Dispensationalism teaches that God deals differently with people at different times, and that the present "church age" will end with the imminent rapture of the saints, followed by seven years of tribulation, and then the final return of Christ and the establishment of His millennial kingdom on earth. This doctrinal view grew from the teachings of the Plymouth Brethren and was popularized by the notes in the *Scofield Bible*.

The fifth influence was a longing for the power and miracles of the New Testament church and the "signs and wonders" of the book of Acts to be restored. Some understood Joel's reference to the "latter rain" (Joel 2:23 KJV), as a prophecy of a restoration of this kind of power in the end times. The understanding that there would be a renewal of these New Testament gifts and power is sometimes called "Restorationism." Several Restorationist movements were active around the turn of the century.

All five of these influences came together in the great Azusa Street Revival in Los Angeles in 1906. This revival continued until 1909 and is usually considered to be the birthplace of modern Pentecostalism.

Events leading up to the Azusa Street revival probably began with Charles Fox Parham, an evangelist who led a revival in Topeka, Kansas, in 1901. Parham equated the "second work of grace" with "baptism in the Holy Spirit," and taught that it was always accompanied by speaking in tongues. Parham insisted that this was normative for all Christians.

Parham's teachings influenced William J. Seymour, a member of a Restorationist group called Evening Light Saints. Seymour went to Los Angeles, where his preaching sparked the beginning of the Azusa Street Revival. The revival continued for three years and attracted many people, especially those from Holiness and Restorationist groups. Numerous denominations originated from the Azusa Street Revival. They include the Assemblies of God, the Church of God in Christ, the Church of God (Cleveland, Tennessee), and the Pentecostal Holiness Church. Aimee Semple McPherson started in the Assemblies of God, but in 1927 broke away and founded the International Church of the Foursquare Gospel. The emphases of the Foursquare Gospel are personal conversion, baptism of the Holy Spirit evidenced by tongues, physical healing, and the imminent second coming of Christ.

Other Pentecostal groups developed from some of the above, but the largest continual Pentecostal denomination since that time has been the Assemblies of God.

The Charismatic Renewal

The charismatic movement began in the 1960s and is considered a "renewal" by participants, because it brings together Christians of various groups and denominations in a unified concern for restoring the power and gifts of the Holy Spirit in today's churches. The term "Charismatic" comes from the Greek *charis*, meaning "gifts, grace, beauty, kindness." In secular literature this word usually refers to people who have special qualities of leadership to charm and influence others, but in theology it refers to spiritual gifts of ministry, service, and worship, inspired and empowered by the Holy Spirit.

As a movement, the Charismatic renewal began with Father Bennett of St. Mark's Episcopal Church in Van Nuys, California (1960). His belief in and practice of the gifts of tongues, healing, prophecy, and others, attracted Christians of many denominations. From there it spread to the Roman Catholic Duquesne University (1967) and finally to many branches of the church.

The Charismatic movement is often confused with Pentecostalism, but each is distinct. There are, of course, similarities. Both believe in the renewal of the gifts of the Spirit in the modern church. But the Charismatic movement differs from Pentecostalism in at least three ways:

1) It is not a separate movement, in the sense of a new denomination. The Charismatic movement spread internally and informally into many different denominations and religious groups without concern for its own organizational structure.

2) Charismatics emphasize a diversity of gifts, not just tongues. In addition, not all Charismatics claim tongues to be normative for all Christians.

3) Whereas Pentecostalism seemed to appeal to certain classes of society, the Charismatic movement includes all levels of social groups.

The Revival of Evangelicalism

The term "evangelical" has been in use for a long time, perhaps since the evangelical revivals and social action in England in the nineteenth century. In the twentieth century, however, it became more prominent.

The evangelical movement was a two-way reaction to religious liberalism on the one hand, and fundamentalism on the other. The latter part of the nineteenth century saw a significant rise of liberal scholars and church leaders who denied the inspiration and authority of Scripture and sought to modify Christian doctrine and belief to be more acceptable to the age of science. This resulted in the denial of miracles and almost everything supernatural.

One result of liberalism was the development of a counter-movement—fundamentalism, a movement to draw believers back to the fundamentals of the faith.

Between 1910 and 1915 *The Fundamentals*, a twelve-volume response to liberalism, was published. It contained ninety articles by sixty-four authors and was distributed to over 300,000 ministers and Christian workers. It defended the "fundamentals" of the faith, including belief in the deity of Christ, the infallibility of the Bible, the need for personal conversion, and similar basic doctrines. Those adhering to these doctrines became known as "fundamentalists," and the movement "fundamentalism." In 1923 the American Conference of Undenominational Churches was formed to provide cooperation and support for the fundamentalist cause. At its annual conference in Cicero, Illinois in 1930, the name was changed to The Independent Fundamental Churches of America. In addition to adhering to orthodox doctrines of the person of Christ, Scripture, salvation, etc., the IFCA also stressed the need for separation from apostasy based on 2 Corinthians 6:17.

Later, in 1941, under the leadership of Carl McIntire, another significant fundamentalist group was formed, taking the name American Council of Christian Churches. Founders of the ACCC were not only concerned about the liberalism in the Federal Council of Churches (now the National Council of Churches), but felt it was improper and unbiblical for fundamentalists and/or evangelicals to be in any fellowship or connectional relationship with either these major liberal movements or with others who are in such fellowship. True biblical separation, they felt, was to break away from both liberals and those who fellowship with them. Membership in the ACCC, therefore, was denied to those churches, denominations, or individuals having any affiliation with the World Council of Churches, the National Council of Churches, the World Evangelical Fellowship, the National Association of Evangelicals, the charismatic movement, or the ecumenical movement.

There were, however, a large number of Christians who agreed with *The Fundamentals* doctrinally, but were not pleased with fundamentalists. Their primary concern about fundamentalists was a seeming lack of graciousness and love toward other Christians who disagreed with them and a lack of concern for social causes and needs. This lack of social concern was sometimes called "the great reversal," because Christians in the nineteenth century were so active in social issues. Now, in the twentieth century, it seemed liberals were more concerned about social needs; whereas, fundamentalists were perceived as being only concerned about saving souls. Whether or not this was true, a large number of Christians chose to be called "evangelicals" rather than "fundamentalists." Evangelicals believe in the inerrancy of Scripture, the need for personal conversion and a life transformed by the Holy Spirit, the return of Jesus Christ, and the need for vigorous proclamation of the Gospel. The movement includes, but is much broader than, the Pentecostal movement. It stresses the importance of social concerns along with, but not in place of, personal conversion.

The evangelical movement received a strong boost from the ministry of Billy Graham and the Billy Graham Association. Graham came to be recognized as both a leader and example of evangelicalism. He was severely criticized by many fundamentalists because he was willing to allow individuals considered liberal to participate in his crusades.

Uncomfortable and not welcome in the more separatist fundamentalist groups, evangelicals formed the National Association of Evangelicals in 1942. The NAE exists as an organization through which evangelicals work together in areas such as education, military chaplaincy, social concerns, missions, political action, and similar kinds of issues. More than forty evangelical denominations joined the association along with a large number of independent churches.

Like the Charismatic movement, "evangelical" as well as "fundamentalist" are terms applied to people with certain beliefs and/or specific Christian sub-cultures. Neither term identifies a denomination. A denomination is a group of churches in the same organization and under a common administration.

Renewal within the Roman Catholic Church

The Roman Catholic Church experienced dramatic changes as a result of the general church council, Vatican II (1962-1965), called by Pope John XXIII.

Vatican II resulted in many changes in the Catholic Church. They include, but are not limited to, encouraging Bible reading and study for Catholics, changes in the mass from Latin to the vernacular, the altar brought forward with the priest facing the congregation, informal greetings in the worship service, congregational singing, and the relaxing of some of the authoritative, almost "superhuman," perceptions of papal authority. Some practices the reformers had so vigorously objected to four centuries earlier (such as the sale of indulgences) were minimized or discontinued. In addition, Pope John XXIII reached out to Protestant and Orthodox Christians by establishing the Secretariat for Promoting Christian Unity.

The fundamental concepts of a papal hierarchy and sacramental theology did not change. Attitudes, however, did change; and therefore the late twentieth century saw some healing between Catholics and Protestants that stands in stark contrast to the enmity of the previous five centuries. Catholics and Protestants studying the Bible together in informal groups became common for the first time in history.

Attempts at Unity

The twentieth century has seen various attempts to bring together the many splintered groups in the church. Those denominations with a more liberal persuasion sought to do this through organizational union (mergers) and cooperative ministries through the National Council of Churches and the World Council of Churches. These attempts became known as the "Ecumenical Movement" and led to several significant mergers of major denominations.

Evangelicals and fundamentalists reacted unfavorably to the ecumenical movement. They objected to the concept of Christian union being simply organizational rather than spiritual. Their primary concern, however, was the liberal influence in the ecumenical movement.

The Challenge of Eastern Mysticism

Disillusioned by the failure of science and education to bring peace and prosperity to the world, many people began to turn toward "spirituality" as the end of the twentieth century approached. Unfortunately, this spiritual renewal was not Christian. It marked a return to the paganism of ancient religious cults and the mysticism of the Orient.

The religious scene in America is undergoing dramatic and sometimes frightening changes. Eastern mystical ideas are attracting many, while others find Islam intriguing. Eastern mysticism sometimes blends with Christianity so those not aware of the differences are being caught up in beliefs and practices that are more occult-like than Christian. As God indicated through the prophet Hosea, "My people are destroyed from lack of knowledge" (Hos. 4:6).

We will study Eastern mysticism and our postmodern culture in Unit Six, Lessons 26—28.

Assignment

If possible, identify your personal denominational affiliation, or the affiliation of your family of origin. (If this doesn't apply, just pick a tradition you're interested in learning more about). In chart form, trace this denomination as far back as you can in order to learn about its origin and development. Be prepared in the next class to be the "expert" about the history and distinctiveness of this denomination. Compare it with at least one other denomination, and describe how the two are different.

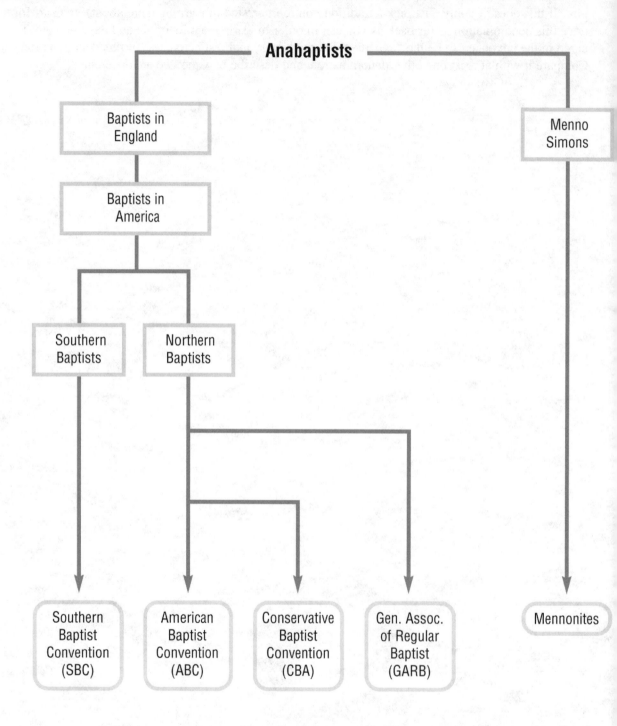

The groups cited above are only a few of the denominations descended from the early Anabaptist movement. Many other Baptist and Mennonite groups and sub-groups exist. Some are ethnic groups, such as German Baptists (North American Baptist Conference), Swedish Baptists (Baptist General Conference), National Baptists, etc. Some are separate because of distinctive beliefs, such as Seventh Day Baptists, Free Will Baptists, etc.

There are also many divisions of Mennonites, ranging all the way from the very conservative Amish to mainline groups such as the Mennonite General Conference.

U N I T

III

Pillars of Faith

LESSON 15

The Nature of God and the Person of Christ

<table>
<tr><td>

Equipment Needed

1) Chalkboard or whiteboard

</td><td>

Teaching Supplies Needed

1) Copies of student lesson 16 to distribute to the class.

</td></tr>
</table>

Lecture

Introduce the "Pillars of Faith" section as a time for each class member to search the Scriptures about the key issues of Christian belief. This will involve students doing some individual research and reflection. It will also necessitate their bringing a Bible to class. An assignment for Bible study will help prepare students for firsthand background of Bible knowledge. This knowledge will enrich class discussion.

Begin this class by asking for responses from student homework. Ask students to volunteer the comments they have written in their homework for each question, and list their responses on the chalkboard. Take each question in order:

1. Who is God?
2. What is God like?
3. Who is Jesus?

If students have been diligent about their preparation, this will stimulate some good discussion because they will have been thinking about these issues.

After this introduction, have students turn to page 176, "Attributes of God." Explain that the term, "attributes," is simply a scholarly name for "characteristics." We are listing the characteristics of God in a systematic way. Explain the difference between "natural" (sometimes called absolute or immanent) and "moral" (sometimes called relative or transitive) attributes. Natural attributes are what God is like in His innermost being, apart from creation. If there were no creation, these characteristics would still define the nature of God. Moral attributes define His *relationship* with His creation. Use this list of attributes as a guide for class discussion.

Explain that this is an example of how theologians have organized information about God. It is called "Systematic Theology," which simply means we look at each subject individually and in an orderly fashion. This class is a systematic study of the nature of God. Subsequent classes in this unit systematically study other subjects of theology.

It is, of course, impossible for us to understand God fully, but we can look at some of His major characteristics one at a time. Compare it to a jeweler examining a diamond, looking through his magnifying glass into one facet at a time.

The moral attributes can be divided further. Truth can be defined as "veracity" (absolute accuracy), and "faithfulness" (He will do what He promises). A map is a good illustration of veracity. If it is a truthful map it will accurately define the landscape. The features "on the ground" will be exactly the way they are depicted on the map.

Love can be divided into grace (God's giving us what we do not deserve), and mercy (not giving us what we do deserve). Holiness, also, can be defined by the two concepts of "justice" (God is entirely just) and "righteousness" (God always does what is right).

Also explain that the study of theology is a bit like learning a new language. Theologians have given names to various beliefs and concepts, which makes it easier to refer to them. The terms are like "handles" on the concepts. Most of these terms come from Greek or Latin and seem strange at first. The more you use them, however, the more familiar they become. As the instructor, you need to be able to define several of these terms. The list of definitions below will help:

Theology: The study of God. "Theos" is Greek for God. "ology" means a branch of learning.

Omnipresent: Present everywhere. "There is no place where God is not."

Omniscient: All-knowing.

Omnipotent: All-powerful.

Transcendent: Above, greater than, and separate from creation.

Immanent: Present with and closely involved with each individual and all of creation.

Paraclete: "One who is called alongside to help" (*Para*: alongside, as in "paramedical," "paralegal," etc. *Clete*: To call). Jesus used this term for the Holy Spirit whom He promised to send.

Discuss the meanings of "transcendence" and "immanence" with the class (Student section, page 176), and be sure they understand the meanings. This understanding is essential to a study of the alternate religions in Unit V.

Likewise, the section on the person of Christ is of great importance. Discuss this topic until you are confident all the class members thoroughly understood it.

When discussing the Holy Spirit, it is quite likely the class will want to explore the meaning of "baptism of the Spirit" and "filling of the Spirit." It is difficult to grasp these terms because people attach different meanings to them. You seldom

---

Sidebar (left column):

Write on the whiteboard as you describe:

Truth
  • Veracity
  • Faithfulness
Love
  • Grace
  • Mercy
Holiness
  • Justice
  • Righteousness

List student responses on the whiteboard.

know what a person means by these words without knowing something about their personal experience and affiliation.

Here are the two most common understandings.

The first has its origins in the Holiness tradition of a "second work of grace," which later was incorporated into a Charismatic understanding of an experience, subsequent to salvation, when the Holy Spirit endows a believer with special gifts and abilities. Such gifts may include speaking in tongues, prophecy, healing, etc. Persons so endowed and enriched are often referred to as "Spirit-filled."

The more traditional understanding is that the baptism of the Spirit is a one-time occurrence at the time of salvation. Those who hold this view refer to 1 Corinthians 12:13, where the term is used in the context of the Spirit placing us into the body of Christ. (The Greek word baptizo, translated "baptized" means literally "to immerse into.") They also call attention to the fact that there is no command in Scripture to be baptized by the Spirit. There is, however, a command to be filled with the Spirit (Eph. 5:18). According to this view, the filling is an ongoing process, not a singular event.

Our purpose in this class is to be sure our students understand the different views, not to promote one or the other. We are educators, not indoctrinators.

Attributes of God go beyond human understanding. It is sometimes helpful to explain that God is separate from and above the "time/space universe" of which we are a part. We cannot conceive of things like eternity or omniscience because our minds only work in time/space concepts. It is like a fish imagining living outside the fishbowl. This is not just a problem for theology. Unbelievers and atheists cannot explain "what was before time" either. Thinking about it is mind stretching, however, and will be a good mental exercise for our students. Remind them that of all the world's holy books, only the Bible provides clues to the existence of a system outside of and beyond our time/space universe, and the Bible's descriptions match what we are just now learning from astronomy and physics.

UNIT III

LESSON 15

The Nature of God and the Person of Christ

UNIT III

This is the first lesson of the "Pillars of Faith" section. In previous lessons we reviewed many differing opinions of scholars and church leaders about theological issues. In this section our purpose is to examine some of these questions ourselves and to ask, "What does the Bible say about this topic?" We will continue to study and compare the interpretations of various scholars, but this is primarily a time to investigate these things for yourself and come to your own conclusions.

Historically, the Bible has been the source of authority for Christians. Lesson 21 will examine reasons why it is logical and appropriate to trust the Bible. Meanwhile, let's assume it is true and trustworthy and go directly to Scripture in our search for answers.

In the study of theology, usually the first questions people ask are "Who is God?" "What is He like?" and "Who is Jesus?" These are fundamental questions because our view of God affects everything else about us.

Do some self-study this week on these questions and also questions about the person of Christ. The study of the person of Christ is called "Christology."

These three key questions are listed on the following pages, along with some Bible references that shed light on the subject. Please find and read these references in your Bible and summarize briefly what you think the Bible says about these questions.

You may not have time to read *all* of these Scripture passages. In that case, pick a few at random from each topic and respond to those. It is better to read one or two from each topic than all of them from only one topic.

Ready? Get your Bible, turn to page 179 in your manual, and let's start!

A group's belief about the person of Christ forms the watershed between orthodox faith and heresy. Because this is such an important subject, we will devote considerable time to discussing it in the next class session.

Before class, think about the nature of Christ and pray for understanding. You may want to review some of the false teachings about Christ that were declared heretical in early church councils. The notes are in Lessons 8 and 9, on pages 105-106 and 115-116. Also review The Nicene Creed discussed in Lesson 9. On the basis of the Scriptures you have read so far, do you think the delegates to the Council of Nicea got it right?

Class discussion will include biblical teaching about the Holy Spirit and the relationship of Father, Son, and Spirit. These deep and mysterious subjects tax our intellectual abilities to the limit. Please pray for God's wisdom in this search for truth.

The following pages summarize some of the major concepts about the nature of God, the person of Christ, and the Holy Spirit. Review them briefly. They will be an important reference in your next class discussion.

Attributes of God

God's natural attributes (Absolute, Immanent)
1) He is a person (possessing intellect, emotions, and will).
2) He is Spirit (Deut. 4:15-18; 5:8; John 4:24),
    As Spirit, He is invisible (Rom. 1:20; Col. 1:15; 1 Tim. 1:17; Heb. 11:27).
3) He is eternal (Deut. 32:40; Pss. 90:2; 102:27; 1 Tim. 6:16).
4) He is omnipresent (Ps. 139; Acts 17:27-28).
5) He is omniscient (Pss. 33:13-15; 139:2; 147:4; Isa. 46:9-10; Matt. 10:29-30; Heb. 4:13).
6) He is omnipotent (Ps. 115:3; Matt. 19:26; Eph. 4:11).

God's moral attributes (Relative, Transitive)
1. He is true (John 3:33; Rom. 3:4; Num. 23:19; Titus 1:2; Heb. 6:18).
2. He is love (Rom. 5:8; 1 John 4:8; Rev. 1:5).
3. He is holy (Deut. 32:4; Matt. 5:48; 1 Pet. 1:16).

In addition to the attributes listed God is also described in the Bible as both **transcendent** and **immanent**.

Transcendence means God is separate from and greater than His creation. He is "exalted . . . above the heavens." (Pss. 57:5, 11; 108:5)

Pantheists deny God's transcendence. They believe God and the universe are the same. Most Eastern religions and New Age religions are pantheistic.

Immanence means God is present with and closely involved in all of His creation. He is personally concerned with each individual and it is possible to maintain a continual relationship with Him. "Even the very hairs of your head are all numbered." (Matt. 10:30)

The Person of Christ

The doctrine of the person of Christ is the foundation of Christianity. Discussion about His nature occupied the earliest church councils, and the denial of either His deity or His humanity has always been declared heretical.

It is the cardinal conviction of the orthodox church that Jesus is fully God and fully man. Consider the decree of Chalcedon (A.D. 451), which states:

> We all with one voice confess our Lord Jesus Christ one and the same Son, at once complete in Godhead and complete in manhood, truly God and truly man...acknowledged in two natures, without confusion, without change, without division, or without separation; the distinction of natures being in no way abolished because of the union, but rather the characteristic property of each nature being preserved, and coming together to form one person.

1) Jesus is believed to be God because:
    His deity is taught in Scripture (John 1:1, 18; John 20:28; Heb. 1:8; 1 John 5:20).

2) He has attributes of God:
    a. He is eternal
        1) Existed before John (John 1:15)
        2) Existed before Abraham (John 8:58)
        3) Existed before the world (John 17:5, 24)
        4) Saw Satan fall from heaven (Luke 10:18)
        5) Existed "in the beginning" (John 1:1)
        6) Lives forever (Heb. 1:12; Rev. 1:18)
    b. He is omnipresent and omniscient

       1) Matthew 18:20; 28:19-20
       2) John 1:48-49; 2:24-25; 4:29; 13:21-26; 16:30; 21:17
       3) Colossians 2:3
   c. He is omnipotent
       1) Revelation 1:8; Hebrews 1:3, Matthew 28:18; Colossians 1:15-17
       2) He has power over disease, death, and nature

3) He exercises the prerogatives of deity
   a. He forgives sin (Matt. 9:1-8)
   b. He executes judgment (John 5:22; Rev. 19:15; Acts 17:31; Matt. 25:31-32)
   c. He is called Lord and accepts worship (Matt. 7:21-22; 14:33; 15:25; 22:41-44; 28:9
     Luke 1:43; 2:11; Acts 16:31; 1 Cor. 12:3; Phil. 2:9-11)
   (Note: God, *only*, is to be worshiped—Exod. 34:14, Matt. 4:10)

Jesus is believed to be fully human because:
   1) The Bible declares Him to be (Phil. 2:5-8)
   2) He "came in the flesh" (1 John 1:1; 4:2-3—the "incarnation")
   3) His sacrifice was that of a man (1 Cor. 15:21)
   4) Scripture calls Him man (1 Tim. 2:5)
   5) He repeatedly called Himself the "Son of man"
   6) He experienced human limitations (hunger, thirst, weariness, temptation, etc.)

The Holy Spirit

It is apparent in Scripture that the Holy Spirit is a person, the third person of the Trinity. He is represented as one who "comes alongside" the believer to guide, comfort, and help. The Holy Spirit was active in creation (Gen. 1:2), and He is the Giver of life in regeneration as well.

The work of the Holy Spirit in the life of the believer includes:
   1) Conviction of sin (John 16:8)
   2) Cleansing from sin (Rom. 8:13)
   2) Assistance in prayer (Rom. 8:26)
   3) Equipping with gifts of service (Rom. 12:3-8; 1 Cor. 12:1-31)
   4) Producing spiritual fruit (Gal. 5:16-26)
   5) Giving assurance of salvation (Rom. 8:16)
   6) Sealing the believer for the day of redemption (Eph. 4:30)
   and much more!

The Holy Spirit is active in the life of every true believer; guiding, convicting, comforting, encouraging, and ministering the presence of Christ. Sometimes the terms "baptism of the Spirit," and "filling of the Spirit" are used to refer to a special work of the Holy Spirit in an individual's life. These terms are variously defined among different Christian groups and can be controversial.

The Trinity

One of the greatest mysteries of our faith is the doctrine of the Trinity. The word "trinity" does not occur in the Bible; it is simply a name given to the belief that Father, Son, and Holy Spirit are separate persons but one God.

How three can be one in the Godhead is a concept that goes beyond our human ability to grasp. That does not mean it is illogical or contradictory. Similar to many mysteries in nature in this age of quantum physics, things sometimes seem contradictory simply because we do not understand them.

In our finite understanding, we do not fully know the meaning of "Godness" (to coin a new word), nor do we understand the meaning of "persons" in relation to God. It is no doubt different than "Tom, Dick, and Harry" in our experience. We simply rest in the knowledge that Scripture clearly teaches that the Father, the Son, and the Holy Spirit are each God. It also clearly teaches that God is one. We can go so far and no further in our understanding of God. We simply stand in awe and holy reverence, remembering God's own declaration; "For my thoughts are not your thoughts, neither are your ways my ways, declares the LORD. As the heavens are higher than the earth, so are my ways higher than your ways and my thoughts than your thoughts." (Isa. 55:8-9).

1. Who is God?   Notes

Genesis 1:1

Deuteronomy 4:35

Deuteronomy 6:4

Deuteronomy 7:9-11

1 Kings 8:60

Isaiah 40:9-31

Isaiah 43:10

Isaiah 45:22

John 17:3

1 Corinthians 8:4-6

2. What is God like?

Numbers 23:19

Deuteronomy 4:15-18

Deuteronomy 32:4, 39

Psalm 27:10

Psalm 90:2

Psalm 139

Isaiah 46:9-10

Matthew 6:25-34

(Cont'd)

What is God like?   Notes

    Matthew 10:28-31

    Matthew 19:26

    John 4:24

    2 Corinthians 1:35

    1 Timothy 1:17

    Titus 1:2

    1 John 4:7-16

    Revelation 21:3-4

3. Who is Jesus?

    John 1:1-4

    John 8:21-26; 48-58

    John 17:5, 24

    Philippians 2:1-11

    Colossians 1:15-20; 2:2-3

    Hebrews 1:1-14

    Hebrews 2:14-18

    Hebrews 4:15

    1 John 5:20

LESSON 16

The Nature of Man and the Means of Salvation

Equipment Needed	**Teaching Supplies Needed**
1) Chalkboard or whiteboard	1) Copies of student lesson 17 to distribute to the class.

Request assignment responses from your student, and list each response on the whiteboard. Pursue each question separately:
1. What is man?
   Be prepared for discussion about the meaning of "image of God." It is usually defined as the moral, rational nature of man—the ability to relate to God, to distinguish between right and wrong, and to be creative.
2. What is man's present condition?
3. How can a man be made righteous before God?
4. How does Christ's sacrifice become effective for me? (What do I have to *do*?)
5. What happens to me when I place my faith in Christ?
6. What does God expect of me as a result of my faith?

This is a very important lesson because it deals with the plan of salvation and how a person becomes a Christian. Some of your students may not have personally trusted in Christ, or they may be depending upon their works to save them. This may be their opportunity to learn the basic elements of salvation.

Lecture

Be sure to stress these basic points:
1. Everyone is guilty of sin. No exceptions. (Rom. 3:23). And "the wages of sin is death" (Rom. 6:23).
2. Christ died in our place to pay the penalty for sin.
3. We can be accepted and forgiven if we repent and place our faith in Christ.
4. True faith is life changing.

You don't need to preach! Just emphasize and clarify these points as students share the results of their study.

There may be a question about how Adam's sin and guilt can be transmitted to us, who were not personally involved in that transgression. It's a complex question, and one for which Scripture does not give a detailed answer. Theologians have proposed several theories, all the way from Adam and Eve's example and the influence of an evil environment to an innate deficiency genetically transmitted from generation to generation. The latter is the most commonly accepted understanding among evangelicals. These various explanations are called "Theories of Imputation."

Write student responses on the whiteboard.

Ask the participants to elaborate on the definitions of the three key terms: Justification, Regeneration and Sanctification: (Page 187 of the Student section)

Justification is a declaration of acquittal. When a judge acquits someone, that acquitted person is free from the penalty of the law, regardless of his actual guilt. A sinner who repents and receives Christ is justified on the basis of Christ's work, not on the basis of his works. This is an extremely important concept, because most people assume they need to earn their salvation. Doing so would be utterly impossible. Some Scripture passages you may wish to study about justification include: Acts 13:38-39; Romans 3:21-24; and Romans 5:1-21.

One result of justification is adoption by God as a member of His family, in line for inheritance (Gal. 4:1-7; Eph. 1:3-5).

Regeneration is the new life given to the believer by the work of the Holy Spirit. This mysterious work is sometimes called "new birth" in Scripture. At other times it is referred to as "being made alive in Christ," "new nature," or the "new man." This new life is implanted by the indwelling Holy Spirit and enables the believer to live a righteous life (2 Pet. 1:3-11).

For background study see John 3:1-8; 1 Peter 1:22-25; and 1 John 3:7-10.

Sanctification is the process by which a person is transformed into the image and likeness of Christ. The sanctified person actually becomes what she was declared to be when justified. The person reflects the image of Christ by a righteous life. This image-bearing is made possible by the work of the Holy Spirit and the believer's obedience to the will of God. The result is a demonstration of the fruit of the Spirit and a Christ like character (Gal. 5:22-25; 2 Pet. 1:3-10)

Christians differ about how this process takes place. Holiness groups, following the teaching of John Wesley, contend it is possible to experience "entire sanctification" in a single spiritual experience subsequent to salvation. Wesley, however, never claimed "sinless perfection," as some of the later Holiness groups did. He saw entire sanctification as a perfection in love (or attitude), out of which the Christian worships God and ministers in love to others. In that sense, his understanding of sanctification was centered on an immediate event followed by a life of holiness. The more traditional view defines sanctification as a lifelong process, not completed until we meet Christ.

This difference in teaching about sanctification and the possibility of living a sinless life is probably based, at least in part, on differing definitions of sin. Some theologians define sin as "any voluntary transgression of a known law." The more traditional definition is "any lack of conformity to the moral law of God," and includes a state of being, not just actions. The latter definition would also include involuntary sin and sins of ignorance; it represents a much higher standard.

Suggested passages for background study include Philippians 2:12-13; Ephesians 2:11-13; 1 Thessalonians 4:3-8; and 2 Thessalonians 2:13.

Illustration

I've found the following illustration, used by a life insurance agent in his presentation, to be helpful in explaining the concepts of justification, regeneration, and sanctification. You may find it useful. He started by drawing a rectangle

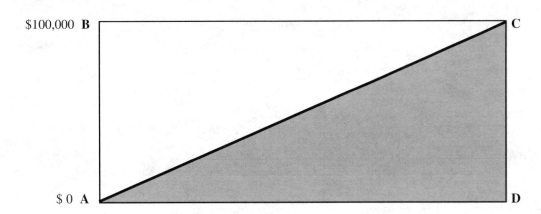

He asked me: "How old are you?"

I said, "Twenty-five." He said the bottom line, (A-D) would represent age, with my current age to the left and age sixty-five to the right. He then asked, "If you were to die tonight, how much money would you leave for your family?"

I said, "None."

He said the vertical line, (A-B) represents the amount of money I had in the bank to leave for my family in the event of my death, and wrote "zero." Then he asked, "How much money do you wish you had in the bank for your family if you were to die tonight?"

I replied, "$100,000."

So he wrote $100,000 at the top of the chart (B). "This," he said, "represents what you want to leave for your family.

"Now," he said, "there is no way you can have that money in the bank tonight without creating an obligation just as large—simply because you don't have it! But here's what I can do for you. If you will just sign this application, my company, with its huge financial resources, will declare you worth $100,000, even though you are penniless. If anything happens to you tonight, your family will have $100,000 in the bank just as if you had earned it and put it on deposit."

He continued his presentation with "Not only that, but you will change your financial habits in the future. Instead of wasting all your money on non-essentials, you will be sending some to my company every month. They will put it on deposit for you. Therefore, the area on the chart (A-C-D) represents a growing 'nest egg' that in reality is all your money. When you reach age sixty-five, you will actually be worth what my company has declared you to be worth for forty years!"

To me it was an amazing illustration of justification, regeneration, and sanctification. You come to Christ, trust Him, receive forgiveness of sin, and He declares you righteous, even if you do not have one righteous act to point to in your whole life! That's justification.

As a result of your justification and the presence of the Holy Spirit's work in your life, your interests and your conduct change. What was dead comes to life. That's regeneration. Now you find you are gradually taking on the nature and character of Christ. That's sanctification.

Finally, when you meet Christ (not at age sixty-five—no illustration is perfect!) you will actually be what He declared you to be on the day of your justification. (Phil. 1:6).

LESSON 16

The Nature of Man and the Means of Salvation

"What is man...?"   (Ps. 8:4)

Knowing the nature of man is important not only in theology but also in all of life. How we construct government, families, relationships, economics, and most everything about us is based on our understanding of the nature of man. In theology, the topic is critical. Is man basically good, not needing salvation? Or is man a sinner by nature and resting under the condemnation of God? If the latter, what provision has God made, if any, for man to be redeemed? These are awesome questions with eternal consequences!

Read the Scriptures referenced below. As you read them, ponder the questions and jot down impressions that come to your mind. Come to the next class session with your mind full of Scripture on this subject, and be prepared for a great discussion.

1) **What is man?** (Scripture uses "man" in the generic sense, meaning the human race. The term does not denote male, as opposed to female)

   Genesis 1:26-30
   Psalm 8:4-8

2) **What is man's present condition?**

   Genesis 3:16-24
   Psalm 143:2
   Proverbs 20:9
   Ecclesiastes 7:20
   Jeremiah 17:9
   John 3:3-5
   Romans 3:10-12, 19, 23
   Romans 5:12
   1 John 1:8

3) In the words of Job, "How then can a man be righteous before God? How can one born of woman be pure?" (Job 25:4)

Isaiah 53:4-6
1 Corinthians 15:3
Mark 10:45
Romans 5:8
Hebrews 9:24-28
1 Peter 2:24
1 John 3:5

4) So, if Christ paid the price for my sin, what, if anything, do I have to do?

John 3:14-18
Acts 16:29-31
Romans 3:28
Romans 5:1
Galatians 2:16, 20
Galatians 3:11
Ephesians 2:8-9
Titus 3:5-7

5) What happens to me when I place my faith in Christ?

John 3:1-8
Romans 8:9-11
Galatians 5:22-26

6) What does God expect of me as a result of my faith?

Romans 6:15-18
Romans 8:12-17
Romans 12:1-8
Ephesians 2:10
Ephesians 4— 6 (Ephesians 4:22-24 is a key passage.)
Titus 3:8

The Nature of Man and the Means of Salvation

Based on your study of Scripture (pages 185-186), you have no doubt come to certain conclusions about the nature of man. After thinking about this subject, write a one or two sentence summary below about the spiritual condition of mankind:

You have also studied Scriptural teaching about the means of salvation, which is centered in the work of Christ. Theologians often call Jesus' death on the cross a "vicarious" sacrifice, meaning it was substitutionary. Jesus represented us on the cross and died as our substitute. Being fully man, He was able to die as a man and represent the human race. Being sinless and perfect, He was able to pay the price for others, since He did not have to pay the price for Himself.

In your study, you saw that Christ's effective work is appropriated by personal faith. This was pictured in the Old Testament whenever the priest would lay his hands on an animal sacrifice, symbolizing the transference of the sin of the worshiper to the animal that was sacrificed. In the same sense, personal faith expresses the confidence that He paid the penalty of our sins. In turn, His righteousness is "credited" to us (Rom. 4:6, 8, 11, 22-24; 2 Cor. 5:19; Jas. 2:23). In the King James Version, the word "credit" is translated "impute." Therefore, this doctrine of the reversal of guilt and innocence between Christ and us became known as "the doctrine of imputation."

The scriptural definition of faith includes agreement to the fact that Jesus is Lord, that He died in our place, and that He rose again. It is more than just intellectual assent, however. (See Jas. 2:14-26.) Saving faith involves a commitment of life to Christ, evidenced by subsequent change in behavior. This change in behavior is made possible by the indwelling Holy Spirit and by the believer's choice to be obedient to the Spirit and the Word.

Theologians use three key words to describe what happens to us when we place our faith in Christ. The words are: Justification, Regeneration, and Sanctification. A brief definition of each word follows:

Justification: To declare righteous. It is like a judge declaring a person to be free from the penalty of the law and restored to favor. Justification relates to guilt and innocence, but is different. A person may be guilty, but still justified in the sight of the law. In that sense, we are all guilty of sin but have been "justified freely" in Christ. God declares us justified by faith. He sees in us the righteousness of Christ because we are "clothed in His righteousness."

Regeneration: The impartation of a new nature. Regeneration is the act whereby the Holy Spirit brings back to life what was dead. We were dead in our sins, but the indwelling Holy Spirit brought us back to life through the new birth. Being "born again" results in our having a new nature with different desires and purposes.

Sanctification: The act or process by which people or things are cleansed and dedicated to God, ritually and morally. In the Old Testament, things (for example, the vessels in the temple used for worship) were cleansed and dedicated to God. They were not to be used for secular use. In the New Testament, the word is used to refer to people who are cleansed and dedicated to God. Believers (the Bible calls them "saints") actually become, through sanctification, what they are declared to be in their justification. There seems to be a "past, present, and future" aspect to sanctification. That is, we *were* sanctified when we came to Christ, we are *being* sanctified in our spiritual walk, and we *will be* sanctified when we meet Christ at His coming.

LESSON 17
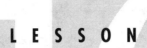

The Doctrine of the Church and Supernatural Beings

Equipment Needed

1) Chalkboard or whiteboard

Teaching Supplies Needed

1) Copies of student lesson 18 to distribute to the class.

Guide the class through the various topics of this week's lesson, encouraging discussion and interaction. Students will no doubt try to relate the organization of their own church or previous churches they have attended, to these scriptural terms and principles. Focus on function (of church officers, etc.) rather than titles. Often the titles of church officers will vary from one church or denomination to another, while the functions of those offices will be quite similar.

In our time, Christians frequently move from one church or denomination to another, and are unfamiliar with the differences in church government. They consequently become frustrated because things are not done the way they were in their last church, which they naturally assume to be the "right" way. Explaining the differences in church government helps build understanding and acceptance.

Lecture

Define church

The Student section explains the meaning of the original Greek word translated "church" in English. *Ekklesia* is the root of the English word "ecclesiastical," meaning "that which relates to the church or church government."

In Greek, "ekklesia" means literally, "called out ones." Ask students to suggest reasons why the church (the people who belong to Christ) might be considered "called out ones."

Our English word "church," comes from the German *Kirche* and Latin *kirika*, which in turn comes from the Greek *kyriake*, meaning "the Lord's house." Unfortunately, many people still think the word "church" means a building. That is just one of the meanings, but in New Testament usage it means the "called out ones" who are in Christ.

Write "Body," "Building," and"Bride" on the board. Under each, list the characteristics of the church suggested by the students. If you're artistic, you may wish to draw a picture of a body, a building, and a bride.

The Student section lists three analogies of the church used in the New Testament: A body, a building, and a bride. Write these three words on the board, one at a time, and ask the class to suggest what each analogy tells us about the church. Write each person's suggestion on the board. Responses might include:

Body: The church is alive! It is an organism, not just an organization. Christ is the Head, and every part of the body, whether visible or unseen, attractive or not, is vital to the body's health. (See 1 Cor. 12 and Rom. 12:3-8.)

Building: We are, both individually and collectively, the dwelling place of God. God's Spirit lives inside us. Just as the Old Testament temple represented the presence of God, so does the church.

Bride: The church should be growing in loveliness, in anticipation of its eternal union with Christ, the bridegroom. The relationship between Christ and the church should be the very closest spiritual union imaginable.

Class members have been thinking about these analogies as part of their assignment, and will probably come up with other suggestions. These are just a few examples to get you started thinking.

Church Officers

Review the titles and functions of the church officers listed on page 193 of the Student section. How do they compare with officers in the student's church?

Point out the vast differences between how titles are used in various churches and denominations. The titles are not important. The functions are. It is probably purposeless and divisive to argue about whether an office should be called "elder," "deacon," "bishop," "pastor," etc. What these officers are responsible to do and their qualifications for that function are much more important.

The terms "bishop" (or "overseer," depending on the translation) and "elder" are often considered synonymous because they seem to be used interchangeably in the New Testament. For example, in Paul's letter to Timothy (1 Tim. 3:1-7) he listed the qualifications of church leaders and calls them bishops (overseers). In his letter to Titus (Titus 1:5-9) he called them elders. Perhaps "elder" refers to the office, and bishop (overseer) refers to the function. In Jewish synagogues, elders exercised oversight. It would be natural for the title to transfer to early Christian churches.

Define the role of deacons and pastors as well, using Acts 6:1-7 as a basis for understanding the origin of the office of deacon. Pastors may have been a separate office or merely a reference to one of the duties of elders.

Ordinances / Sacraments

Carefully distinguish the difference in meaning between ordinances and sacraments, as defined on page 194 of the Student section. Point out that the terms are used loosely in our time, and most people aren't aware of the difference in meaning. Consequently, not everyone who calls these rituals sacraments believes in "sacramental theology."

This was a big issue during the Reformation. Ask students to recall the conflict we saw in the church history section between the papacy and some of the reformers about the significance of the mass. Do the mass and other sacraments actually dispense grace, or are these rituals only a remembrance and symbol of spiritual truth?

Perhaps some of your students have experienced churches that practice the ordinances or sacraments differently than their present church. Allow opportunity for them to describe that practice.

Church Government/Organization

Refer to the Student section, page 194, for a description of the three major forms of church government. Draw the diagram shown on the following page on the board as you discuss each. Ask students to share their comments (from their assignments) about the advantages and/or disadvantages of each form.

Angels

The Student section lists considerable information about characteristics and activities of both "good" and "evil" angels. Use remaining class time to review this list and, if time permits, ask students to look up some of the references and read them to the class.

Draw diagram comparing the three forms of church government.

UNIT III

Church Government

In the Episcopal form, authority flows from top to bottom (for example, in the Roman Catholic Church, from the pope and cardinals, to archbishop, to bishop, to parish priest, to church members). The Roman Catholic Church is the best example of a pure form of Episcopal church government.

Pope and Cardinals

Archbishops

Bishops

Parish Priests

The Faithful

In the Congregational form, authority rests within the congregation, and church officers are chosen by and responsible to the membership.

Officers	Congregation	Officers

The Presbyterian form reflects a combination of the two. Church members select representatives to the Presbytery. They in turn send representatives to the Synod, which chooses representatives to the General Assembly. Authority then flows downward from the General Assembly, through the same channels, to the local church.

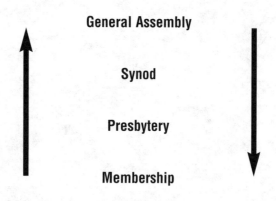

General Assembly

Synod

Presbytery

Membership

LESSON 17

The Doctrine of the Church and Supernatural Beings

This lesson covers two subjects; the church and supernatural beings (specifically, angels). The biblical teaching about each is summarized below. As you read this section, also look up the Bible references given and reflect on their meaning and their implications.

The Church

The word translated "church" in our English versions of the New Testament, comes from the Greek word *ekklesia*. It means "the called out ones." The Bible uses the term to refer to both the church universal and to local groups of believers. In both cases, the term applies to those who are "in Christ."

The New Testament uses several analogies to describe the church. The three most important are:

1) A body (1 Cor. 12; Eph. 4:4; Col. 3:15)
2) A building (1 Pet. 2:5; Eph. 2:20; 1 Cor. 3:9, 16-17)
3) A bride (Eph. 5:25-27, 31-32; 2 Cor. 11:1-2; Rev. 19:7; 22:17)

Church Officers

The New Testament seems to imply a very simple organization in the church. In fact, the church is represented as an "organism" rather than an "organization." The officers referred to include:

1) Bishops and elders. The two terms seem to be used synonymously. The word "bishop" means "overseer." Elder is probably a carryover from leaders of Israel in Old Testament times who were overseers in the synagogues. Examples of the mention of elders and bishops are: Philippians 1:1; 1 Timothy 3:1-7, and Titus 1:5-9

2) Deacons, from the Greek *diakonos*, meaning "helpers." Acts 6:1-7; Romans 16:1; 1 Timothy 3:8-13.

3) Pastors. The word means "shepherd." It is translated as pastor only once in our English versions (Eph. 4:11). The same word occurs more than a dozen times in the New Testament, however, and is usually translated "shepherd," referring to Christ.

The simple form of the early church, then, seemed to include elders/bishops who had the general oversight of the church, deacons who assisted them, and pastors who tended to the spiritual needs of the flock. Teachers are also mentioned as an important part of the leadership but as a function rather than as an officer.

The church gathered regularly in homes for teaching, worship, and fellowship (See Acts 2:42-47). When they met, they frequently observed the Lord's Supper. Baptism was practiced for new believers.

Ordinances / Sacraments

Most Protestant churches continue to observe the Lord's Supper and Baptism as the two "ordinances" of the church. Some add foot washing as an ordinance. A few (such as the Friends) do not believe these ordinances were intended to be observed literally but have only spiritual significance. The Roman Catholic Church believes there are not two, but seven sacraments to be literally observed.

Some churches refer to these observances as "sacraments," while others prefer the term "ordinances." There is a significant difference. An ordinance is defined as "a ritual that illustrates and brings to memory a spiritual truth." A sacrament, on the other hand, is "a ritual that, when properly administered, confers grace upon the recipient." Those who prefer the term "ordinance," do so because they do not believe the ritual actually confers any special grace. It simply pictures or commemorates a spiritual truth. Those who prefer the term "sacrament" tend to believe the ritual in and of itself confers some spiritual grace or power. This belief is called "sacramental theology."

Church Government / Organization

A difference exists in the form of church government practiced in various denominations. The three major forms of church government are:

Episcopal: The authority of the church flows "from top down." The theory is that Christ makes His will known through the leadership of the church, with directives and guidance in matters of faith and practice being passed down through a hierarchy. The Roman Catholic Church is the best example of the Episcopal form.

Congregational: The authority of the church rests in the congregation. The theory is that Christ makes His will known through the congregation collectively. They in turn come to consensus in matters of faith and practice and choose leaders to direct and organize the work and to serve as teachers, pastors, and officers. The officers, then, are actually servants of the congregation.

Presbyterian: This form of church government is a hybrid of the other two. The name Presbyterian" comes from the Greek *presbuteros*, which means "elder." Elders govern the church, but they are chosen by the congregation or congregations.

The form of government a church or denomination adopts is often determined by both tradition and the situation surrounding the congregation. Scripture does not seem to be clear or precise about the exact form to be followed. It has been said that a church (or denomination) tends to adopt a form of church government similar to the government of the nation in which they are founded. There seems to be historical support for that assumption.

The important thing to remember is that, whatever the form, Christ is the head of the Church and the Church consists of the body of believers who belong to Him. He is cleansing and purifying the church, preparing it for the day the Church will be united with Him forever, just as a bride is prepared for her wedding day.

Angels

The Bible clearly teaches the existence of supernatural spiritual beings called "angels" (from the Greek *angelos*, meaning "messenger") that exist both in our universe and in the presence of God. The study of these creatures is fascinating, and has captured the imagination of many in our culture.

UNIT III

Unfortunately, the "angel fad" has been sadly commercialized and has brought with it some unbiblical teaching about angels.

One thing to be remembered is that humans never become angels when they die. Angels are an entirely separate creation. Also, angels are not always good. There are good angels and evil angels. Scripture calls the evil angels "demons." They live in a state of rebellion against God under the leadership of Satan. God has not provided a plan of redemption for them. They are under His condemnation, and He will consign them to eternal doom.

Let's begin with a brief review of the characteristics of angels in general. The following list, with a few Scripture references as examples, should provide some insight:

1) They are incorporeal—do not have physical bodies (Heb. 1:14; Eph. 6:12).
2) They are able to appear in various forms (Ps. 104:4; Heb. 1:7; Exod. 3:1-2; Luke 1:11-13).
3) They are "asexual"; not a race (Matt. 22:30).
4) They are created beings (Ps. 148:1-5).
5) They will never die (Luke 20:34-36).
6) They are exceedingly powerful (2 Thess. 1:6-7).
7) They are a great multitude (Rev. 5:11; Deut. 33:2; Ps. 68:17; Dan. 7:9-10).
8) They are organized, and some have leadership titles (Matt. 26:52-53; 1 Thess. 4:16; Jude 9).

The activities of the "good" angels include:
1) Worshiping God (Ps. 29:1-2)
2) Serving God (Ps. 103:20; Heb.1:7)
3) Guiding the affairs of nations (Dan. 10; 11:1; 12:1)
4) Watching over churches (Rev. 1:20; 1 Cor. 11:10)
5) Assisting individual believers (1 Kings 19:3-9; Ps. 91:9-14; Dan. 6:21-22; Matt. 4:10-11; Heb. 1:14; Matt. 18:10; Luke 16:22; Gen. 48:15-16)
6) Guiding and encouraging God's people (Matt. 28:5-7; Acts 8:26; 27:23-24)
7) Protecting God's people (Gen.19:1-13; Dan. 3:28; Acts 5:17-20; 12:5-11)
8) Executing God's judgments (Acts 12:23; Rev. 15:1; 16:1)
9) Accompanying Christ at His return, gathering the saints to meet Him, and executing judgment on unbelievers (1 Thess. 4:16; Matt. 13:39-50; 24:31)
10) Rejoicing in God's work (Job 38:4-7; Luke 15:10)

At some point in the past, Lucifer, a beautiful angel of light, rebelled against God, and many of the angels joined in his rebellion. He is referred to in Scripture by numerous uncomplimentary names, including Satan, Devil, Beelzebub, Belial, the Dragon, the Wicked One, Serpent, Tempter, The God of this World, Prince of this World, Prince of the Power of the Air, and The Evil One. His followers, called "demons" or "evil spirits" are under the same condemnation as Lucifer (2 Pet. 2:4; Jude 6). Their activities include:
1) Opposing and frustrating God's work (Dan. 10:12-13; Eph. 6:12; Mark 4:15; Matt. 13:37-39)
2) Possessing individuals whose personality and will are set aside and the evil spirit controls them (Mark 1:21-28; 9:14-27)
3) Promoting false religions (2 Thess. 2:9-10; 1 Cor. 10:18-20)

Angels are not to be worshiped! See Colossians 2:18 and Revelation 22:8-9.

UNIT III

Assignment

Write a sentence or two in response to each of the following questions. Be prepared to share your answers with the class:

1) Think about the analogies used in Scripture to describe the church. In what ways is the church like:

    — A body?

    — A building?

    — A bride?

2) What advantages / disadvantages do you see in each of the three major forms of church government?

    — Episcopal

    — Congregational

    — Presbyterian

UNIT III

LESSON 18

The Return of Christ and the Doctrines of "Last Things"

UNIT III

Equipment Needed	Teaching Supplies Needed
1) Chalkboard or whiteboard	1) Copies of student lesson 19 to distribute to the class.

Lecture

1. Begin this class with student feedback from the Bible reading assignments:
   - Isaiah 9:6-7
   - Daniel 2:44-45 and 7:27
   - Philippians 2:10-11
   - Revelation 19:11-16; 21; 22

   Write student responses on the board and discuss.
   Suggested discussion questions might include:
   - What are the basic elements involved in the Lord's return?
     Possible responses could be: He will rule on David's throne; it will be an eternal kingdom; it will be "in the time of those kings" (Dan. 2:44); *everyone* will bow to Him, etc.
   - What effect should the knowledge of His return have on us?
     (You may wish to refer to passages such as Matt. 24:42-51; 25:13; Heb. 10:36-37; and Titus 2:11-15.)

2. Discuss the significance of how heavily the topic of Christ's return permeates all of Scripture. Refer to the quotation from *Signs of the Times* in the Student section, page 201.

3. Define "Eschatology." *Eschatos* is the Greek word for "last." Eschatology includes a broad range of subjects, including the Lord's return, personal immortality, heaven and hell, etc.

4. Refer to the characteristics of Christ's return given on page 201 of the Student section (Sure, Sudden, Spectacular, Secret). How do these truths shape our expec-

Write student responses on the whiteboard.

tations? Do they change any perceptions students now hold about the second coming?

5. Discuss the three major events associated with Christ's return: The Rapture, the Tribulation, and the Millennium. Review the discussion of each of these events in the Student section.

6. Note the three major views concerning the Millennium, and discuss each. (The amillennial, postmillennial and premillennial positions)

Draw diagrams of pretribulational, midtribulational and postribulational views.

7. Explain the three major premillennial views regarding the Rapture and the Tribulation. Draw charts as you explain each. For an example of charts for each of these views, see page 200 of this Leader's section. Refer to the arguments for each view in the Student section, pages 203-205.

It is not our purpose in this course to endorse or promote any of these views, but to be sure our students understand them and the reasons given in support of each position. Probably the most commonly accepted view among evangelicals is the premillennial, pre-tribulational position. This may be due in part to the fact that dispensational theology became very popular in the late 1800's. Dispensational theology teaches that God deals differently with people during various dispensations of time.

The church age, called "the Dispensation of Grace," extends from Pentecost (some dispensationalists use a different starting point) to the Rapture. Since dispensational theology draws a sharp distinction between Israel and the church, the pre-tribulational view fits it well. Dispensationalists believe that when the church age ends (at the Rapture) the Jewish clock "begins ticking again," and the fulfillment of all the kingdom prophecies given to Israel in the Old Testament will be realized. This view was popularized in the Scofield Bible notes and has been widely accepted during the past century. Our students need to know, however, that this interpretation is of comparatively recent origin.

The fact that various conflicting views exist should not be allowed to detract from the basic message of the Lord's return, which is where this lesson started and where it should conclude. We feel it is important for our students to be familiar with these various positions, because there is so much being published and taught today, sometimes dogmatically, by various authors and teachers.

It may be well, at this point, to remind our students about the nature of prophecy. God doesn't tell us about future events so that we can make charts. He tells us these things so we can have hope, be faithful, and look forward to Christ's return. Often the details don't make sense until it happens.

Eschatology also includes the study of personal immortality. Scripture is clear that the dead will be raised; the righteous to reign with Christ and the unsaved to eternal punishment. Between an individual's physical death and the resurrection, the saved are apparently with Christ in heaven while the lost are suffering in hell. Jesus gave a real-life description of individuals in heaven and in hell in Luke 16:19-31.

The period of time between death and the resurrection is sometimes called the "intermediate state." During this time we exist as disembodied, but fully conscious

UNIT III

spirits. At the return of Christ, the spirits of the saints who have died will return with Him and will inherit new bodies—"the same," but "different:" (See 1 Cor. 15:35-58.) Believers still alive will be instantly changed (1 Thess. 4:13-18; 1 Cor. 15:51-52).

The experiences and environment of God's people in the eternal future is mysterious and fascinating. There is mention of reigning with Christ (Rev. 20:6; 22:5), and never again experiencing mourning, tears, death, or pain (Rev. 21:4).

Suggested Chart of Pre-tribulational and Post-tribulational views:

The Pre-tribulational View:

The "Church Age"	Christ returns *for* the church	Tribulation	Christ returns *with* the church	The Millennium
	(The "Rapture")	Seven yrs.		1,000 yrs.

Note: The Mid-tribulational view is essentially the same as the Pre-tribulational view, except that Christ would return in the middle of the tribulation rather than before the tribulation.

The Post-tribulational View:

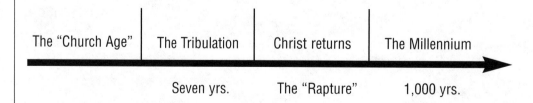

The "Church Age"	The Tribulation	Christ returns	The Millennium
	Seven yrs.	The "Rapture"	1,000 yrs.

LESSON 18

The Return of Christ and the Doctrines of "Last Things"

The return of Christ to receive and reward His people, destroy evil, and establish His eternal kingdom, is the ultimate goal of history. It is the blessed hope of the church (Titus 2:13) and the fulfillment of dozens of prophecies permeating both Old and New Testaments. Read the following passages and jot a note about what impresses you most in each prophecy:

Isaiah 9:6-7

Daniel 2:44-45 and 7:27

Philippians 2:10-11

Revelation 19:11-16; 21; 22

Paul Lee Tan, in *Signs of the Times*, states: "Both the Old and New Testaments are filled with promises of the Second Coming of Christ. There are 1,845 references to it in the Old Testament, and a total of seventeen Old Testament books give it prominence. Of the 260 chapters in the entire New Testament, there are 318 references to the Second Coming, or one out of 30 verses. Twenty-three of the 27 New Testament books refer to this great event...for every prophecy on the First Coming of Christ, there are eight on Christ's Second Coming." [13]

The study of "last things" is called "eschatology," from the Greek word *eschatos*, meaning "last." As one might expect, many different interpretations and understandings exist concerning end time events. A few things, however, are certain. Among these are the facts that Jesus' return will be:

- **Sure.** It is foundational to the whole biblical message.
- **Sudden.** "In a flash, in the twinkling of an eye" (1 Cor. 15:52)
- **Spectacular.** You won't miss it! (Matt. 24:27)
- **Secret.** No one knows *when* it will happen (Matt. 24:36).

Several elements are associated with His return. The most significant are the Rapture, the Tribulation, and the Millennium. Read about each of these in the passages referenced below:

The Rapture

This word does not occur in the Bible. It is a term theologians use to refer to the event described in 1 Thessalonians 4:13-18, 1 Corinthians 15:51-52 and possibly Matthew 24:30-31; 40-41. When Jesus appears in the sky, there will be a resurrection of those who have died in Christ. They will rise to meet Him. Then living believers will meet Him in the air and be changed instantly.

The Tribulation

Various prophecies in both the Old and New Testaments refer to a future time of "great tribulation". The best summary of this event is in Jesus' discourse in Matthew chapter 24. It is probably described figuratively throughout most of the book of Revelation (chapters 4–18), although some interpreters think this section of Revelation describes spiritual warfare in general, rather than the Tribulation specifically. Daniel 12:1-2 refers to this event.

The assumption that the Tribulation will last seven years comes from an interpretation of the time schedule given in Daniel 9:20-27. This is a rather complex description of "seventy sevens," or 490 years decreed for the Jewish nation. Four hundred and eighty-three years were fulfilled prior to the crucifixion. It is thought the final "seven" may be this last terrible persecution. In Hebrew, the word "week" and the word "seven" are the same word. That's why you sometimes hear this referred to as "Daniel's seventieth week." There is also frequent reference to three and a half years, so some people think the tribulation will be only three and a half years long.

All this can become quite complex. Fortunately, you don't need to understand it all to be saved. In addition, keep in mind that much of this subject (how long the Tribulation will be, the interpretation of Daniel 9, etc.) is quite speculative. But, as scholars, we should have some knowledge of these various interpretations. It is quite certain that there *will* be a time of tribulation in the future because several Bible prophecies converge on that issue.

The Millennium

The word "millennium" is Latin for "one thousand years." In theology, it refers to a period when Christ will personally rule the entire earth, in fulfillment of various prophecies in both the Old and New Testaments.

The only mention of one thousand years is in Revelation 20. Scholars debate whether the thousand years should to be taken literally or is symbolic of a long period of time. Whatever the Millennium's length, the description in this chapter is awesome. Satan will be locked up, and the resurrected saints will rule with Christ. At the end of this time, Satan will be released and he will gather all nations against Jerusalem for a final battle. Apparently, the righteous are resurrected at the beginning of the "thousand years" and the lost will be resurrected at the end. The lost will then face eternal punishment.

Read about this coming Utopia in the following Old Testament passages:

Psalm 2
Isaiah 11:1-9; 32:1-5; 65:17-25
Jeremiah 33
Daniel 7:13-14
Micah 4:1-8
Zechariah 9:9-13; 14:6-21

In what order do these events occur? Here Bible teachers' opinions differ. The first difference involves the Millennium and represents three major views:

Amillennialists think the Millennium should be understood symbolically, not literally. They believe biblical references to a millennium represent the power of the Gospel over the world system. They believe in the future imminent return of Christ, followed by the judgment and the dissolution of this world.

Postmillennialists believe the world will become increasingly better as the Gospel is preached and will culminate in the Millennium. After this millennium of 1,000 years of peace, etc., Christ will return and establish His eternal kingdom.

Premillennialists believe Christ will return around the time of the Great Tribulation. At the end of the Tribulation He will establish His kingdom on earth and reign with His saints for 1,000 years.

Premillennialists divide into three sub-groups. Pretribulational Premillennialists believe the Rapture will take place just before the Tribulation. The raptured saints will be in heaven with Christ during the Tribulation. They will return with Him after the Tribulation to inaugurate the Millennium and to celebrate the "Marriage supper of the Lamb."

Midtribulational Premillennialists believe basically the same as Pretribulationalists, except they expect Christ to return at the middle of the Tribulation (three and a half years into it) instead of at the beginning.

Postribulational Premillennialists expect Christ to return after the Tribulation but before the Millennium.

Nearly all Premillennialists interpret the seven-year Tribulation and one-thousand year Millennium literally.

Are you wondering what arguments Pretribulationalists and Posttribulationalists use to support their positions? If so, you may wish to peruse the lists of some of the major arguments of both groups on the following pages. The Midtribulational view is basically the same as the Pretribulational, so there is not a separate list for that view because most of the same arguments would apply.

When there is this much disagreement among Bible scholars, it's quite reasonable to assume none of them have all the truth. When Christ comes, we'll all know how it happened and it will seem obvious. Meanwhile, we are commanded to be faithful, to be aware of the prophecies, and to be constantly watching for His return.

Arguments for a Pretribulation Rapture

1) The tribulation is an outpouring of God's wrath against His enemies. Therefore, the very nature of this time militates against God's people being present, for He would be directing His wrath against His own.

2) The "Restrainer" of 2 Thessalonians 2:6-7 is probably the Holy Spirit. The influence of the Spirit, indwelling believers, is a restraint against the outbreak of evil that characterizes the tribulation. When believers are removed in the Rapture, that restraining influence will also be gone.

3) The church in Philadelphia (Rev. 3:10) is told it will be kept "from the hour of trial that is going to come upon the whole world." This must refer to the Tribulation. The Philadelphia church, like the church in any age, is given the promise of escape from this "hour" by being taken out in the Rapture.

4) There is a break between chapters 3 and 4 of Revelation. Chapters 1—3 relate events contemporary with John, and chapter 4 begins with prophecies about the future. John is instructed to "Come up here…" (Rev. 4:1). This is an indication that the Rapture occurs at this point, prior to descriptions of the tribulation.

5) There are many mentions of the church in the first three chapters of Revelation, but no mention of the church after that. In addition, the twenty-four elders of chapters four and five imply both Israel and the church are represented in heaven and the "great multitude" of 7:9-17 implies that the raptured saints have arrived in heaven.

6) Numerous "imminency passages" teach that Christ may return at any moment. A posttribulation rapture would place the return of Christ and the rapture at least seven years away, denying the clear biblical teaching of immanency.

7) The judgment seat of Christ requires time. This could happen during the Tribulation.

8) The coming of the Lord is said to be at a time of peace and safety, not at a time of Tribulation.

9) The Tribulation is the last "seven" (or "week," depending on the translation) of Daniel's prophecy (Dan. 9:24-27). This prophecy has to do with Jewish, not Gentile history. The Jewish dispensation and the church dispensation should be kept separate. Therefore, the church will not be on earth during the tribulation. *

10) Posttribulationists argue that Matthew 24, Jesus' discourse on end-time events, makes no mention of the Rapture prior to the Tribulation. But Matthew 24 is Jewish truth, referring to the Jewish nation, not the church. That is the reason Jesus does not mention the Rapture, an event that applies to the church. *

*Dispensational Theology

The last two arguments, above, presuppose dispensational theology. Dispensationalism is a system of Bible interpretation systematized by J. N. Darby, a Plymouth Brethren theologian, in the mid 1800s and popularized by the Scofield Bible. It holds to various different dispensations (time periods) during which God deals differently with His people. In dispensational theology it is held that the Jewish dispensation and the church dispensation must be kept separate. It is believed the Rapture signals the end of the church age (the "Age of Grace") and the reinstatement of the Jewish age, which had been interrupted at the beginning of the church age. For someone who does not hold to dispensational theology, arguments 9 and 10 would carry little weight.

Arguments for a Posttribulation Rapture

1) Scripture clearly teaches that Christ will return with His saints to establish His kingdom after the tribulation. On this, all premillennialists agree. However, there is no teaching of an additional return "for" His saints prior to the Tribulation. This can be asserted only on the basis of inference. According to universally accepted principles of debate, the person making the affirmation must bear the burden of proof. In other words, those asserting that Christ will return before the Tribulation are obligated to produce scriptural evidence of such a coming. If such proof cannot be found, then we are left with the postribulation coming, upon which we all agree.

2) An unbiased reading of Matthew 24 and parallel passages (Mark 13 and Luke 21) places the end-times in clear chronological perspective. The events of the Great Tribulation are followed by the coming of Christ. There is no other "coming" mentioned—a glaring omission, even if this is only "Jewish truth." Many Christians interpret Matthew 24:30-31 and 40-41 as a reference to the Rapture. If this is true, it makes the posttribulation Rapture position all the stronger.

3) Second Thessalonians 2:1-12 clearly teaches that "our being gathered to Him" (the Rapture) will not occur until after the Antichrist is revealed. Apparently false teachers had alarmed the Thessalonian Christians by claiming the Rapture had already occurred and they missed it (2:1-2).

Paul assured them this was not the case and reminded them that the Rapture will not occur until after the Antichrist is revealed and proclaims himself to be God. (2:3-4).

Pretribulationists interpret the one "holding back" the power of lawlessness (the "restrainer") in verse 6 as the Holy Spirit indwelling believers. The indwelling Spirit, it is assumed, will be taken out of the way in the Rapture because Christians will be removed. This is a long leap of inference. Had he meant that, Paul would have said it. However, if he was referring to the Roman system of law and order, there was good reason for being subtle about it. Indeed, we are beginning to see the dissolving of that system of law and order in our own day, making possible the dictatorship of the Antichrist.

4) It is clear in Scripture that those in Christ will be resurrected at the time of His coming (1 Thess. 4:16). Revelation 20:4-5 obviously refers to the resurrection of the just after the Tribulation and calls it the "first resurrection." To say this means the "second phase" of the first resurrection, as pretribulationists do, is to bend the simple meaning of a statement in order to make it fit a superimposed doctrine.

5) The only coming of Christ mentioned in Revelation occurs in chapter 19. To read the rapture into 4:1, as pretribulationists do, is an unwarranted inference.

6) There are many parallels between the plagues in Egypt and the judgments of the Tribulation. So much so that the former seems to be a "type," or picture of the latter. It is to be noted that while the Lord protected His people from the more severe judgments in Egypt (Exod. 8:22-23; 9:22-26; 10:22-23, for example), He did not take them out until it was all over. The claim that the church cannot endure the judgment of God is a weak argument, for God's people have always suffered along with their nation when it was being judged for sin. Nevertheless, He may well protect His people from the more severe judgments during the Tribulation. In addition, Christians have never been promised immunity from the wrath of man directed against God and His people (Matt. 5:11-12; 10:22), and much of the persecution of the Tribulation will be exactly that.

7) The early church fathers make no mention of belief in a pretribulation Rapture. In fact, they thought they were in the Tribulation. Justin Martyr, Tertullian, Irenaeus and others talk about the coming of the Lord and the Rapture of the church after the man of sin is revealed and the tenfold division of the empire takes place. Belief in a pretribulation Rapture is of recent origin, growing out of a dispensational system of interpretation introduced in the 19th century and popularized by the Scofield Bible notes.

UNIT III

UNIT
IV

Defending Your Faith

LESSON 19

Is There a God? If So, Is He a Loving God?

Equipment Needed	Teaching Supplies Needed
None	1) Copies of student lesson 20 to distribute to the class.

Lecture

Introduction to the Study of Apologetics:

Apologetics is "the branch of theology having to do with the defense and proofs of Christianity" [6]. It is **not** to "apologize" for the faith, as some mistakenly assume, even though the roots of the words "apologize" and "apologetics" may have some early etymological connection.

The biblical basis for the science of apologetics comes from 1 Peter 3:15, "Always be prepared to give an answer to everyone who asks you to give the reason for the hope that you have. But do this with gentleness and respect." Other passages instruct us to "contend for the faith" and "persuade men" about the truth of the Gospel. Apologetics is an essential part of our faith.

Apologetics provides answers to the question; "Is Christianity credible in this age of new scientific discoveries?" As Christians, we make some profound claims about our faith. We contend that a man rose from the dead and that many other miracles occurred in history and are even possible today. We maintain that a personal, loving God created the universe and exists today. We hold to the authority and "inspiration" of an ancient book as our supreme guide in faith and practice. Are these beliefs intellectually defensible? Apologetics responds with a resounding yes.

Our purpose in apologetics is to help remove sincere intellectual barriers to the Gospel and to show that the Christian faith is an intelligent faith. We do not turn off our minds when we come to faith. We can show that our faith rests on a firm foundation of truth.

Honest reasoning is sometimes difficult to achieve because people opposed to the Gospel are often hindered from thinking logically about spiritual matters because of a "spiritual darkness" or "blindness." The Bible speaks of this in Ephesians 4:17-19 and other passages. This blindness, or "hardening of the heart," has nothing to do with a person's IQ. It has a spiritual cause. In apologetics we often find ourselves "toe to toe" with the Devil himself, and we must realize this is a spiritual battle as well as an intellectual undertaking (Eph. 6:12)

Generally attitudes toward the Gospel fall into three categories.

1. *Believing the Gospel is irrational.* People holding this attitude see the Gospel as senseless, contrary to reason, an absurd belief. An example is the statement by Robert Blatchford, an English journalist;

> I claim that the heavenly Father is a myth; that in face of a knowledge of life and the world, we cannot reasonably believe in Him. There is no heavenly Father watching tenderly over us, His children. He is the baseless shadow of a wistful human dream. I do not believe in a God. The belief in a God is still generally accepted...but in the light of scientific discoveries and demonstrations, such a belief is unfounded and utterly untenable today." [7]

Blatchford has since died and changed his mind. But his statement adequately represents the attitude of those who believe the Gospel is irrational.

2. The second group *believes the Gospel is non-rational.* They think spiritual things are not subject to reason. This is common in Eastern mysticism and in New Age thinking. The Guru Maharaj Ji, for example, said:

> "Ignorance is only created by the mind, and the mind keeps the secret that you are something Divine away from you. That is why you have to tame the mind first. The mind is a snake and the treasure is behind it. The snake lives over the treasure, so if you want that treasure, you will have to kill the snake. And killing the snake is not an easy job." [8]

This group is much more difficult to deal with than group one because they do not accept reason as a means to discern truth. They are on an entirely different "playing field."

3. The third group *believes that the Gospel and reason, logic, and good thinking, are compatible.* They are willing to weigh evidence, search for the truth, and determine whether there are "reasons to believe."

Scripture clearly presents the Gospel as rational. The Bible tells us to use our minds, to reason, to examine evidence. One of the great positives of the Christian faith is that it is based on real happenings, to real people in verifiable history. (See 1 John 1:1.) We are invited in Scripture to use our senses to determine the truth of biblical claims.

Below is a list of Scripture passages that speak about the importance of using our minds in determining truth. You may wish to have class members read some or all of them:

> Matthew 22:37
> Hebrews 8:10
> 1 Peter 1:13
> 2 Peter 3:1
> 2 Corinthians 4:1-6

2 Corinthians 11:3
Romans 1:21, 28
Ephesians 4:22-23

A clarification: When we speak of the importance of reason and the use of our minds, we are *not* talking about "Rationalism." Rationalism is a philosophical belief that rejects revelation and the supernatural and holds that human reason is the only source of knowledge. Rationalism is an anti-Christian belief system.

What we *do* insist on, as Christians, is that there are good and sufficient reasons to believe what we believe. This does not mean we understand or can explain everything we believe, but good logic will bring a person to recognize a very high degree of probability that what we believe is true. We are convinced there is much stronger evidence supporting our faith than there is for unbelief. Author Clark Pinnock says it well in his book, *Set Forth Your Case:* "Faith is not believing what you know to be absurd. It is trusting what, on excellent testimony, appears to be true." [9]

Evidence is crucial to faith. The Apostle Paul, for example, says: "...if Christ has not been raised, your faith is futile…" (1 Cor. 15:17).

Our position, then, is that Christianity is based on evidence that is both internally and externally consistent. (Internal evidence means it is self-consistent. External evidence means it does not contradict facts we know to be true from other sources). Reason is not a substitute for faith; it is a basis for faith. Or to say it another way, there is good reason to believe what we believe.

When we say apologetics can demonstrate a "high degree of probability" about the truth of our beliefs, we do not mean the evidence is somewhat short of convincing. Rather, we do not claim to completely "prove" our assertions because of the nature of evidence. Usually, when people talk about "proof," they are referring to the scientific method, which has to do with concrete, observable, measurable, repeatable events. When discussing something as abstract as theology and the existence of God, it does not conform to the scientific method. You cannot repeat or observe creation or most of the events of history, and abstract concepts are not measurable. You cannot measure out five pounds of love or three feet of hope. The Student's section (page 213) touches on how difficult (impossible!) it is to "prove" the obvious. It is necessary to start with certain assumptions that cannot be proven. That's why we use the term, "high degree of probability," when referring to theological concepts.

Apologetics is a broad subject because there are so many facets to it and the questions seem endless. The more you and your students can read on the subject, the richer class discussion will be. A few recommended resources are listed below:

- *Why I Believe* by James Kennedy
- *Handbook of Christian Apologetics* by Peter Kreeft & Ronald K.Tacelli
- *Evidence that Demands a Verdict* by Josh McDowell
- *Scaling the Secular City* by J. P. Moreland
- *The Universe Next Door* by James W. Sire
- *No Doubt About It* by Winfried Corduan
- *The Fingerprint of God* by Hugh Ross

- *Show Me God* by Fred Heeren
- *Why Believe?* by C. Stephen Evans
- *I Don't Have Enough Faith to Be an Atheist* by Norman L. Geisler and Frank Turek
- *The Case for Christ* by Lee Strobel
- *The Case for Faith* by Lee Strobel
- *The Case for a Creator* by Lee Strobel
- *To Everyone an Answer.* Francis J. Beckwith, Wm. Craig, and J. P. Moreland, editors

Obviously, you will not be able to read all of the recommended books before teaching this section, but if any of them are available to you or your students from a church library or other source, take advantage of the opportunity to read whatever you can for background information. The list does not exhaust the resources. Many additional texts are available on the subject of apologetics.

Suggested Format for Teaching Lesson 19

Introduce the subject of Apologetics, drawing from the above material, in whatever way you deem best for your class. Then review the classical arguments for the existence of God from pages 214-215 of the Student section. This discussion can slide into deep and abstract philosophical concepts. Each of these classical arguments has several versions that developed through history. This is one of those times you may need to remind students this is a *survey* course. We want our students to gain familiarity with each of the arguments so we have an organized concept in mind about how to answer objections. If students want to delve more deeply into the subject, recommend the reading list, above, for their own personal study.

Discuss the "problem of evil" (page 216 of the Student section). Work through the five points on page 216. Have volunteers read the passages under points 4 and 5. This should stimulate considerable discussion.

Ask the class to respond to the statement at the bottom of page 216 in the Student section—"Is God, Himself, cruel, even *evil*?" Think through these issues carefully before class so you can guide students in clear thinking. These are weighty subjects that require focused attention.

If time permits, divide the group out into pairs. Ask one to role play a skeptic, and the other to roleplay a Christian defending his/her faith. The student assignment was to be "ready to give an answer," and this exercise will sharpen their readiness. Allow about five minutes, then ask them to reverse roles. This is a technique you can use in any of these four lessons on apologetics, but it's best not to use it every time.

LESSON

Is There a God? If So, Is He a Loving God?

The traditional name for this part of our study is "Apologetics." Apologetics is defined in Webster's New World Dictionary as "the branch of theology having to do with the defense and proofs of Christianity." We have recently studied about the truths we believe. Now, how do we defend these truths against unbelievers who challenge us?

Even though we "walk by faith," the Bible commands us to think through the reasons for our faith. Many things about God and the Christian life lie beyond our present understanding, but there are nevertheless good *reasons* to believe these truths of Scripture. We need to know those reasons and be able to explain them to others.

The key Bible verse for the study of Apologetics is 1 Peter 3:15—"Always be prepared to give an answer to everyone who asks you to give the reason for the hope that you have. But do this with gentleness and respect."

We are most commonly challenged on one or more of the following five questions:

1) Is there a God?
2) If there is a God, is He a *good* and *loving* God?
3) Is Jesus God?
4) Did Jesus actually rise from the dead?
5) Is the Bible reliable?

The next three lessons deal with each of these questions in the above order.

Is there a God?

The unbeliever or skeptic will argue that the concept of a personal God is a hangover from medieval days when people tried to explain the mysteries of nature by imagining a creator. Modern science, they will say, has ruled out such archaic ideas. Belief in God is just a crutch for weak people.

The most popular idea in our time, however, is not the classical denial of God mentioned above, but the idea that we are *all* god. We and the universe are one is a popular notion, but it denies that a loving, holy, personal God exists and is separate from us—a God with whom we can and must relate on a person-to-person basis.

Both of the above groups would contend that we cannot *prove* the God of the Bible exists. In one sense, they are right. Not because there isn't abundant evidence, but because, as every philosopher knows, obvious things are the most difficult to prove. Take, for example, the question of your own existence. Do you *really* exist? How do you know? Maybe it's just an illusion. Maybe you are just a spirit imagining bodily existence. How can you *prove* your existence to me? This gets us into questions about the reliability of our senses and all sorts of deep philosophical considerations.

In order to function as human beings we all have to start with some basic assumptions. Philosophically, we are Christian Realists. That means we *assume* we exist, are able to think, and that our senses are ordinarily valid. That is, when we are awake, conscious, and in reasonable health, what we see is actually there, what we hear is an actual sound, and we have the capacity to think and reason. All of this is an assumption. It cannot be "proven" because it is outside the realm of science. Philosophers call it an "a-priori assumption." Most of the rest of us call it common sense.

Common sense tells us that everything has a cause. Some things have an intelligent cause, and others are just the result of some inanimate force or action. Any normal person looking around at our universe would conclude the vast evidence of design indicates an intelligent cause. It makes sense that this intelligent cause is a god, and the Bible description of God fits the evidence exactly.

So who, or what, caused God? Nothing! Besides that, God made the universe out of nothing.

Isn't that contradictory? No, because the concept of causation is something inherent in our time/space universe. Here, everything is caused. God is outside of our time/space universe and separate from it. In eternity, where God is, things are different, because in that realm apparently time and space do not exist in the same way they exist in our universe. God exists in eternity without beginning or end and without cause.

Confused? Of course, because we're dealing with concepts that go beyond what our minds can grasp. But what we really *need* to know about all this is that where we live, everything has a cause; and that the universe with all its intricate design calls for an intelligent cause.

Theologians and philosophers love to organize arguments and give those arguments impressive sounding Greek and Latin names. So down through the ages they have developed four classical arguments for the existence of God. They are called the "Cosmological Argument," the "Teleological Argument," the "Anthropological Argument," and the "Ontological Argument." It's a neat, organized way to answer the question "How do you know there is a God?" You will be able to impress people if you remember these dignified sounding titles for the arguments, but the important thing is to know, in plain language, what these arguments are. A brief summary of each follows.

The Cosmological Argument

The word "Cosmos" may ring a bell with you. It's Greek for the universe. It means more than just a collection of stars and planets, but also the fact that it's an orderly system. It's not just a collection of rocks and sparks thrown together.

We've already discussed how everything in our universe has a cause, so what is the cause of the cosmos? Common sense tells us that everything that exists not only had a cause, but a cause greater than itself.

Many scientists and philosophers used to say that the universe is eternal—it's always been here. That's not a popular view anymore, even among unbelieving scientists and philosophers. We've learned an awesome number of new things about the universe in recent years. One of those things is that the universe is expanding from what seems to be one central point. That, along with a mass of other facts provides evidence that the universe is not eternal. It had a beginning—exactly as the Bible says ("In the beginning…"). If so, who or what is the "beginner?" No explanation fits as well as "In the beginning *God created…*"

When you are dealing with an unbeliever, don't be on the defensive all the time. Ask what his/her explanation of the origin of the universe is. What alternative is there? You'll hear some pretty weak ideas.

Recent developments in astronomy and physics have caused many scientists to take another look at the "God concept." New evidence for the "Big Bang Theory," especially, points to an intelligent creator. George Smoot, of the Lawrence Berkeley Laboratory in California, well known for his discoveries in astronomy, says "There is no doubt that a parallel exists between the big bang as an event and the Christian notion of creation from nothing." [14]

Smoot is not the only scientist coming to that conclusion. Even more exciting is the growing consensus that the universe not only had a creator, as the Bible says, but an *intelligent* creator. That's what the "Teleological Argument" is about.

The Teleological Argument

The Teleological Argument is the argument from design. Whereas the Cosmological Argument simply states the universe has a cause outside itself (we maintain that cause is God), the Teleological Argument goes a step further and seeks to establish the fact that this cause is an *intelligent* cause —a person.

Everywhere you look in creation there is evidence of intelligent design. The science author, Fred Heeren, relates how Sir Fred Hoyle, the British astrophysicist, had his "atheism greatly shaken" when he calculated how impossible it is that the resonance of carbon could exist by chance. As a result, he wrote in the November, 1981, issue of *Engineering and Science:* "A common sense interpretation of the facts suggests that a superintellect has monkeyed with physics, as well as with chemistry and biology, and that there are no blind forces worth speaking about in nature. The numbers one calculates from the facts seem to me so overwhelming as to put this conclusion almost beyond question." [15] Sir Fred Hoyle does not claim to be Christian, but he is at least honest with the facts!

If the resonance of carbon indicates an intelligent creator, what about the numberless other, and even more impressive, evidences of design? It would take a million books to try to describe them! Consider, for example, the human DNA. Every cell in our bodies contains a blueprint of the structure of that body. The information contained in this blueprint, if printed in book form, would be the equivalent of 1,120,000 pages. The cell that contains this information is 1/2500 of an inch in diameter, but if the DNA string were stretched out it would be six feet long. Talk about miniaturization! Is it logical to assume all this "just happened"? And we haven't even begun to talk about the stars!

Because of the incontrovertible evidence of design in nature, a growing number of researchers and teachers in the scientific community are promoting "Intelligent Design Theory." This is a recognition that the universe could not possibly be the result of blind chance. The only logical explanation of origins must include the concept of intelligent design.

The Intelligent Design Theory does not necessarily require that God be the explanation of the intelligence in question, and not all who adhere to the theory are theists. Some pull in other explanations of intelligence (for example, extra-terrestrial creatures). But the *best* and *most logical* explanation of design is to assume a God, such as the one described in the Bible, is the Creator of the universe. The growing interest in Intelligent Design Theory in scientific and educational circles is certainly a step in the right direction.

The Anthropological Argument

Anthropos is the Greek word for "man." The Anthropological Argument asserts that the nature of mankind points to a creator who has a moral consciousness.

No matter where you find man, you see him possessing a moral consciousness. It is a universal occurrence in all healthy humans. Even though various cultures differ on what they consider to be right or wrong, they all agree that there *is* a standard of right and wrong. How do you explain this universal moral consciousness? The simplest and best explanation is that there is a creator, Himself moral, who created mankind in His image.

Note the progression of these three arguments. Each builds upon the previous one. Together they are powerful:

> The Cosmological Argument—The universe has a cause, a creator.
> The Teleological Argument—This creator is intelligent, a person.
> The Anthropological Argument—The creator is a moral intelligence.

The Ontological Argument

The Ontological Argument is ancient and comes in several forms. Some people consider it to be vague and unimpressive. Others insist it is the most powerful of all. Use it if you're comfortable with it. Otherwise, skip it.

Ontology has to do with the study of the nature of things. It is the very nature of humans to assume the existence of an infinitely perfect being. Since we are able to conceive of such a being, and since every culture has such a conception, there must be a reality to match the concept.

Is God really good and loving?

"Proving" the existence of God is one thing. Establishing the fact that He is, as the Bible says, a good and loving God, is more difficult. Whereas the unbeliever's problem is explaining order and design in the universe, the believer's problem is to explain the existence of disorder and injustice.

The ten o'clock news any day of the week proclaims injustice and disorder. Good people suffer and evildoers prosper. Natural evil (earthquakes, floods, tsunamis, tornadoes, etc.) abound. Moral evil (murders, deceit, robbery, etc.) is a daily diet in our newspapers and newscasts.

Even nature, so perfectly designed, is "red with tooth and claw." The philosopher, John Stewart Mill, wrote "...in sober truth, nearly all the things which men are hanged or imprisoned for doing to one another, are nature's everyday performances...killing, the most criminal act recognized by human laws, nature does once to every being that lives; and in a large proportion of cases, after protracted tortures such as only the greatest monsters whom we read of ever purposely inflicted on their living fellow creatures ...nature impales men...casts them to be devoured by wild beasts, burns them to death, crushes them with stones like the first Christian martyr, starves them with hunger, freezes them with cold...all this nature does with the most supercilious disregard both of mercy and of justice, emptying her shafts upon the best and noblest indifferently with the meanest and the worst." [16]

No one can disagree with Mill. That's how it is in the world. So where is God? Did He not promise to protect us? To "be with us, even unto the end of the world?" "The Lord is my shepherd, I shall not want…"

For many people, this problem is too big to handle. They conclude that if there is a God, He either doesn't care (He is not a loving God) or He can't do anything about it (He is not omnipotent).

What is our answer? It's probably the most difficult apologetic problem for us Christians. It's called the "problem of evil."

Does the Bible provide any answers? We believe it does. Study the five points below, read the references in the Bible, and see what you think.

1) God created everything perfect. It was His intention that His creation live in peace and joy, experiencing eternal life and complete health. He also desired fellowship with His creation. This fellowship was to be an interaction between Him and creatures that were free to either worship Him or not. If they were not free, their worship would not be real. They would simply be puppets. Therefore, God created man with the ability to choose, told him about the results of obedience, and warned him about the consequences of disobedience.

2) God's perfect creation was disrupted by rebellion, when both mankind and some of the angels chose to use their free will against God. This distorted God's purpose and was the cause of both moral and natural evil. It is the natural outcome of separation from God.

3) Therefore man and the fallen angels are ultimately responsible for the moral and natural evil in the world. The line of responsibility goes back to the creature, not the Creator.

4) God is in the process of cleansing the earth of evil and bringing justice. Find and read the following references:
   - Psalm 73:1-28—*Ultimately* God will bring justice.
   - Romans 8:18-21—Even natural evil will one day come to an end.
   - Revelation 20:11—21:5—This is God's ultimate goal.
   - Matthew 25:31-46—Judgment is still future.
   - 2 Peter 3:9—What is the difference between "patience" and "slowness?"
   - Luke 16:19-25—God will some day bring *personal* justice to everyone.

5) During this interim period, God allows evil to exist. Sometimes the presence of evil around us strengthens us and, by contrast, demonstrates the glory of God. An example of this is the encounter of Moses with Pharaoh. Also read James 1:2-4, 12.

But what about the charge that God, Himself, is cruel, even *evil.* He orders his servants to kill seemingly innocent people, drowns nearly the entire human race, exacts horrible punishments on unbelievers,

UNIT IV

slays a man for gathering sticks on the Sabbath, dispatches otherwise "good" people to an eternal hell just because they don't believe certain doctrines, etc. The philosopher, Bertrand Russell, said: "There is one very serious defect to my mind in Christ's moral character, and that is that He believed in hell. I do not myself feel that any person who is really profoundly humane can believe in everlasting punishment." [17]

It is true that Jesus believed in hell, and not just as a passing mention. The Gospels record more of His teaching about hell than about heaven. Is this, indeed, a "very serious defect...in moral character?" What is an appropriate Christian response to these charges?

Several important questions need to be raised in the Christian response:

1) What is the definition of "good?" From where does the critic derive a standard of ethics and morality higher than God, to which God is supposed to be subject and accountable? Consider Romans 9:14-29: "Is God unjust? Not at all! ...who are you, O man, to talk back to God? Shall what is formed say to him who formed it, 'Why did you make me like this?' Does not the potter have the right to make out of the same lump of clay some pottery for noble purposes and some for common use?..."

2) Does God not have a "right" (as the Creator) to exact punishment on a rebellious creature? Should it not be expected that if God is, indeed, absolutely righteous and holy that He would despise and punish sin? Is not the appropriate question: "Why are some saved?" rather than "Why are some punished?"

3) Is there the possibility of a higher purpose or eventual positive outcome in what we perceive as "cruelty?" Consider many of the Old Testament prophecies that thunder the judgment of God upon a wicked people, but almost universally end with statements of forgiveness, restoration, and healing. Through the agony of exile, for example, Israel was forever cured of idolatry.

4) Does not the evidence of God's grace and mercy infinitely outweigh any charges of perceived injustice and "cruelty"? Consider, for example, God's patience in allowing the heathen people occupying the land of Canaan 400 more years to repent before the invasions under Joshua (Gen. 15:12-16), or the love evident in the passion of Christ, in that "while we were still sinners, Christ died for us" (Rom. 5:8). The many acts and words of Jesus showing compassion and forgiveness toward sinners demonstrate a God of love, not a capricious tyrant.

5) In the words of Abraham when he was responding to God's announcement of judgment upon Sodom and Gomorrah, "Will not the Judge of all the earth do right?" (Gen. 18:25). We can trust God's judgment upon unbelievers, even upon those who never heard. Lee Strobel, in *A Case for Christ,* quotes D. A. Carson: "Hell is not a place where people are consigned because they were pretty good blokes but just didn't believe the right stuff. They're consigned there, first and foremost, because they defy their Maker and want to be at the center of the universe. Hell is not filled with people who have already repented, only God isn't gentle enough or good enough to let them out. It's filled with people who, for all eternity, still want to be at the center of the universe and who persist in God-defying rebellion. What is God to do? If he says it doesn't matter to him, then God is no longer a God to be admired. He's either amoral or positively creepy. For him to act in any other way in the face of such blatant defiance would be to reduce God himself." [18]

In the contentious matter of the heathen who "never heard," it is well to remember that God is righteous in judging people. The Bible implies He takes into account the light people have received and that there are degrees of punishment just as there are degrees of rewards (see Rom. 2:1-16; 1 Cor. 3:10-15; Luke 12:47-48). Only God can sort this out.

These are deep and heavy subjects. Reflect on these things in preparation for the next class session.

Assignment

First Peter 3:15 gives two directives about apologetics:

    1) Be ready always.
    2) Speak with gentleness and respect.

In order to be ready, memorize the names of the three primary arguments for the existence of God (cosmological, teleological, and anthropological). Know the basics of each well enough to use it in a reasoned, gentle, and respectful manner.

In your own words, write a paragraph or two in response to each of the following questions posed by critics. Be prepared to interact with others in class about your responses:

1) How do you know there is a God?

2) If God exists and is both loving and all-powerful, why does He allow bad things to happen?

3) Isn't God, Himself, cruel? The Bible says He killed people for minor offenses and sends people to an eternal hell just because they don't believe (or even know about) the right doctrines!

LESSON 20

Is Jesus God? Did Jesus Rise from the Dead?

Equipment Needed

1) Chalkboard or whiteboard

Teaching Supplies Needed

1) Copies of student lesson 21 to distribute to class.

Lecture

Introduction

Ask for responses to the diagram on page 223 (the first page of this lesson in the Student section). Does anyone know what it represents?

Actually, it's an ancient symbol for the Trinity. The Father (PATER), Son (FILIVS) and Spirit (SPVS) are all God (DEVS). But the Father is not the Son or the Spirit; the Son is not the Spirit or the Father; and the Spirit is not the Father or the Son.

Christians have believed this teaching about the Trinity since the beginning of the church. But in our age, the "man on the street" has difficulty accepting the idea that Jesus is God or that He literally rose from the dead. Ask the class for ideas and opinions about why this truth is so difficult for the modern person to accept.

The deity of Christ and His resurrection are the cornerstone of the Christian faith. We seek to help our students think through the reasons to believe this extremely important truth and to defend it before people who may not believe the Bible in the same way we do.

Aut deus aut homo malus

Guide students through the "*aut deus aut homo malus*" argument. That's an impressive Latin phrase for "Either God or a bad man." The argument is explained in the Student section. Write the syllogism on the board and work through it with the students.

Write syllogism:
1. Jesus was either God or a bad man.
2. Jesus was not a bad man.
3. Therefore Jesus is God.

Advise students they may start with either premise #1 or #2, depending on how it best fits into the conversation taking place. Usually the discussion will center on what a good person Jesus was, so it leads directly into premise #2. Most people will agree that Jesus was a great ethical teacher and influenced the world for good. This insight can be strengthened by referring to quotations such as those given in the Student section (pages 223-224) and other statements that may come from the students' reading or yours. Encourage discussion about Jesus being recognized as a great moral teacher.

Then move to premise #1, calling attention to the claims Jesus made for Himself. Because of these claims, Jesus could not be a good man if He is not God. He is either God or a liar. But how could the world's greatest moral teacher be a liar?

Skeptics may seek to escape from this dilemma by proposing the alternatives of "lunatic, guru or myth." Walk through these alternatives with the class and examine the likelihood of each. The Student section gives some ideas about how unreasonable each of these "explanations" really is. Ask students to add their own insights and responses.

The only reasonable alternative is that Jesus is, indeed, God.

The Resurrection

Discuss the three questions on page 226 of the Student section. Students should have these crucial questions well in mind when discussing the resurrection with skeptics. Often the best defense of a position is a well-worded question, presented with respect, kindness, and concern.

Discuss the four theories some people use in their attempt to explain away the resurrection. Have students share what they wrote for each. Possible responses might include:

1. For the Hallucination theory:
    • The women at the tomb were surprised and startled at Jesus' appearance, Mary thinking it was the gardener. The scene was dramatically different from someone working up a hallucination.
    • The disciples were not expecting a resurrection. They were in grief, hidden away in fear.
    • How could that many people be hallucinating at once? (over 500; 1 Cor. 15:6)
    • Why did the "hallucinations" suddenly stop—all at the same time—forty days after the resurrection?

2. For the Myth theory:
    • There simply wasn't enough time for a myth of this proportion to develop.
    • The written records are by contemporaries. There is no record of any dissenting views by contemporaries.
    • Where is the body? Why is the grave empty?

3. The Conspiracy theory
    • The supposed "conspirators" were all willing to die for the truth of their witness. Not one denied the story, even when facing martyrdom.

- How could it be that the disciples changed so dramatically from fearful fugitives in hiding to outspoken, fearless apostles, if their witness wasn't based on reality?
- The tomb was sealed and guarded by Roman soldiers. The soldiers would most likely be punished by death if they allowed someone to steal the body.

4. The Swoon theory
   - Anyone abused, beaten, and crucified as Jesus was would not simply rest for awhile and regain consciousness.
   - Roman soldiers attending crucifixions knew when a person was dead. They were certain Jesus was dead before they removed Him from the cross.
   - The tomb was sealed and guarded. How could Jesus have emerged, even if He did revive in the cool tomb? The guards would certainly have prevented that.

Encourage students to share stories of encounters they may have had (or are currently having) with someone who denies the deity and/or the resurrection of Christ. Ask class members to share suggestions of how to be the best witness in these specific situations. Include these concerns as you conclude the class with prayer.

LESSON
20
Is Jesus God? Did Jesus Rise from the Dead?

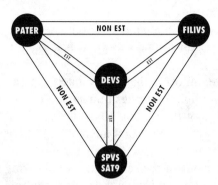

In this lesson we're concerned about convincing those who don't believe the Bible to be an authoritative, divinely inspired, document. So, what do you say to them? Is there evidence outside the Bible we can point to?

This question is extremely important because the nature of Christ and His resurrection is the central pillar of the Christian faith. Note 1 Corinthians 15:14-19: "...if Christ has not been raised, our preaching is useless and so is your faith. More than that, we are then found to be false witnesses about God.... And if Christ has not been raised, your faith is futile; you are still in your sins. Then those also who have fallen asleep in Christ are lost. If only for this life we have hope in Christ, we are to be pitied more than all men."

That heavy statement deserves our rapt attention. The subject of the deity of Christ and His resurrection are related, but each is so weighty that this lesson has two parts: 1) the deity of Christ, and 2) His resurrection.

The most common argument you will encounter goes something like this; "Jesus was a good man and a wonderful teacher, but He was not God." That argument is fallacious and illogical. There is a classical argument to refute it. The Latin title for this argument is *Aut deus aut homo malus*, meaning, "Either God or a bad man." The argument maintains that it is impossible that Jesus was a good man but God, and it is based on the following syllogism:

1) Jesus was either God or a bad man.
2) Jesus was not a bad man.
3) Therefore, Jesus was (is) God.

Let's start with the second premise, "Jesus was not a bad man." We start there because almost everyone will agree with us. Consider, for example, the following quotations from famous people who are well qualified to make judgments about historical figures:

"Measured by its fruits in the human race, that short life has been the most influential ever lived on this planet. As we have been at pains to point out, the impress of that life, far from fading with the passing centuries, has deepened. Through Him millions of individuals have been transformed and have begun to live the kind of life which He exemplified...Gauged by the consequences which have followed, the birth, life, death, and resurrection of Jesus have been the most important events in the history of man. Measured by His influence, Jesus is central in the human story." [19]

Those are the words of Kenneth Scott Latourette, the Director of the Department of Religion in Yale Graduate School, and one of the greatest church historians of our time. Consider, further, the following statement by Napoleon:

"I know men; and I tell you that Jesus Christ is not a man. Superficial minds see a resemblance between

Christ and the founders of empires, and the gods of other religions. That resemblance does not exist...Everything in Christ astonishes me. His spirit overawes me, and his will confounds me. Between him and whoever else in the world, there is no possible term of comparison. He is truly a being by Himself. His ideas and sentiments, the truth which he announces, his manner of convincing, are not explained either by human organization or by the nature of things...I search in vain in history to find the similar to Jesus Christ, or anything which can approach the gospel. Neither history, nor humanity, nor the ages, nor nature, offer me anything with which I am able to compare it or to explain it. Here everything is extraordinary." [20]

We could fill many pages with similar quotations from keen observers of human nature, but one more statement seems to summarize what most people, Christian or non-Christian, would accept. This quotation is from Philip Schaff, an American theologian:

"Jesus of Nazareth, without money and arms, conquered more millions than Alexander, Caesar, Mohammed and Napoleon; without science and learning, He shed more light on things human and divine, than all the philosophers and scholars combined; without the eloquence of the school, He spoke words of life such as were never spoken before, nor since, and produced effects which lie beyond the reach of orator or poet; without writing a single line, He has set more pens in motion and furnished themes for more sermons, orations, discussions, works of art, learned volumes, and sweet songs of praise than the whole army of great men of ancient and modern times. Born in a manger and crucified as a malefactor, He now controls the destinies of the civilized world, and rules a spiritual empire which embraces one-third of the inhabitants of the globe." [21]

These observations and many more like them by other observers support premise #2 in our syllogism; "Jesus was not a bad man." But what does this have to do with premise #1, "Jesus was either God or a bad man"?

In answer to that question, think about the claims Jesus made about Himself, as witnessed by historians and his closest followers:

1) He said He lived before Abraham.
2) He said He is Lord over the Law of God.
3) He claimed to be the source of eternal life.
4) In His relationship to the Father, he claimed:
   to know Him is to know the Father.
   to see Him is to see the Father.
   to receive Him is to receive the Father.
   He and the Father are "one."
   He is the *only* way to the Father.
   to hate Him is to hate the Father.
   to honor Him is to honor the Father.
5) He forgave people's sins, while acknowledging only God can do this.
6) He accepted worship.
7) He had the authority and power to "send the Holy Spirit."

Now, if the above claims are *not* true, then Jesus is *not* a good man. He is a deceiver of the worst kind.

Consider the observation of C. S. Lewis, the well-known Christian apologist, writer and teacher. He wrote in *Mere Christianity:*

A man who was merely a man and said the sort of things Jesus said would not be a great moral teacher. He would either be a lunatic—on a level with the man who says he is a poached egg—or else he would be the Devil of Hell. You must make your choice. Either this man was, and is, the Son of God: or else a madman or something worse. You can shut him up for a fool, you can spit at Him and kill Him as a demon; or you can fall at His feet and call Him Lord and God. But let us not come with any patronizing nonsense about His being a great human teacher. He has not left that open to us. He did not intend to. [22]

Of course, Jesus could have been lying about who He was. Or could He? Consider the statement of Christian apologists Peter Kreeft and Ronald Tacelli, in the *Handbook of Christian Apologetics:*

If...Jesus was a liar, then he had to have been the most clever, cunning, Machiavellian, blasphemously wicked, satanic deceiver the world has ever known, successfully seducing billions into giving up their eternal souls into His hands. If orthodox Christianity is a lie, it is by far the biggest and baddest lie ever told and Jesus is the biggest and baddest liar.

...we have never known anyone who thought Jesus was a deliberate liar. That would be more bizarre than calling Mother Teresa a party animal. [23]

This argument is compelling. It places an unbeliever in the dilemma of either taking the position that Jesus is a "bad man," or admitting that He is God. If a bad man, how does one account for the fact that His teachings are recognized around the world as having the highest of moral and ethical standards?

People familiar with debate and logic, when faced with a dilemma of this sort, will seek to "escape between the horns of the dilemma." That is, they will avoid selecting either of the two alternatives by suggesting a third possibility. Perhaps Jesus was not a liar, but was honestly deceived into thinking He was God. This is sometimes expressed as; "Liar, Lunatic, or Lord of all?"

But is it rational to consider someone like Jesus a lunatic? Seriously, how could an insane person accomplish what Jesus accomplished? His wisdom amazed the greatest minds of the time, and He displayed superb balance in His personality. There is such a thing as a "divinity complex," but the profile of such a personality is totally opposite of Jesus. And lunatics just do not produce the kind of results that Jesus did.

But the possibilities are still not exhausted. Maybe Jesus never said any of these things. What if all of it was just a myth that developed after He died and the story was promoted as truth by Bible writers? Now the question becomes, was Jesus Lord, liar, lunatic, or myth?

Lesson 21 delves into the question of whether the Bible is a reliable record of what really happened, so let's hold that question until then. Suffice it to say here that all the witnesses who wrote about Jesus agreed on what He claimed about Himself and on the nature of His personality. Then nearly all of these witnesses died a martyr's death without changing their statements. That's a pretty strong indication that their testimony is true.

One more possible escape route for the unbeliever—Maybe the record is true, but what Jesus *meant* was that He is God in the same way all of us are God. Jesus was a "New Age Pantheist," or "Guru."

No one who knows Jewish doctrine would believe that for a moment. Jesus was a Jew, and the Jews just don't believe in that kind of nonsense. If this was what Jesus meant, He contradicted Himself repeatedly when talking about the nature of God as a person separate from His creation. Besides, the scribes and Pharisees would have picked up on that very quickly and said something about it. Instead, they sought to stone Him because "...he was even calling God his own Father, making himself equal with God" (John 5:18). They knew *exactly* what He meant!

There are only five possible alternatives. Review them and practice your answer for each. Come to the next class session prepared to give a brief answer to each of these theories:

---

1) Jesus never claimed deity . . . . .MYTH THEORY
2) Jesus claimed deity and
    a. He meant it mystically . . . . .GURU THEORY
    b. He meant it literally and
        1) He knew it was false . . . . .LIAR THEORY
        2) He didn't know it was false .LUNATIC THEORY
        3) It is true . . . . .HE IS LORD!

(Above chart modified from Peter Kreeft and Ronald K. Tacelli, *The Handbook of Christian Apologetics*, InterVarsity Press, 1994, p. 171)

The *strongest* argument of all for Jesus' deity is His resurrection. But did it really happen? That's the subject of the second part of this lesson.

Did Jesus Really Rise From the Dead?

The question of Jesus' resurrection is central to our Christian faith. "He is risen!" was the flag of the primitive church, and the message they carried to the world. As we saw in 1 Corinthians 15:12-19, if Jesus did *not* rise from the dead, the entire structure of our faith collapses. The word "gospel" means, literally, "good news." The good news the early church and the apostles and evangelists proclaimed was the fact that Jesus rose from the dead (Acts 17:18; 1 Cor. 15:3-4).

So, did it really happen? Those who deny it have some heavy explaining to do. There are several questions they must answer:

1) How do you explain the origin of the church, which spread rapidly across the empire, if the central message they proclaimed was not true? After all, these were contemporaries to the event.
2) How do you explain the willingness of the witnesses (the apostles) to suffer a martyr's death for the truth of their message? It seems, if it were not true, that at least *one* of them would have flinched!
3) Why did hardened skeptics (the Apostle Paul, for example) do such a sudden reversal of their belief about the resurrection?

Skeptics will usually resort to one or more of four different theories to try to explain the resurrection away. The four theories are listed below. Think about them this week, and write a sentence beside each one telling how you would respond to that argument. Be prepared to share your thoughts with your class.

1) The "Hallucination theory." This theory maintains that Jesus didn't actually rise from the dead, but His disciples *wanted* this to happen so badly that they hallucinated. They actually *thought* He rose from the dead, but He didn't.

2) The "Myth Theory." Jesus didn't actually rise from the dead, but with the passing of time the myth of His resurrection grew and finally was incorporated into the writings we call the Gospels.

3) The "Conspiracy Theory." The disciples stole Jesus' body and claimed He had risen.

UNIT IV

4) The "Swoon Theory." Jesus wasn't actually dead at the time of His burial. The coolness of the tomb allowed Him to regain consciousness. He then exited the tomb, much to the astonishment of everyone who thought He had risen from the dead.

These are about the only possible options other than simply accepting the fact of His resurrection.

To accept the resurrection of Jesus is to affirm His deity and the validity of everything He taught. It is also the foundation of all our hope for eternity and our relationship with God today. No other single issue is as important as this!

UNIT IV

LESSON

Is the Bible True and Reliable?

Equipment Needed	Teaching Supplies Needed
None	1) Copies of student lessons 22-24 to distribute to the class.

Lecture

Most students in evangelical churches hold to a high view of Scripture, including the inspiration and inerrancy of biblical texts. However, you may need to caution the students about "leading" with the insistence on inerrancy when in a witnessing or apologetics situation. Witnessing attempts can bog down in endless and pointless arguments about things like a supposed inconsistency in the text that are minor, unimportant, and usually explainable. The point at issue is not how many angels the women saw at the tomb or the chronological order of events in the Gospels, etc., but whether the Bible is a reliable record of historical events and a trustworthy guide for faith and practice.

For this reason we advise avoiding terms such as "inerrant" or "literal" when speaking with skeptics about the Bible. It is better to turn attention to the unusual things about this book (literally, this spiritual library) that show its uniqueness. The best defense is often a well-worded and timely question. After explaining one or more of the six defenses given on pages 231-233 in the Student section, it may be much more powerful than "preaching" to ask the skeptic for his explanation of these matters.

The goal in dealing with skeptics is simply to establish that the biblical record is reliable, trustworthy, and unique. There is no other book like it in the world. Therefore, it deserves a closer look. Belief in its inerrancy can come later.

Also clearly define the meaning of "inspiration," as translated in 2 Timothy 3:16 in some versions (*King James*, for example). Inspiration is often misunderstood to mean "dictation," with the assumption that we claim God dictated all of Scripture and the human writers were simply instruments (like a stenographer) writing it down. That's not what the term means. The word in original Greek means to "breathe in." We still use the term that way in a medical context. Inspiration is to breathe in. Expiration is to breathe out.

This means God breathed into the Scripture. Human writers wrote from their own experience and observation, but the Holy Spirit influenced their writings in a mysterious way to keep them from error. That is why each writer wrote according to his own personal style. Scripture is, therefore, the faultless product of both God and man.

In teaching this lesson, begin by emphasizing the importance of external evidence—evidence from outside the Bible—when dealing with skeptics. Spend some time with the internal evidence summarized on page 231 in the Student section. Then allow plenty of time for discussion of each of the six external evidences (pages 231-233 in the Student section). Any reading on these subjects you can do in advance of this lesson will enrich class discussion.

Student assignments ask which of the six defenses the students feel are strongest, and why. As you review each of these defenses in class, ask those who selected that defense to share their reasons. Encourage students to draw from their own experience and reading with examples of how the trustworthiness of Scripture is supported by evidences from other sources. Usually, the most convincing defense when speaking with others will be what convinced the person herself. As students share these testimonies, class members will help each other sharpen up their presentations. Roleplaying, again, can be helpful.

Ask students to share their responses to question #2 in the student assignment (page 233). Encourage honesty in sharing any doubts or confusion about the subject of the Bible's trustworthiness.

Since this subject is exhaustive (having to do with everything from the writing to the preservation, copying, and canon of Scripture), it deserves more study than is possible in a survey course. You may wish to recommend the book list on page 211-212 of this Leader's section, and/or other books you may know about. Consult your pastor and church librarian for help in making these recommendations.

LESSON 21

Is the Bible True and Reliable?

The question of the accuracy and reliability of the Bible is extremely important in Christian apologetics, because what we know and believe about God is based on what the Bible tells us. If the Bible is untrustworthy, even in matters of history and geography, we cannot be sure it is true and dependable about spiritual issues, either. Jesus said, "I have spoken to you of earthly things and you do not believe; how then will you believe if I speak of heavenly things?" (John 3:12) The same can be said of the Bible. If it isn't accurate about things we can test, how can we depend on what it says about things that cannot be seen or tested?

Evidence for the Bible's authority is both internal and external. Internal evidence (what it says about itself) builds a strong case for inerrancy. Consider the following:

1) It claims to be "inspired" ("God-breathed"; 2 Tim. 3:16).
2) The writers claimed to speak from God (Hab. 2:2; Jer. 36; Acts 1:16; Mark 12:36; Rom. 1:1-3).
3) The New Testament refers to the entire Old Testament as being the authoritative Word of God (Rom. 3:2).
4) The apostles considered their New Testament writings as the Word of God having divine authority (1 Thess. 2:13; 1 Cor. 2:13; 14:37; Gal. 1:8).
5) Jesus held a high view of Scripture, considering it to be absolute authority:
   a. He considered all Scripture to be the authoritative Word of God (Matt. 5:18-19; Luke 16:17).
   b. He staked His claim to be the Messiah on Scripture (John 5:39, 46; Luke 24:27, 44; Matt. 11:1-5; Isa. 35:5).
   c. He claimed the words of Scripture to be the actual words of God (Matt. 19:4-5: "the Creator...said..."; cf. Gen.2:24)
   d. He used the phrase "it is written" as final authority (Matt. 4:4, 7, 10; Matt. 21:13; 26:24).
   e. He saw His own teaching as possessing the same weight of divine authority as the Old Testament.

In our present study, however, we are defending the truth of Scripture against those who do not yet believe it. Therefore, they would dismiss all of the above statements as being "circular arguments." They would be right. We are using the assumed authority of the Bible to prove the authority of the Bible, and that is not good logical reasoning. Even what Jesus said about the Bible is only accurate if the Bible is accurate in reporting His words. Therefore, we must move to *external evidence* (what we can learn from sources outside the Bible) to show the Bible's credibility.

When we look at external evidence, what do we find? Interestingly, we find *strong* evidence that this book is most unusual—unique among the books of the world. Much of what the Bible reports in history is verifiable by other sources, and those sources support the position that the Bible is amazingly accurate.

As apologists, we should be familiar with the following six defenses:

1) The Bible best explains the nature of man and the universe.

Philosophers and scholars have wondered for millennia why the nature of man is so self-

UNIT IV

contradictory. On the one hand, man is the crown of creation. He is able to design and construct ingenious machines and understand his environment, all the way from the atom to the far reaches of the universe. He can create, philosophize about, and manage things like no other creature on earth. Yet, he can be unbelievably cruel and self-destructive. Nearly every great invention of man is ultimately used for destruction.

How can this be? Why would such an intelligent creature act so ignorantly and selfishly? Only the Bible gives an adequate explanation. It states that man was created in the image of God, but that image was marred by sin and rebellion. No other religious or philosophical system provides an answer as adequate as the Bible's description of mankind.

2) The Bible fits what we know to be true from other sources.

Every week brings new discoveries from the fields of archeology, history, astronomy, physics, and other sources that affirm the truth of the Bible. Other books written during the time when the Bible was written are riddled with fanciful ideas and myths about creation, the planets as gods, etc. Hindu holy books speak of civilizations on the moon and sun. Babylonian sources number the stars at 3,000 total. Yet, the Bible is free from all these errors. It even declares the stars to be "numberless, like the sand on the seashore," and prohibits the worship of stars and planets. Why is one ancient religious book so different from the rest and so free from error?

One by one the scientific theories that contradict the Bible are falling into disrepute as we learn more about our universe. The awesome evidence of intelligent design, all the way from stars to atoms, is affecting how scientists view our universe. New evidence that the universe actually had a beginning is replacing the old ideas of the eternality of matter, and bringing science into line with the Bible which declares *"In the beginning* God created…"

This subject is vast and deserves extensive study. In this survey course we can only mention it in passing, encourage your further research, and declare our conviction that the trend is toward growing harmony between the claims of Scripture and the findings of science.

3) Divine inspiration is the only way to explain Bible prophecies.

In his book, *Why I Believe,* Dr. D. James Kennedy states "In all the writings of Buddha, Confucius, and Lao-tse, you will not find a single example of predicted prophecy. In the Koran…there is one instance of a specific prophecy— a self-fulfilling prophecy that he, Muhammad himself, would return to Mecca. Quite different from the prophecy of Jesus, who said that He would return from the grave. One is easily fulfilled, the other is impossible to any human being." [24]

The Bible is filled with amazing, specific prophecies about people, nations, cities, and events. Often the prophecies are the exact opposite of what ordinary expectations would be, yet they have been fulfilled *exactly* the way the prophet stated. Concerning the life of Christ alone, 330 prophecies relate to His birth, family, death, circumstances, and other very specific details of His life. Each one has been fulfilled with precise accuracy. How do you explain this, apart from assuming this book is of divine origin?

4) The Bible is unique in its remarkable preservation.

Entire nations have tried repeatedly to destroy the Bible. Yet, it lives on, and today is the world's best-seller. Not only has it survived, but it has been preserved with an accuracy unrivaled by any other ancient book.

The exciting discovery of the Dead Sea Scrolls gave us copies of portions of the Old Testament that were more than 1,000 years older than any previously available. Yet, there were only a few very minor differences (mostly spelling and punctuation) from the copies already in hand.

5) The unity of the scriptural writings is best explained by a superintending divine intelligence.

The Bible is not one book. It is a library of sixty-six books bound together in one volume. What is truly extraordinary about that is the way all these books, written over a period of almost 1,500 years by forty different authors—writing in different nations, different cultures, different languages, and separated by centuries of time—yet all agree!

How often could you walk into a library, choose two books on the same subject, and have them agree in nearly every detail? The fact that occasionally a skeptic gets excited because he thinks he found a "contradition" in the Bible is proof of its amazing unity. A supposed "contradiction" is so rare it makes news.

The best, most logical, explanation of this miraculous unity is to assume the same divine intelligence was at work in the writing of all the books.

6) The Bible's effect on individual lives is unparalleled by any other writing.

Occasionally someone will testify to a life-transforming experience as a result of reading a particular book. But the number of lives transformed, and the depth of that transformation, as a result of reading the Bible, is infinitely greater than any other book. There seems to be a "power in the Word" that goes beyond the information transmitted, as though there is a spiritual power at work in the mind of the reader.

The Bible is its own best commentary on this spiritual power. In it, God says: "As the rain and the snow come down from heaven, and do not return to it without watering the earth and making it bud and flourish, so that it yields seed for the sower and bread for the eater, so is my word that goes out from my mouth: It will not return to me empty, but will accomplish what I desire and achieve the purpose for which I sent it" (Isa. 55:10-11).

Assignment

1) Of the six defenses of Scripture given on pages 231-233, which do you feel is the strongest? Why?

Can you think of any other arguments for the trustworthiness of Scripture?

2) What is your own personal view regarding the inspiration and inerrancy of Scripture?

How did you come to this conclusion?

U N I T
V

Alternative Religions

LESSONS 22-24

Alternative Religious Movements and Practices

Equipment Needed	Teaching Supplies Needed
None	1) A sign-up sheet for students to choose the religious movement they will research. 2) Copies of student lesson 25 to distribute to the class.

Lecture

Lesson 22 is devoted to a discussion about alternative religions in general and the "Five-Point Test of Truth," as a guide for discerning truth from error. There are no lesson plans or student handouts for Lessons 23 and 24 because students are assigned specific religious movements to research and to report their findings to the class. The reports will be given and discussed in those two lessons.

The class discussion will be enhanced if someone in your congregation or acquaintance (perhaps in your class) has experienced involvement in a cult or alternative religion. Invite them to share their testimony, with emphasis on characteristics of that particular group and how they were brought out of it.

Follow the student material in presenting this lesson. Lead the class in discussing:

1. The reasons cults and alternative religions appeal.
2. Discuss the definitions of the terms "cult," "orthodoxy," "alternative religions," and "new religions" as the terms will be used in this class.
3. Ask for student responses to the Scripture readings listed on page 242 in the Student section.
4. Spend most of the class time discussing the Five-Point Test of Truth. Remember the objective in this unit is not so much to learn about specific alternative religions as it is to develop skill in determining truth and recognizing heresy.
5. Assign a religious movement to each student to research and report. The reports should summarize the history and beliefs of the religious group and analyze those beliefs using the Five-Point Test of Truth. There will be many other incidental facts about each of these groups that will be interesting to report, but each student should be sure to put the major emphasis on analyzing the group's core beliefs. These five points will lead to those core beliefs.

In assigning religious movements to students, do not be limited by the list of suggestions on page 239. (Page 245 of the Student section) There are more than a thousand groups to choose from, and students may have a reason to study one that is not on the list.

Based on the number of students in your class and the time available, inform class members about how much time is allowed for each report.

The best source of information about belief systems is the Internet because it is current, free, and provides access to both primary and secondary sources. The Student section suggests doing a search on the Internet for the group they are studying. It also recommends the Watchman Fellowship website (www.watchman.org). Watchman Fellowship is a Christian apologetics and discernment ministry. It maintains over 10,000 files and a research library of over 25,000 books and periodicals on cults and new religious movements.

If students pull up the current Watchman Fellowship "Index of Cults" on their website, they will be overwhelmed by over 1200 listings. Some will have intriguing names and raise their curiosity to research. That's fine, but we recommend your class reports stay with the most common cults, because students are most likely to encounter them. Which cults are most common depends to some degree on your location. The list on page 239 are most prolific in the United States. The list includes cults of Christianity, those in some way related to Christianity, or seem to have an appeal to some nominal Christians. But the list also includes some non-Christian belief systems as well as some that fully conform to orthodox Christian belief.

There is a vast field of non-Christian cults and religions students may wish to explore because of a special interest (such as Zen Buddhism, Nation of Islam, Hare Krishna, est. Training, etc.). If this happens, use your best judgment about whether you consider such research to be relevant to the needs of your class.

Be sure someone is assigned New Age. Point out that New Age is not a "cult," as commonly defined. It is more of a social and religious movement but the movement has such an impact on current religious thinking that it needs to be analyzed. Put one of your best researchers on this topic. It would be well for that student to give his or her report first, because some others will involve "New Age Cults," which will be better understood if the class already has some insight into the characteristics of New Age thought.

If some of the students do not have access to the Internet, we suggest that you (or another student) access it for them and print some information to help them with their research. Of course, any additional information available to students through books, their church libraries, interviews, etc. should be encouraged.

We suggest you prepare a "sign-up sheet" with a list of the groups you wish to assign and have students sign beside the cult of their choice. Some may have a special interest in a specific group because a friend or family member is involved in it. Such requests should receive priority. Be open to expressions of interest in analyzing any belief systems not on your list. It is fine for students to study a group we may not ordinarily classify as a cult or alternative religion because the purpose of this exercise is to discern truth from error. For example, some evangelical observers consider Seventh Day Adventism a cult. Others do not. Groups like this are great for students to analyze, come to their own conclusions, and explain the reasons for their conclusion to the class.

Suggest to students they may wish to review their notes from Unit III, "Pillars of Faith" (Lessons 15-18) as background before attempting their analysis.

As time allows, you may wish to read up on a specific religious group and conclude this class by analyzing it, using the Five-Point Test of Truth. This class exercise will help students become acquainted with the process.

Suggested Religious Movements for Student Research

Note: Not all of the groups listed below fit into the definition of new or alternative religions. It is your task as the researcher to determine whether the group you are studying is, or is not, consistent with orthodox Christian belief. Also, not all of these are cults of Christianity (for example, Islam, Bahai's, etc.), but they are included because of current popular interest.

- Christian Science
- Unity School of Christianity
- Unification Church (The "Moonies")
- Swedenborg Foundation
- Messianic Judaism
- The Church of Scientology
- Transcendental Meditation
- Unitarianism
- Worldwide Church of God
- Nation of Islam
- Freemasonry
- Word-Faith Movement
- Oneness Pentecostalism
- The Family of Love (Children of God)
- Mormonism
- The New Age Movement
- The Way International
- The Amish
- Islam
- Jehovah's Witnesses
- Bahai
- Christian Identity Movement
- Eckankar
- Yoga
- Quakers
- Seventh Day Adventism

LESSONS 22-24
Alternative Religious Movements and Practices

During the past several weeks we have studied doctrines commonly believed by Christians of all denominations (Pillars of Faith) and the reasons why we believe these basic truths (Apologetics). Now it is time to look around us and examine other belief systems, many of which deny or modify some of these basic doctrines.

Most people are startled to realize how many such belief systems exist. Some observers claim an average of one new religion comes into existence each day. Some of these cults claim to be Christian. Others derive from Buddhism, Hinduism, Islam, etc. There are certainly plenty of choices available for people who are seeking an alternative religion.

The past century has seen a literal explosion of new religions and new forms of old religions. Sociologists ponder why this is true. One reason, no doubt, is the tolerance toward other religions, which has almost become a religion in itself in Western culture. People don't get burned at the stake anymore for having a heretical belief (at least not in the Western world). This is an obvious encouragement to those who like to believe and teach heresy. But there are other reasons for this development as well.

Observers point out new religions appeal to people for several reasons. These reasons include:

1) Easy "black and white" answers to theological, social, and personal problems. Thinking through issues and finding one's own answer based on biblical principles demands hard work. It's much easier to just follow a religious leader's rules. Many people are attracted to that kind of authoritarianism.
2) Meeting personal emotional needs. Religious leaders know that the route to a person's heart (and commitment) is through a feeling of love and acceptance within a group. Everyone needs to feel accepted by others, and those with an identity crisis or an emotional problem are especially vulnerable.
3) New religions make a special effort to leave a good impression on society by focusing on one or more things they do well; often something the traditional church is *not* doing well at the time. Ironically, a group will frequently demonstrate an extraordinary ability to excel in something that was its greatest weakness at its founding. For example, Jehovah's Witnesses' founder, Charles Taze Russell, despite his fraudulent claims of Greek scholarship, was shown in court to be nearly totally ignorant of Greek. His followers today, however, love to preface their deviant interpretations of Scripture with, "The original Greek says" or seek to impress people with their scholarship. Many people find such supposed knowledge of Greek to be impressive. In a similar vein, Mormons, whose founder's practice of polygamy was anything but supportive of the traditional family, place great emphasis today on "family values". Thus, a group's effort to compensate for weaknesses creates a strength that people admire.

Definitions

Orthodoxy—A belief system is considered "Orthodox Christianity" if it conforms to the traditional, historic beliefs of the Christian church as established by the early church councils and maintained by the consensus of "mainline" denominations which hold to the authority of Scripture. The "Five Point Test of Truth" given below is a very brief summary of what we consider the essentials of orthodox Christian belief.

New Religions—The term "New Religions" as used in this study refers to religions which are relatively recent in America and the Western world.

Alternative Belief Systems—Belief systems which in some significant doctrine or practices are different than traditional, orthodox, Christian belief or practice in what is considered "mainline" Christian denominations.

Cult—The word "cult" is difficult to define, and probably not the best word to use. The dictionary definition of "cult" is simply "a system of religious worship or ritual…" or "devoted attachment to, or extravagant admiration for, a person, principle, etc." By this definition almost any religious system could be called a cult. The meaning of the word is so broad that it is nearly meaningless. In common usage, it is often used to refer to a splinter group that has broken away from a larger group because of one or more distinctive beliefs. In recent years, it is frequently used to refer to a group that falls under the spell of some persuasive leader who exercises extraordinary, almost hypnotic, control over its members.

If one defines "cult" as a splinter group from an existing religion, there are cults of Christianity, cults of Islam, of Buddhism, Hinduism, etc. We regard a cult of Christianity as "a religious group, claiming to be Christian, but denying one or more cardinal doctrines of historic Christian faith."

In addition to alternative religions, we will also study the "occult" in Lesson 25. The word, occult, means "hidden" or "obscure." In religious use it refers to mysterious spiritual activities many consider to be of satanic or demonic origin.

The Bible warns against false doctrine and occult practices. Read the following passages and reflect on the seriousness of these warnings. After reading all of them, write a sentence or two about your impressions. Specifically, what does the Bible tell us to avoid? How can we discern the true from the false?

> 1 John 4:1-6
> Galatians 1:6-9
> Matthew 7:15-23
> Matthew 24:23-17
> 2 Timothy 3:1-9
> Deuteronomy 18:9-13

The Five-Point Test of Truth

There are many "red flags" to watch for when we encounter a religious system, including things like unusual devotion to a human leader, isolation from the traditional Christian community, inappropriate control over the adherent's personal life and thought, claims of some "special" knowledge that only they possess, etc. But our interest here is primarily on their belief system. How can you tell biblical doctrine from that which is false and misleading?

The task of sorting truth from error is difficult because false teachers mix enough truth with their message to make it sound appealing. Sometimes groups quote Scripture copiously, but "twist' it just enough to make it seem to fit their false teaching.

As a guideline for sorting truth from error, we suggest the following "Five-Point Test of Truth." For background, you may wish to review the basic doctrines we studied in the "Pillars of Faith" section.

1) What is the basis of their authority?

They will often *claim* their authority is the Bible, but is it, really? Ask yourself, where did this new revelation come from? Was it the result of some vision or insight of only one individual? That is always a red flag. Beware of subjective experience, extra-biblical sources of information, miracles not publicly verifiable, or secret information denied to all others. They usually claim to be the only ones to possess this knowledge and the only place one can receive salvation. When they quote Scripture it is frequently with a meaning different from what has been commonly believed by the great body of scholars throughout church history. Sometimes they accomplish this by giving words new definitions.

2) What do they teach about the nature of God?

Is their description of God consistent with the Bible's representation of God as the Creator, separate from us and the rest of His creation, yet involved intimately with His creation (both immanent and transcendent)? Is He defined as a person who is omnipotent, omniscient, and omnipresent? Do they hold to the scriptural definition of the Trinity as three separate persons; eternally co-existent, but one in essence?

3) What is their view of the nature of man?

Is man viewed as a direct creation of God, separate from Him, responsible to Him, and in need of salvation? Or do they hold a pantheistic view in which man is god, a part of god, or evolving into becoming a god? Pantheism is incompatible with Christian truth. Do they describe man as unique among the animal kingdom by virtue of being created in the image of God? Do they recognize the impact of universal sin in the human race and the fact of standing under condemnation because of sin – therefore needing salvation?

4) What do they say about the nature of Christ?

This is listed in our outline as #4, but it is probably the #1 question to ask. The doctrine of the person of Christ is basic to the Christian faith. It was the first doctrinal question discussed by the ancient church, and is first in importance.

5) What do they teach as the means of salvation?

Many groups will have a system of works in place as a "ladder" to God, with the teaching that performing this series of works will earn your salvation. It may be knocking on doors and selling literature, as with Jehovah's Witnesses, or by building a good karma, as with Theosophy. All of these systems will deny the simple and precious truth of Scripture that Christ already paid for our salvation, that acceptance with God is possible *only* through Him by faith, and that salvation is a free gift of God's grace to those who believe.

The next several lessons will explore specific religious groups and practices. The purpose of this study is not so much to learn about each one as to develop skill in discerning truth from error. For this reason, learn this "Five-point Test of Truth" well and practice applying it to teachings you hear about.

In the next class session you will be asked to choose a group to study and report back to the class about:

1) The historical background and distinctiveness of this group.
2) How do the teachings of this group compare with the "Five Point Test of Truth? On the basis of that comparison, does it stand in the tradition of orthodox Christian belief? Why or why not?

You may be interested in choosing a group to study that you or someone in your family or circle of friends have some experience with, and therefore you would benefit by further study about their teachings. Otherwise, just choose one that sounds interesting to you. Your instructor will seek to avoid duplications among class members, so it would be well for you to have several groups in mind to choose from. You will find a list of suggested groups on page 245. of this section. Do not be limited to this list. Also, keep in mind that not every group on this list is an "alternative religion." Some on the list will conform to historic orthodox Christian doctrine and will pass the "Five Point Test of Truth" with flying colors! Your task is to determine which category fits the group you are studying. The purpose of this exercise is to gain experience in evaluating a belief system to determine whether or not it conforms to Scripture and orthodox Christian belief.

Your instructor may have suggestions for sources from which you can research information about these groups. The best source is the Internet, because:

1) You can have access to a huge volume of information.
2) You can directly access "primary sources,' (the websites of these groups) to confirm their teachings, rather than being limited to "secondary sources" (people who aren't on the "inside" of the group but have written about them), and
3) It's free!

It is best to use both primary and secondary sources. Primary sources add validity to your research because you get your information directly from the group itself, and secondary sources help you notice things you may otherwise overlook.

Do a search of the Internet for both primary and secondary sources. An excellent secondary resource is Watchman Fellowship, Inc., an apologetics ministry that maintains a file of hundreds of religious groups. Their website is: www.watchman.org.

If you do not have access to the Internet, please inform your instructor, who will attempt to provide resource information for you about the group of your choice.

Your instructor will schedule a time for you to give a report on your research, and will inform you about how much time you will have to give your report. It will be an enjoyable experience. It will also be "heart-wrenching" to hear everyone's report and learn how many false beliefs are embraced by so many people.

Suggested Religious Movements for Student Research

Not all of the groups listed below fit into the definition of new or alternative religions. It is your task as the researcher to determine whether the group you are studying is, or is not, consistent with orthodox Christian belief. Also, not all of these are cults of Christianity (for example, Islam, Bahai's, etc.), but they are included because of current popular interest.

- Christian Science
- Unity School of Christianity
- Unification Church (The "Moonies")
- Swedenborg Foundation
- Messianic Judaism
- The Church of Scientology
- Transcendental Meditation
- Unitarianism
- Worldwide Church of God
- Nation of Islam
- Freemasonry
- Word-Faith Movement
- Oneness Pentecostalism
- The Family of Love (Children of God)
- Mormonism
- The New Age Movement
- The Way International
- The Amish
- Islam
- Jehovah's Witnesses
- Bahai
- Christian Identity Movement
- Eckankar
- Yoga
- Quakers
- Seventh Day Adventism

UNIT V

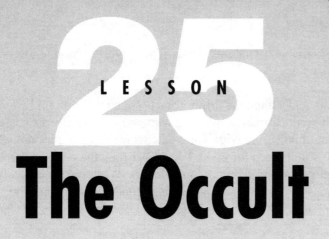

LESSON 25
The Occult

Equipment Needed	Teaching Supplies Needed
None	1) Copies of student lesson 26 to distribute to the class.

Lecture

If all your students have not had an opportunity to present their reports in previous lessons, use the first part of this lesson to finish them. The study of the occult is simply an extension of the previous study on cults. However the difference is that occult practice reflects satanic and demonic activity more directly.

It is important in this lesson to achieve balance. Some Christians tend to deny the existence and influence of evil spirits or to focus too much on this subject—blaming every hardship in life on the influence of Satan and evil spirits. The latter focus usually leads to the fear of evil spirits and preoccupation with resisting the occult. This focus turns a believers' attention toward Satan rather than toward Christ. Either extreme is unfortunate, unbiblical, and a hindrance to effective discipleship.

Occult practice varies all the way from innocent-appearing parlor games to actual worship of Satan. Review some of these practices with the class, as listed on pages 249 and 250 of the Student section. If one or more class members object to the inclusion of a specific practice as part of the occult, a proper response would be to simply say, "Many Christians do consider it to have occult overtones." Often by the end of the lesson class members will modify their opinion.

As you review the list of occult practices, ask what experiences, if any, class members have had with occult games. Many games flood the market in addition to those listed on page 249 of the Student section. What influences, if any, did the involvement with these games have on the participants?

Practice #2 on the list (séances, channeling, and mediums) is part of spiritism, the belief in communication with the dead. It is also called necromancy. Channeling is often associated with attempts to communicate with "ascended masters," supposedly those of the dead who have experienced evolutionary advancement and are therefore more knowledgeable and wiser than the living.

Psychic readers are practitioners who claim to have supernatural powers to discern facts about a person's past lives, present relationships, and information otherwise not discernable by natural means. They claim to be able to give advice for a fuller, happier life.

Help students understand the differences between what might be termed "ordinary" occult practices, paganism, and white witchcraft. People sometimes question what could be wrong with white witchcraft, since it does not seek to harm anyone and is motivated for good. For a Christian, the concern involves not just a White Witch's motivation, but the fact that the White Witch is involved in the same practices as other witches—practices condemned in Scripture. Regardless of "which witch it is," witchcraft practices are not compatible with Christian faith.

Ask students to share their one- or two-sentence summary (page 252) of what the Bible teaches concerning the occult. Allow plenty of time to discuss specific passages they found interesting, informative, or provocative. Since some people think the Bible doesn't have much to say about the occult, working through this list of references should put that idea to rest.

As students summarize and share the Bible teaching about the occult, note the repeated prohibitions against looking to nature (creation) for guidance. It is reminiscent of Romans 1:25, which speaks of those who worship and serve created things rather than the Creator. It is important for students to understand why God prohibits occult practice. In addition to the obvious one—the satanic influences and invitation to evil spirits—in much occult practice, people look to things in nature (stars, tea leaves, etc.) for guidance instead of coming to the Lord or searching Scripture.

This class lesson can be greatly enriched by the testimony of someone who has past occult experience and is now a Christian. If you are aware of such a person in your congregation or community, you may wish to invite that person to share her story in this lesson.

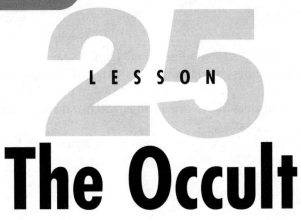

LESSON 25

The Occult

Definition

The word occult means "hidden, secret, sinister, beyond comprehension, dark, or mysterious." When used in a religious context, it means the practice of magic arts, usually involving contact with evil spirits (demons) and/or Satan. The definition of occultism includes certain practices of divination, superstition, and magic.

Various Levels of Occult Practices

Occultism ranges all the way from dabblers in the occult to actual Satan worshipers. Many people, even Christians, nibble at the fringes of the occult for entertainment or thrills without realizing they are actually practicing occult arts. Examples would be people who live by astrology charts, read tea leaves, or play occult related parlor games. The "deep end" of the occult is the worship of Satan. Between these two ends of the spectrum is a vast array of witchcraft and pagan practices, some of which involve direct and purposeful contact with Satan and/or evil spirits and surprisingly, some practitioners who do not even believe Satan exists.

The motivations for involvement in the occult include:

1) Seeking thrills;
2) Attempting communication with a deceased love one;
3) Gaining power over others;
4) Promising of wealth, romance, pleasure, or prestige;
5) Foretelling the future.

Examples of Occult Practices
Many activities and practices may have occult involvement. Some of the major ones are:

1) Occult games: such as the Ouija Board, Dungeons & Dragons, Magic the Gathering, and many others.
2) Séances, channeling, and mediums
3) Fortune-telling: tea leaves, palm readings, crystal balls, tarot cards, etc.
4) Psychic readers
5) Astrology
6) Horoscopes
7) Voodoo

Paganism

The definition of a pagan used to be "someone who is not a Christian, Muslim, or Jew." Now a revival of ancient pagan practices called "Neo-Paganism" (New Paganism) is upon us. New Paganism claims to be a restoration of the earliest world religion. Although it is related to the occult, it is somewhat different from the practices described previously. Pagans worship the earth as "Mother Goddess." Usually they are animists, believing spirits inhabit inanimate objects. They do not worship Satan. Many pagans do not even believe Satan exists.

The family of paganism includes Wicca, witch doctors, medicine men, herbal magic, shamanism, and various kinds of sorcery.

"White" Witchcraft

Those who call themselves "White Witches" follow practices similar to those of pagans, but they insist they use their powers only for good. They seek to deflect some of the bad things of "black witchcraft" and claim to use their witchcraft to bring healing and other good things to people. They are not necessarily anti-Christian. In fact, they often appeal to statements in Scripture in support of their practices.

White witches use sorcery and "white magic" to affect healing and seek to be in touch with "ascended masters" through séances and mediums to gain information that will help bring understanding or resolve problems. Some do not want to be called "witches," preferring the title "channelers."

The "Occult Explosion"

The past few decades have witnessed a dramatic increase in occult practice around the world. The growth is so significant that some observers are calling it the "Occult Explosion." Many see it as a fulfillment of prophecies about the "end times" (for example, Rev. 9:20-21).

Occultism was a major part of community life in Europe during the high Middle Ages and also in some other parts of the world (Africa, etc.). In the West, it almost disappeared with the advance of science, but it is making an aggressive comeback today.

Evidence of this revival of occult/paganism is everywhere. Browsing any secular bookstore will reveal endless best-selling titles with occult overtones. Occultism permeates popular music, especially music that appeals to youth. Many TV programs, video and computer games, toys, and role-playing games reflect occult images and ideas. The popularity of the Gothic subculture in many high schools reflects teens' interest in the occult.

Part of the appeal of the occult is the excitement of connecting to supernatural power. Occult powers are real, and many people in this sterile secular culture (and some in dead churches) have never experienced anything supernatural. Therefore, they find the mystery and power of the occult attractive. A significant number of professionals and wealthy individuals are involved in the occult.

Another reason for its popularity is that occult leaders and writers promise great benefits for those who practice the magic arts. These benefits include everything from wealth and power to romance and pleasure. Many of those who practice the occult do, in fact, experience such power. Sadly, they ultimately learn that occult power is temporary and often leads to despair, spiritual slavery to Satan, and even suicide. A growing number of murders, suicides, and other violent behaviors in recent years are reported to have been, in some way, associated with occult practice.

What Does the Bible Say about the Occult?

The answer is, "a lot!" On the next two pages is a list of some of the references to occult practice mentioned in the Bible. In preparation for class discussion, please find and read each of the passages referenced in the list. The references appear in biblical order to make the task of finding them easier. When you have finished reading these passages, write a sentence or two summarizing what you think the Bible says about occult practices.

- Leviticus 19:31

- Leviticus 20:27

- Deuteronomy 4:15-19

- Deuteronomy 17:2-5

- Deuteronomy 18:9-14

- 1 Samuel 28

- 2 Kings 21:1-6

- 2 Kings 23:24-25

- Job 31:26-28

- Isaiah 2:6

- Isaiah 8:19

- Isaiah 19:3

- Isaiah 44:24-25

- Isaiah 47:11-15 (This passage makes a prophecy against Babylon, considered by many to be the ancient "home" of the occult.)

- Jeremiah 10:1-2

- Jeremiah 14:14

- Jeremiah 27:9-10

- Daniel 2:1-12

- Daniel 5:5-8

- Micah 5:12

- Zephaniah 1:4-6

- Acts 19:18-19

- 2 Corinthians 11:13-15 (Could this passage have any application to "White Witchcraft"?)

- Galatians 5:19-21

- Revelation 9:20-21

- Revelation 21:8

Having examined these passages, try to write a one- or two-sentence summary telling what the Bible teaches about the occult:

Sometimes people have certain experiences or unusual powers that seem to lie beyond the ordinary but may not be an occult practice. We call them "paranormal experiences." They may include an apparent telepathy, premonitions about future events, unusual discernments, prophetic dreams, etc. Not everyone who experiences these things is practicing the occult. We simply do not understand every aspect of human behavior, so we must be careful about labeling an experience as demonic or associated with the occult just because it seems strange. Sadly, many people have been falsely accused.

Additionally, we Christians need not fear satanic power. We are assured that "the one who is in you is greater than the one who is in the world" (1 John 4:4). Rather than fear those involved in the occult, we need to reach out in love, sharing the joy of Christ. Many of these people are seeking a spiritual reality to fill the emptiness of their lives, but they're looking for fulfillment in the wrong places!

U N I T
VI

Postmodern Culture

LESSON 26
Postmodernism

Equipment Needed	Teaching Supplies Needed
None	1) Copies of student lesson 27 to distribute to the class.

Lecture

The goal of this lesson is to help students understand the transition taking place between modern and postmodern worldviews. The concepts imbedded in this transition are not easy to grasp. For your own preparation, it would be very helpful if you have access to *The Death of Truth* by Dennis McCallum (Bethany House Publishers). You can teach this unit without McCallum's book, obviously, but if you can read it prior to teaching this unit you will find it very helpful.

We state in the student's material— and you will want to emphasize this—that as Christians we do not identify with either modernism or postmodernism. We must evaluate both in the light of Scripture and a *Christian* worldview. From a Christian perspective, both modernism and postmodernism have some good and bad features.

The challenge in this unit will be to explain the meaning of "worldview" clearly and to present the postmodern worldview accurately and understandably. The terms, themselves, will be new to many people. But almost everyone is in some way influenced by postmodern attitudes.

A worldview is simply a statement of how people see their world. James Sire, in *The Universe Next Door*, suggests a worldview answers five basic questions:

1. What is prime reality—the really real?
2. Who is man?
3. What happens to man at death?
4. What is the basis of morality?
5. What is the meaning of human history? [10]

The answers to these five questions define the basics of a person's worldview. Peripheral to these questions is a host of modifiers and descriptors that further define how people see their world.

After beginning with a brief explanation of the medieval worldview, we contrast that with the modern worldview, and conclude by showing the changes taking

UNIT VI

place as our culture moves from a modern to a postmodern mindset. The Student section follows this order.

QUICK COMPARISON CHART

Modernism	Postmodernism
Revere Science	Distrust Science
Primacy of Reason and Logic	Rejection of Reason
Goal = Progress	Goal = Equality of Power
Existence of Objective Truth	Relativism / Subjectivism
Respect for Authority	Individualism / Tolerance
"Sin" = Error	"Sin" = Intolerance
"Melting Pot" American culture	Multiculturalism
Optimism	Pessimism

Have students turn to the "Quick Comparison Chart" on page 262 of the Student section. Discuss each of these eight topics thoroughly, asking class members to respond with their own opinions about whether the chart accurately describes characteristics of today's culture. Introduce the chart by acknowledging that this is a *general* description of *trends* in our culture. We are not saying everyone follows these trends. But the changes in culture seem to be moving in these directions. Older members in your class will be the most perceptive in discerning and describing the changes.

Note the first item on the chart and discuss the shift in public opinion about science. In modernism, science was virtually worshiped. It was seen as the vehicle through which utopia was coming. Science, it was thought, would eventually find solutions to all our problems and give us control of our environment. Through science we would conquer disease, live a life of comfort, and lead the way to a better world. This attitude produced a spirit of superiority, even arrogance, as "developed" nations like the United States saw themselves as better than others because we were more technologically advanced.

In contrast, many people today are disillusioned with science. It hasn't solved all our problems. Instead, it has brought us pollution, horrible weapons of war, a sterile "chemically based" health care system that has lost its warmth of personal caring, and many other miseries. Technological advances have not made us "better." In many ways, it is perceived, the native tribesman in his grass hut with a mud floor is happier than we are with all our technological wizardry.

The second item on the chart concerns how logic is perceived. Modernists held logic and the powers of reason in the highest regard. But today there is a growing suspicion of reason because, it is pointed out, everyone's so-called "logic" is colored by personal biases. There really is no such thing as pure reason. Emotion (feeling) is more important than reason.

The third item contrasts the modernist goal of seeking to "get ahead"—progress—with the postmodernist goal of "getting along." The conquistadors and early Americans were out to conquer and subdue. Postmodernists are more concerned with making sure everyone has equal power. Therefore the "marginalized" (for example; minorities, women, homosexuals, etc.) must be brought up to equal power with the mainstream.

The fourth item is about the rejection of absolutes. Einstein's theory of relativity in physics and astronomy has spilled over into other disciplines, including ideas about morality. In the modernist era, truth was considered objectively real and out there to be discovered. Today, truth is thought to exist only in the mind, not "out there." It is subjective and relative. My truth is true for me and your truth is true for you. It is of no great concern if the two "truths" are contradictory. It is therefore inappropriate for you to "judge" my truth. Rather than "discoverers of truth," we are "creators of truth."

The fifth entry in the chart contrasts the respect for authority in the modernist era with the individualism of today. Sometimes called the "me generation," people today are less concerned about conformity to rules or submission to authority. It is expected that if I deviate from the accepted "norms" of society, others have an obligation to be tolerant of my ideas and behaviors. In fact, tolerance has almost become a religion in itself.

This relates to the next topic—the definition of sin. In modernist thought "sin" was a violation of the law of God and/or the law of the land. It was to be in error. Today, intolerance is considered as bad as or worse than to violate the law. Christians are often accused of being intolerant because we say Christ is the only way of salvation and because we criticize certain behaviors we consider immoral. On the positive side, the trend toward tolerance has helped to reduce the prejudice and injustice that was common in much modernist behavior.

All of these trends have reshaped the image of America. America used to be considered the "melting pot," where immigrants were expected to "Americanize" in language and culture. Now that notion is criticized because it is thought it destroys other cultures and robs minorities of their ethnic heritage. Instead, the trend is toward encouraging various ethnic groups and sub-cultures to retain their distinctiveness and preserve their language and culture. This has given rise to the "hyphenated American" (African-American, Asian-American, German-American, etc.)

Generally speaking, modernist culture was optimistic—especially in the nineteenth and early twentieth centuries. Science was literally exploding with findings and discoveries to improve people's lives. America was seen as the "shining light on a hill" to bring progress and peace to a waiting world. American values, especially American Christian values, were considered superior to those held in other places.

Postmodernist culture, in contrast, is generally pessimistic. Americans are engulfed in self-criticism and American (especially American Christian) influence in the world is often judged to be intolerant and inappropriate. The rejection of absolutes has resulted in moral confusion, culture wars, and despair.

Next week's lesson will focus on the impact postmodern thought is having on various disciplines in our culture. All this is leading up to discussion about the effect postmodernism is having on the church and our Christian witness, and finally suggestions about how we, as Christians, can effectively relate to this rapidly changing culture.

In their assignment, students were asked to find examples of postmodern thinking in the media and in conversation with others. Encourage them to continue bringing examples to class the next two weeks.

As you distribute the student materials for Lesson 27, call attention to the content. It provides a brief summary of the impact of postmodern attitudes in science, medicine,

ERA COMPARISON CHART			
	Medieval	Modern	Postmodern
"Truth" is:	• Faith / Belief in teachings of church	• What is objectively true	• Subjective / Personal
The "heroes" are:	• Clergy / Kings • Knights • Philosophers	• Scientists / Soldiers • Researchers • Inventors / Explorers	• The "marginalized" • Athletes • Entertainers
The "bad" people are:	• Heretics • Infidels • Heathen	• Superstitious • Kings • Savages	• The arrogant, powerful, polluters • Europeans • Conquistadors
"Production" is by:	• Hand Tools	• Machines	• Computers

UNIT VI

psychotherapy, education, history, literature, and law. If any of the students are involved in one of these disciplines, ask them to reflect on the statements made here in relation to their own experience. Have they noticed a shift from modern to postmodern attitudes in their work or professions? Give them an opportunity to respond in the next class lesson.

LESSON 26
Postmodernism

The purpose of this study is to gain a better understanding of the culture we live in and to learn how we can best relate to this culture as Christians.

The term "postmodernism," is new to many people. So is its meaning. But even though you may not be acquainted with the word, you are well acquainted with postmodern culture, perhaps without even knowing it. Some of your attitudes and values have been shaped by postmodernism. So have some of your frustrations. You are very much aware that "times have changed," but it's difficult to define the changes. It's even more difficult to explain or understand the reasons for the changes.

In defining postmodernism, it is perhaps best to start by stating what it is *not:*

- Postmodernism is not some cult or religious belief. It is not something that was "started" by someone or promoted through an organization. It is not anything you "join."
- There is no "postmodern conspiracy" out there that is seeking to take over the world or win converts.
- Postmodernism is not a political movement, even though it greatly affects politics. It also affects religion, the arts, literature, the writing and teaching of history, law, science, and other aspects of our culture.

So, then, what is it?

The Meaning of "Postmodernism"

Postmodernism is a name for the "mood" or "mindset" of people in America today. Each generation has a different way of looking at things. Philosophers call this a "worldview." It's a person's (or society's) philosophy of life. Sometimes many successive generations have a similar worldview.

Not everyone at any given time or place holds the same worldview. There are probably as many different worldviews as there are people alive. Yet, there seems to be a prevailing mindset in a culture at any given time, and it is appropriate to say that people living at the same time in the same part of the world, *generally* tend to think a certain way. Usually the way they see things (their worldview) is different than the way their grandparents did.

There seems to have been a dramatic shift of worldviews during the past twenty years in America. The change has happened more rapidly than at any previous time in history. People today view reality and truth much differently than they did twenty years ago. Consequently, if we are not aware of the change, we will be very confused by the culture and ineffective in ministering to people today.

As we discuss these changes, remember that as Christians we are not identifying with either modernism or postmodernism. Rather, we stand aside from both and seek to understand and critique them. There are good and bad things about modernism, and there are also good and bad things about postmodernism. Remember, also, that we're talking about the *general* mindset of people in our culture. Not everyone in America fits the description. Some do, some do not—some more, some less. But everyone in America *is* to some degree affected by these changes.

To gain perspective, we will compare three worldviews: the medieval, the modern, and the postmodern. The Western world has gone through these three changes in this order. The shift from medieval to modern ways of thinking took place very slowly over hundreds of years. The shift from modernism to postmodernism, on the other hand, has been occurring with alarming speed!

Medieval Worldview

During medieval times people assumed the world was the center of the universe. They assumed God was the Creator of the world and all that is in it, and man was ultimately responsible to Him. They looked upon the church as the supreme authority in matters of truth and falsehood and understood that the church derived its determination of truth from both Scripture and tradition. The church defined what was "good" and "bad," and people generally accepted the church's teachings as absolutes.

Medieval people believed reality included both the world of sensory experience and the spiritual sphere of good and evil spirits. Occurrences in the visible world of sensory experiences were often seen to be results of powers in the spiritual realm. This led not only to being open to ideas about good and evil spirits but also to almost extreme superstition.

Reality was both objective and knowable (that is, truth was truth, and it was the same for everybody). The church determined what was true for most people. The church's greatest rival for power was the state. But people would generally obey the church and/or state because they felt authority and a "chain of command" were essential to social order.

Important changes began to take place in the fifteenth, sixteenth, and seventeenth centuries. The mood of the Western world gradually shifted, bringing the beginning of what we call the "modern" period.

The "Modern" Worldview

Advances in science, especially astronomy, caused people to change their perception of the world. The world was no longer assumed to be the center of creation, but a peripheral speck of dust in a vast, uncharted universe. God began to recede in their thinking. If He existed at all, He was thought to be far, far away.

Science and human reason were bringing so many wonderful advances and new discoveries into human experience that people began to almost worship science. "Scientific evidence" became more important than the authority of the church. Science and reason were perceived as the ultimate tools for the discovery of reality and control of the environment. The superstitions of medieval times were looked down upon with disdain. Science was understood to be based on objective logic and experiment and therefore free of superstition and bias.

Progress was seen to be inevitable. It was a very optimistic time. Western culture was assumed to be "better" than other cultures because it was more scientifically advanced.

Man was no longer seen to be subject to either church or governmental authority unless (in the case of the church) an individual chose that particular church, or (in the case of government) the rulers were democratically chosen. Man was viewed as autonomous, and the "captain of his own fate." Man was to be governed by laws democratically determined, and the law was to be impartially administered and not influenced by the opinions or feelings of rulers or judges.

The authority of the church to determine "right" and "wrong" gradually diminished. Ethics and the determination of good was based on one or more differing principles, including the nature of man, the "greatest good for the greatest number," or the collective determination of a particular social group. Each individual was left to determine his own system of ethics as long as his actions did not harm others.

Education was seen to be a system of transmitting unbiased knowledge, universal values, and useful skills. The things taught were to be objective truths (things that are true whether you believe them or not).

In order to accommodate to science, many church leaders and writers began to "revise" ancient beliefs to make them look respectable to the scientific age. For example; miracles, the resurrection of Christ, inspiration of the Scriptures, and similar supposed evidence of divine intervention in this world were downplayed. Those who did this came to be known as "modernists."

During the age of modernism, Western culture became dominant in power in the world because of technological advances. In many ways, including the military, the ministry of missionaries, and educational endeavors, the advanced technology and methods of the West were "exported" to nearly every part of the globe. Hardly anyone doubted that Western ways were "better."

Whereas it took several hundred years for medieval culture to be "modernized," we are now seeing a radical, very rapid, shift to "postmodernism." Postmodern, of course, means "after modernism." The basic principles of modernism are being challenged. Postmodern concepts began in academic circles, but are filtering down through educational systems and the media to our own neighborhoods. If the world seems "upside down" to you, it's probably because you are viewing a postmodern world from the perspective of a modern mindset.

What Is Postmodernism?

In a postmodern worldview, people are not seen as autonomous, independent thinkers. We are all the product of our culture. We *think* our ideas and opinions are our own, but in reality we are so shaped by our culture that it is impossible for us to think objective ideas.

Truth is relative and is different in various cultures and languages. There is no objective "right" or "wrong" that applies to everyone. For this reason, objective justice is impossible. Laws are enforced by people, and people reflect their own cultural biases. There is no objective standard of "good" or "bad."

Because of this underlying principle, postmodernists insist Western culture cannot be called "better" than any other culture. To make such a claim is pure arrogance.

In addition, there is no such thing as objective science. Every scientific interpretation is filtered through the bias of the interpreter. A person's subjective impression is just as "true" as so-called "scientific fact."

The modernist idea of "progress" is seen as only a justification for European cultures to dominate and exploit other cultures. All cultures are of equal value and are equally "right" or "true." To seek to unify cultures is to exploit those of lesser power by those of greater power. Therefore, "right" and "wrong" are not moral judgments, as modernists contend, but "right" is equality of power.

Education should not be an exercise in transferring objective truths to others. First of all, no such objective truth exists. Even if it did, it is impossible to communicate it because we are all imprisoned within our own language. The task of education is not to transfer information, but to create experiences and build self-esteem in the student as a basis for developing his own "constructs." A construct is the reality each person builds for himself, within the context of his own culture and experience, and is "true" for him.

Does this sound confusing and illogical? It does if you have a modernist mindset, which most of us have. You may want to read this section over several times and concentrate on the differences between modernist and postmodern mindsets. To help with this process, the following comparison charts contrast some of the differences between a modern and postmodern thinking. Use it as a quick and relatively easy way to pinpoint the major differences.

We will talk about this extensively in class. In subsequent lessons we will look at the influence postmodernism exerts on law and government, history writing, literature, science, medicine, psychotherapy, and the church.

In preparation for the next class, watch for evidences of postmodern thought in various media. As you listen to TV and radio, read newspapers and magazines, and visit with acquaintances, be aware of the expressions of postmodern thought. If you come across examples, be prepared to share them with your class.

Modernism	Postmodernism
Revere Science	Distrust Science
Primacy of Reason and Logic	Rejection of Reason
Goal = Progress	Goal = Equality of Power
Existence of Objective Truth	Relativism / Subjectivism
Respect for Authority	Individualism / Tolerance
"Sin" = Error	"Sin" = Intolerance
"Melting Pot" American culture	Multiculturalism
Optimism	Pessimism

ERA COMPARISON CHART

	Medieval	Modern	Postmodern
"Truth" is:	• Faith / Belief in teachings of church	• What is objectively true	• Subjective / Personal
The "heroes" are:	• Clergy / Kings • Knights • Philosophers	• Scientists / Soldiers • Researchers • Inventors / Explorers	• The "marginalized" • Athletes • Entertainers
The "bad" people are:	• Heretics • Infidels • Heathen	• Superstitious • Kings • Savages	• The arrogant, powerful, polluters • Europeans • Conquistadors
"Production" is by:	• Hand Tools	• Machines	• Computers

LESSON 27

The Effects of Postmodern Attitudes in Science, Medicine, Psychotherapy, Education, History, Literature, and Law

Equipment Needed	Teaching Supplies Needed
None	1) Copies of student lesson 28 to distribute to the class.

Lecture

Those older than thirty have noticed some very rapid changes in cultural attitudes during the past decade or two. What has happened?

The general "mood" of the culture has changed and is affecting every aspect of our society. To get a "feel" of this impact, this lesson looks briefly at seven different professions (science, medicine, psychotherapy, education, history, literature, and law) to gauge the impact postmodern thinking has on each discipline.

Part of the assignment for this week was to watch for examples of postmodern attitudes expressed in the media or in conversations with others. Give students an opportunity to share any observations they may have.

Discuss each of the seven segments in order. If any students are professionals or paraprofessionals in one of these areas, be sure to ask them to evaluate what is said here from their own perspective:

Science

The postmodern view is that science cannot be objective. Every scientific observation is interpreted through the scientist's mind which has been affected by his beliefs. His beliefs in turn have been formed by his culture and language.

Medicine

Note the trend in medicine toward alternative therapies. There is a decreasing trust in traditional medicine—the "biochemical model." Ask students to comment about their observations concerning this trend. What are some of the reasons?

Psychotherapy

Modern therapists generally seek to help a patient become aware of faulty

UNIT VI

assumptions they are making and help them adjust to objective reality. In post-modern therapy, the therapist does not directly challenge the patient's perception of reality because that perception is, in fact, reality to the patient. To assume the therapist's construction of reality is more "true" than the patient's is arrogant.

Education

In modernist practice, the task of educators was to transmit unbiased knowledge. Educators were seen as authorities in their subject fields. In postmodern theory educators are facilitators who help students develop their own "constructs." It is believed that reality is not "discovered," but is "constructed" in the mind of the student. All constructions of reality are of equal worth.

History

In the modernist era history was considered to be an objective science, involving research into what *actually happened* in the past. In postmodern practice, history is seen as what people *think* happened. History writing (and re-writing) is a politi-cal exercise, giving legitimacy to a certain group of people or a particular idea. What *actually* happened in the past is of secondary importance. The result is often a distortion of facts. Incredibly, for example, an alarming number of Americans now think it is possible the Holocaust never happened!

Literature

Postmodern theory holds the reader, not the author, to be the authority over a text. The important thing is what it means to the reader. It is thought that because of the limitations of language and reader bias, it is impossible to know what the writer actually meant. When applied to Scripture, this concept has profound impli-cations.

Law

Law is not considered to be an objective standard of right and wrong. Laws are made and enforced by people who are biased. No judge can be entirely objective because no person can be fully objective. Therefore, law is often an attempt by the powerful to subjugate the "marginalized." To prevent this, the legal system should concern itself with equality of power among the adversaries in a dispute.

Conclusion

Inform students that today's brief summary of postmodern influence in the various professions was for the purpose of gaining more insight into the *trends* in our cul-ture—the way people are beginning to think. What we have learned so far in this unit is background to the next lesson; the impact of postmodernism on the church and on our Christian faith. Call attention to page 275 of the Lesson 28 assignment. Note that, in preparation for the next lesson, they are asked to jot down some thoughts about how our approach to people with the Gospel needs to be different than it used to be—or does it? What impact, if any, does postmodern thought have on our Christian witness? It's important that class members do some serious thinking about this.

LESSON 27

The Effects of Postmodern Attitudes in Science, Medicine, Psychotherapy, Education, History, Literature, and Law

Our culture tends to accept basic principles of postmodern thought. These principles may be summarized, at least in part, as:

A growing rejection of moral absolutes, believing moral truth is relative to the situation. Numerous surveys and polls seem to indicate a rising acceptance of the idea that moral truth is relative. A flexible ethic based upon the circumstances is replacing unchanging moral absolutes. Even Christians are experiencing this change. Many of the behaviors that were unacceptable a generation ago are now tolerated.

A diminishing of the importance of logic, reason, science, etc., claiming pure reason and research are impossible because "truth" is different for each of us. The assumption is that our own experiences and understanding (our "constructs") color our interpretation of data. Each person's feelings and/or understanding is "truth" to that person. It is considered impossible, therefore, to determine an absolute "truth" which is the same for everyone.

In keeping with principle #2, above, it is therefore wrong to judge anyone else's understanding of truth. To claim one's own ideas or religion is better than another is condemned as the height of arrogance.

There is a growing tendency to consider equality of power among all groups and classes of people to be one of the highest virtues. Since European culture has been dominant in America for centuries, postmodern activists seek to diminish the values, heroes, rights, etc., of white European males and enhance the privileges of the "marginalized" (minorities, women, homosexuals, etc.). Pride in one's heritage and personal self-esteem among marginalized people are considered to be essential in order to reach this goal. Multiculturalism (the co-existence of multiple, equally powerful, and equally respected cultural entities, empowered to preserve their unique reality) is favored over the modernist "melting pot" concept. The melting pot is increasingly viewed as the subjugation of marginal cultures to white European constructs.

Personal feelings of satisfaction are increasingly valued as more important than the pursuit of progress, or the attainment of some objective goal.

Cultural trends usually begin in circles of higher education through the writings and teachings of philosophers, theologians, educators, etc., and through time are communicated to the population at large through the media, entertainment, educational institutions, and other forms of mass communication. Most observers feel the five trends listed above are well on their way to acceptance by the majority of people in our culture. This doesn't mean, of course, that everyone around us is "postmodernized," to coin a phrase. Most of us are evangelical Christians. Our "subgroup" is more resistant to postmodern ideology than the culture at large. Nevertheless, we need to understand our culture in order to minister to it effectively.

The growing influence of postmodern concepts is affecting all aspects of our culture. A few examples of these trends in several disciplines are:

Science

In some ways, scientists are probably least affected by postmodernist concepts than their contemporaries in other disciplines. After all, it is difficult to be subjective about a chemical formula or a principle of physics. However, in recent decades, the theory of relativity in astrophysics has shaken the previous confidence in absolute laws. We now know time and space are relative. Two observers can have contradictory data yet both can be right, depending on their perspective.

Science is rapidly changing, and in the overall culture there is a trend toward disillusionment with science, emphasizing the failure of science to provide a better world. The "successes" of scientific progress are often considered sterile and do not provide for people's basic emotional and spiritual needs. To the contrary, it is pointed out, technology has resulted in hectic lifestyles, insane competition, and contributed to pollution of the environment and exploitation of minorities and tribal people.

Postmodernists claim science can never be truly "objective." Not only is there the question of relativism, discussed above, in addition, every researcher filters the data through his/her own biases. The assumption that logic and reason can determine some objective truth is dismissed as a "European construct."

Many postmodernist interpreters claim Western society has used science to dominate other cultures by claiming we are "better" because we are more "scientifically advanced," when in fact primitive cultures are just as "good."

The practical outcome of this minimizing of science is less public funding of scientific research and a diminishing role of science in colleges and universities. Science and logic are being replaced by metaphysical studies.

Medicine

Just as there is disillusionment with science, postmodernist culture is also rejecting, to some degree, the "biochemical model" of medicine. Traditional medicine is seen as an outgrowth of Western mentality; "materialistic, male-dominated and cold." A "holistic model" is replacing it as a system intended to minister to the "whole" person, not just the chemistry of the body.

As a result of this change, an explosion of interest in alternative therapies is occurring as evidenced by Eastern mystical remedies, therapeutic touch, acupuncture, and a wide variety of "spiritual" healing methods.

Psychotherapy

Simplistically stated, in the modernist era, a therapist was expected to help a client recognize wrong patterns of thinking and guide her toward what was "right." In a postmodernist context, on the other hand, the therapist is to recognize there is no universal "right" or "wrong." To a large extent, whatever is "right" for the individual is acceptable.

The therapist's "construction of reality" is not to be assumed as "better." She is just as "culture bound" as the patient. The therapist's role is not to confront or "correct" the patient's thinking, but to offer alternative language to replace the label the patient has placed on her feelings. It is assumed that concepts such as "mental illness" and "mental health" are constructs created by culture through language. No objective standard exists to define what is mental health or illness. Practices such as homosexuality, polygamy, etc., are not subject to "right" or "wrong" judgments. To call them such is just to reflect culturally derived prejudices.

As in each of the disciplines discussed here, please remember we are trying to briefly define the basis of *trends* in our culture. This does not mean most therapists in psychotherapy or most teachers in education, etc., have accepted or are practicing these methods. What we are describing is a movement, a trend, in these directions in our culture.

Education

The educational system is greatly affected by the social forces in our culture. It cannot be otherwise. The educational system is at the heart of a nation's culture, and is therefore influenced by parents' attitudes, community attitudes, educational theory, politics, religion, and every facet of society. To some degree, the educational system forms the attitudes of a culture. To an equal degree, the culture forms the

UNIT VI

concepts and attitudes of the educational system.

Among the trends in our culture that educators are forced to wrestle with is the concept of "multiculturalism." Schools are perceived as a tool to empower the marginalized. Many postmodernist theorists feel the educational system is obligated to correct perceived injustices. As part of this corrective, educators are to build self-esteem and pride in each student's ethnic and cultural roots. This affects how testing is perceived (is the test fair to all ethnic groups?), how the curriculum reflects history, society, literature, and language—even, for example, accepting African American language as equal to and just as valid as "the king's English." Sometimes heroes of ethnic groups replace traditional American heroes in the pictures and literature of schools.

In a postmodernist school environment, "political correctness" is a major issue facing teachers and administrators, and the attempts to provide pure equality result in issues such as "mainstreaming" students not cognitively able to learn at the same level as the rest of their class. This practice is sometimes enforced, even against the wishes of parents.

Part of the postmodernist trend is diminishing competition in education, fearing the negative effect on the self-esteem of underachievers. An extreme example is the admissions policy of the nursing program at Cuesta College in California. It considers grades as an "artificial barrier" to nursing progress, according to their chancellor. So admission to the program is now determined by lottery rather than by prior grades or achievements.

As a sweeping generalization of postmodern trends in education, it might be said that educational methods are shifting from a teacher-centered to a student-centered system. As with most trends, there are probably both good and bad aspects to this change.

History

If you accept postmodern tenets, there is no such thing as reporting "how it really was" in the past. Every historian, it is claimed, interprets historical events on the basis of his own biases. Historical research, therefore, can never describe objective events, only the perceptions of the author. No events in history are more "important" than any other. When a historian names an event in history as important, he is not reflecting an objective reality, only the historian's own bias.

Unfortunately, say postmodern observers, history books and articles in our "Euro-centric culture," have been used as a weapon of the dominant culture to exert power over the marginalized. Postmodern historians, therefore, see their responsibility as correcting the unequal distribution of power caused by the biased reporting of previous historians. History writing is seen as an exercise in politics. Much of the history writing of the past needs to be "deconstructed" because it was written by the politically powerful—the rich, white, males.

Literature

In pure postmodernist theory, the author is not considered to be the authority over the meaning of a literary work. The author, in fact, may be unaware of the meaning. The reader is the authority of the text's meaning for herself. Meaning is subjective, not objective. Texts need to be "deconstructed," meaning the text needs to be separated from the political, religious, and social bias of the author. The author's "meaning" in the text can never be fully known. The reader must inject her own meaning. This is the only "reality" the reader will ever be able to determine.

Law

Consistent with the basic principles of postmodernist theory, it is thought there is no such thing as objective, fair, politically neutral law. The interpretation and enforcement of law is done by *people,* but people are affected by their cultural and religious biases. Postmodern theorists claim no society is governed by law, even when they think they are. It is governed by people who use law as a weapon of political power. Neither written codes of law or judges who interpret them can be truly objective. Both represent biased attitudes and reflect their own culture.

In the past, those in power have used law to oppress the marginalized—the poor and minorities. It is the task of postmodern judges to equalize power rather than to seek some objective standard of right and wrong.

Assignment

Become familiar with the characteristics of postmodern thought. Watch for examples of postmodernism in the media or in your conversations with others. If you notice any such evidences of postmodern thinking, tell us about it in the next class session.

UNIT VI

LESSON 28

The Effect of Postmodernism on the Church

<table>
<tr><td>

Equipment Needed

Chalkboard or whiteboard

</td><td>

Teaching Supplies Needed

1) Copies of student lesson 29 to distribute to the class.

</td></tr>
</table>

Lecture

Discuss each of the three statements on page 273 of the Student section. Ask for illustrations from student observations. If they are at all alert, they should have found many illustrations from the media and conversations with others. "Letters to the editor" in daily newspapers are sometimes rich sources of information about how people in our culture are thinking.

Proceed to the discussion on pages 273-275 in the Student section. Point out there are good features in postmodernist trends as well as very serious concerns. Help students see the importance of affirming what is good (from a Christian worldview) while at the same time being appropriately concerned about non-Christian and anti-Christian characteristics of the culture. We must be honest in our evaluations and careful to not make a blanket condemnation of everything related to postmodernism.

The most important part of this study in postmodernism is the conclusion students come to in their responses on the bottom of page 275. How can we define an effective Christian witness in a postmodern culture? Ask students to share their insights and discuss them together.

Divide your class down into groups of four to discuss the following questions:

1. How does the prevalence of postmodern attitudes in our culture affect our Christian witness?

Write group responses on the board.

2. How, if at all, should our methods of sharing the Gospel be different in a post-modern era than it was in a modernist era?

UNIT VI

Write group responses on the board.

3. What examples can they share of effective ways to relate to unbelievers with a postmodern mindset?

Allow plenty of time for the groups to discuss these questions. Then have one person from each group give a short report of their conclusions. Write the conclusions on the board and discuss them as they are given.

Inform students that the next lesson has additional suggestions about how to relate to postmodern culture as a Christian. They should study it thoroughly in preparation for the next lesson.

UNIT VI

LESSON 28

The Effect of Postmodernism on the Church

Just as postmodern attitudes have affected science, medicine, psychotherapy, education, history, literature, and law, they have also affected the church. Postmodernism factors into the way Christians think about themselves and the attitudes of those outside the church toward our Christian witness. Postmodernism affects the church in several ways. The list below is intended to start us thinking about how these changes in our culture impact our work as Christians. As you read this list, other observations may come to mind, or you may think of examples from your own experience that illustrate one or more of these points. If so, jot them down and share them with the class.

1) In our postmodern culture, telling someone else her religious belief is wrong or that Christianity is better, is seen as the very worst "sin." To judge another person's reality is thought to be intolerant. Therefore, because we Christians believe our faith is superior to other religions, we are considered intolerant, arrogant, and conceited! How *dare* we say our religion is "better." Likewise, when we declare Jesus is the *only* way to the Father—that He is "*the* way, *the* truth, and *the* life"—we are accused of being intolerant of other people and their religions. The result has been to silence the witness of many Christian people.

2) In a postmodern mindset, missionaries are considered to be "destroyers of culture" because they tell people of other cultures that Christianity is better. So what was previously honored as one of the highest and noblest callings (being a missionary) is now held in disrepute. The effect has been to actually convince some missionary agencies that they should no longer seek to convert people. Their mission has changed to some vague humanitarian goal.

3) The Christian concept of absolute truth—that truth exists whether you believe it or not—is now considered naive and old-fashioned. Even many Christians don't think such a thing as objective, absolute truth exists. Everything is considered relative. Therefore, when we talk about things like the Ten Commandments or other "laws of God," we are turned off as being simple-minded and unsophisticated.

Observations about Postmodernism from the Perspective of a Christian Worldview:

Despite the problems, there *are* some good things about postmodernism. Consider the following:

1) Science and technology will not bring in utopia. Christians have always maintained that the major

UNIT VI

human problem is internal—in the human heart. As C. S. Lewis once said, "Education merely makes man a more clever devil." So maybe postmodernists are bringing a corrective to the worship of science and technology.

2) European cultures have often unjustly dominated—even destroyed—other cultures. Sometimes the church and its missionaries have confused Christianity with Western culture, thinking the two were synonymous. Consequently, they have unwittingly destroyed some very good things in pagan cultures.

3) Other cultures do have many excellent qualities. In certain ways they may be better than ours. We shouldn't call other cultures "good" or "bad" simply on the basis of their technological progress or scientific knowledge.

4) It is true that the "American dream" has sometimes been a nightmare for those deprived simply because of their ethnic identity. Power has not been equally distributed nor even fairly distributed.

5) All of us, including scientists and historians, are more subjective than we would like to believe. Our conclusions are significantly affected by our biases.

6) Reason and logic *don't* always lead us to truth. As Christians, we have an explanation for this. It's called universal sin, which affects man's ability to be totally unbiased and truthful. In addition, we know reason and logic, as good as it may be, is inadequate to understand ultimate truth. For that, we need revelation from God. Human reason is a good ladder, but it's too short!

7) Our legal system *is* often unjust, and there is ample evidence of the more powerful in our society abusing that power by discriminating against the weak.

8) There *is* more to reality than the sterile modernist worldview would have people believe. We need to open our minds to the spiritual world.

On the other hand, there are some things about postmodernism that we, as Christians, find alarming. Consider, for example:

1) Postmodernism calls attention to the reality of subjectivism in determining truth, but its conclusions go too far. It may be more difficult to determine absolute truth or real events than we may have assumed, but this fact doesn't mean objective truth isn't out there. It is absurd to insist that reality exists only in the mind of the observer.

2) By reducing the individual to a mere "node on his culture," postmodernism destroys individual responsibility. Now, everything I do wrong is someone else's fault. In fact, there is no objective "wrong." The extreme relativism of postmodernism obliterates any objective ethical and moral standard. This is totally incompatible with Scripture and with the Christian worldview.

3) The postmodernism attempt to equalize power among cultures and groups within a culture is not only impossible, but the very attempt is dangerous. Multiculturalism is creating a renewed conflict between ethnic groups and other sub-cultures. Racial conflict is again on the rise. Instead of focusing on blending and healing, antagonistic groups are wrestling for political power. Because of human nature (which only Christians can adequately explain), each group is seeking—not equality of power—but dominance.

4) In some cases, to say that a practice is "right" for its culture, while "wrong" for another culture, is illogical and ridiculous. But since postmodernists deny the existence of absolute truth, they find

themselves caught in illogical absurdities. For example, why is killing six million Jews "wrong" for Nazis? Why is killing a thousand of your cult followers "wrong" in Uganda? Or is it? How do you know?

5) Logic and reason are *not* just "Eurocentric concepts". Even the most mystical person (anywhere in the world) uses logic and reason to direct her practical daily activities.

6) Postmodernists use logic and reasoning to promote and defend their views that logic and reason are invalid. The natural human mind (not just the Eurocentric mind) would conclude that postmodernists discredit themselves with contradictions. For example, why should the Feminist Movement be empowered to share more of the values males now enjoy? Is it better to be male? But we are told there is no objective "better" or "worse," "good" or "bad." Where did *this* objective truth come from if there is no such thing as objective truth?

7) The practice of "deconstruction" in literature, history, and science, while having some value in understanding and adjusting for the author's biases, is dangerous and dishonest when carried to the postmodern extreme. Rewriting history, for example, is legitimate and appropriate when new facts are discovered or known facts were previously misrepresented. But to rewrite history for the sole purpose of redistributing power today is dishonest and wrong.

8) For Christians, the postmodern challenge to the ethical, moral, and spiritual superiority of the Christian message is one of our greatest concerns. We believe it is *better* to be a Christian and have faith in Christ than, for example, to be a Satanist. We send missionaries around the world because we believe it is "good" (and for *their* good) to convert people to Christ. Postmodernists say we are intolerant destroyers of culture.

Assignment

In the light of this appraisal of trends in our culture, how should Christians approach people who have a postmodern mindset? How should our approach be different from what it was during the modern era? Or should it be different? List whatever observations come to mind and be prepared to share these suggestions with the class.

U N I T

VII

Effective Discipleship in a Postmodern Culture

Serving Christ Effectively in a Postmodern World

Equipment Needed

None

Teaching Supplies Needed

1) Copies of student lesson 30 to distribute to the class.

Lecture

Your students have spent months studying the heart of the Christian faith—its history, doctrines, and defenses against heresy. In recent weeks you have studied the culture we live in and current trends in that culture. This lesson attempts to bring the two together. Just how do we, as informed Christians, serve Christ effectively in our culture?

The message we proclaim never changes, but our culture constantly changes. Therefore, we must periodically review just how we can best relate the unchanging message to the constantly changing culture. That's what this lesson is all about.

Introduce this class lesson by explaining its purpose. Relate it to the last class lesson. In that lesson class members worked on suggestions of how best to relate, as a Christian, to people in a postmodern mindset. Today's lesson follows that theme with additional suggestions. However, this is not to be considered "the word of the experts" after the amateurs have tried it! The real experts are your class members. They know *their* culture best. The seven points in today's lesson are to be viewed as additional suggestions given by others.

Discuss each of these seven points in order. As you do, expect class members to share personal and practical experiences and questions. Statements like: "I work with this person who…" are common in this lesson and should be welcomed and encouraged. You may choose to give class members some time to help one another by offering practical suggestions for such situations.

After reviewing each of these seven points, ask class members to share what they have written for their assignments (page 283). What changes does each of your

UNIT VII

INSTRUCTOR

LESSON

29

class members, personally, seek to make in order to be a more effective witness for Christ? Encourage interaction as the class responds to each person's goals. Class members should help one another make their goals realistic and effective.

The next lesson asks for more self-examination but on a personal discipleship level. It will be the last lesson of the series, so plan ahead! Read for that lesson in the Leader section now. You may wish to do something special for the closing lesson.

LESSON 29

Serving Christ Effectively in a Postmodern World

The purpose of this study of postmodern culture is to gain enough understanding to present the Gospel clearly, in love, and to avoid needless offense. There are no "experts" on this subject. Your own experience, observations, and insights, together with those of others in your class, are important. You know best what the culture in your community is like.

In follow up to the discussion you had in your last class session, read and consider the suggestions below. After reflecting on these seven points carefully, combine them with the conclusions your class came to in your last session. Then write a brief summary of what changes you can make in your own approach toward unbelievers to make your witness more effective.

1. Lead with your testimony and weave your doctrinal beliefs into it.

The point here is that postmodern culture is more interested in your experience than your belief, so try to communicate on that level. What difference does your relationship with Christ make in your personal experience? Are you finding peace, satisfaction, fulfillment, joy, etc., as a Christian?

In sharing your faith with others, use "I" messages rather than "you" or "they" messages, and try to keep your statements positive rather than negative. For example, compare the two approaches below. The scenario is that of a Christian talking to a friend about Mormonism (or talking to a Mormon about Mormonism):

Example A:
"Mormons are wrong because they deny the deity of Christ, claim He is the spiritual brother of Lucifer, and base their salvation on works. They (you) believe good Mormons become gods, and that is clearly in conflict with what the Bible says."

Example B:
"The reason I could not be a Mormon is because I could never do anything different than worship Jesus as God. My relationship with Jesus is very personal, and I serve Him because He paid the price for my sins. What I see in the Bible is that we are all His creation and that there is now and always will be only one God."

Example A is doctrinally correct and may be appropriate for someone asking a direct question, such as: "What's wrong with Mormonism?" But *generally* speaking, in our current culture, Example B would be received better because:

    1) It does not directly attack anyone; therefore, it is less likely to be perceived as "arrogant."

2) It is based on one's own experience and perceptions, so there is nothing to argue about. This is how *you* feel. No one else can deny the validity of your feeling. It is *your truth!*

3) It opens the door to further discussion. It invites the question, *"Why* do you feel this way?"

2. Be sure what you do and say is motivated by a sincere concern for the other person's good.

In our postmodern culture, people are wary of "scalp hunters" (religious fanatics who simply want to add another scalp to their trophy case). They can smell insincerity a mile away!

Too often our evangelistic efforts have seemed like we were only interested in adding another number to our list of converts. Instead, we need to be focusing on sincerely helping others in their spiritual journey.

3. Allow time for your witness to have an effect in the lives of others.

The Czech theologian and Christian educator, Comenius (1592-1670) once said, "We have a tendency to want to plant trees instead of seeds." It may have taken us many years to come to the conclusions we have and to get our lives somewhat straightened out. Yet, we naively assume someone else should buy the whole package instantly.

Postmodernists are pragmatists. They want to know, "Does it work for *you.*" Moreover, they want more than you just saying it does. They want to observe your life. Do *you* know joy? What kind of morality do *you* display? What are *your* priorities? Do you *really* care about them? An old cliché states: "They don't care how much you know until they know how much you care." That's especially true in the postmodern era.

4. Emphasize assurance, certainties, and confidence.

Postmodern culture is philosophically and morally adrift. Having rejected moral absolutes and objective truth, many people are given to despair and hopelessness, lacking purpose in life. As Christians, we have a positive message of hope that we can share with others. We have a worldview that inspires confidence and puts meaning back into life. We know history and world events are not just circumstances falling together by blind chance, but that it all has a purpose guided by a divine hand. This divine purpose also includes each individual life. Our culture desperately craves this kind of assurance and meaning. That's why some Christian books on this theme are bestsellers. God has given us a great open door to connect with postmodern people.

5. Emphasize the emotional aspect of your testimony.

Our culture tends to mistrust logical arguments and wave truth claims aside with "whatever works for you." But there is an insatiable hunger for emotional satisfaction. "Make me feel good," seems to be the universal cry. Self-help books on positive emotional experience sell briskly.

Do you find emotional satisfaction in your relationship with Christ? If so, communicate it to your world. People usually make decisions based on emotion, then use logic to maintain their position. That's human nature. People will hear you better if you communicate on the "feeling" level.

A warning is in order here. We don't try to "sell" our Christian faith on the claim that everything will be wonderful and our problems are over if we put our faith in Christ. That is not true. Neither is it biblical. Nevertheless, our relationship to Christ brings a joy and satisfaction (regardless of circumstances) that the world simply cannot offer. That's what we want to communicate.

6. Understand and feel into postmodern issues.

Concern for the environment, equality of power, kindness to animals, building self-esteem, political correctness, multiculturalism, etc., are important issues to many in our culture. They should also be an essential part of our concerns. But, hopefully, we can be positive about these issues and speak knowledgeably about them without being caught up in the excesses that sometimes characterize activists. If we are to properly relate to people around us we need to be fair, open-minded, informed, and honest about the things that matter to them. We should not needlessly offend our culture.

7. Don't compromise truth.

Christians in the past sometimes made the mistake of trying to accommodate their faith and their doctrinal beliefs to the culture, thinking that would make them more acceptable and gain converts. For example, in the modernist era some Christians abandoned belief in miracles because it didn't fit the modernist mindset. This approach did not result in greater acceptance and respect. Churches and denominations that took this approach actually declined in membership, in contrast to those who remained true to biblical truth and realized growth in membership.

We shouldn't be moral relativists just because people around us are. We shouldn't hedge on the definition of God and the person of Christ in an effort to be more acceptable to New Agers, etc. We shouldn't abandon evangelism or missions because some think it is "arrogant" to claim Christianity is better than other religions. Even though we may lead with testimony rather than doctrine, we must never allow the "pillars of faith" to be compromised.

Assignment

Now that you have had an opportunity to examine the basics of our Christian faith and taken a glimpse at the culture we live in, try to bring all of this together into the practical. What changes do you want to make in your own life and witness as a result of all this study? How do you think you can be more effective in understanding and relating to your culture?

Think it through carefully and prayerfully. Then write a paragraph or two reflecting your conclusions. Be prepared to 1) share your conclusion with the class, and 2) meaningfully interact with other class members who will also share their personal thoughts and goals on this subject. Help them to evaluate their conclusions, as they do the same for you.

LESSON 30
Guarding Your Heart

Equipment Needed	Teaching Supplies Needed
None	1) Copies of the Certificate of Completion to distribute to the class.

Lecture

Finally! Rejoice with your students about "finishing the course!" Yet, there will probably be a tinge of sadness if your class disbands after this lesson. You have built relationships that will last for years.

Make this lesson special. Here are a few suggestions:

1. You might want to have a party. Have several people bring refreshments and use the last part of the class to visit and eat.

2. *Before* you party, be sure to discuss the five characteristics of a disciple. This is a very important lesson, so don't minimize the instructional part of it. Share some practical suggestions about your own experience (for example, how do you maintain a consistent Bible study program? How did you get involved in ministry opportunities? Etc.). Ask students to share with each other about the same issues and covenant to pray for each other.

When honest, most Christians express difficulty maintaining consistent study of Scripture. (Item #3, page 288 in Student section). An assignment for this lesson is to read Psalm 1 and Psalm 119. Psalm 119 is a long chapter (the longest in the Bible!), and it's all about the benefits of feeding on the Word. Read this chapter before class and note the rewards that come from feasting regularly on God's Word. Discuss these in class. Ask if any class members have found an effective way to maintain this vital discipline. What suggestions can they give for the rest of the class?

Psalm 1 is also an excellent passage to discuss in terms of the value of meditating on the Word of God and the results of being rooted in the Word, in contrast to the one who ignores the Word. Ask for student responses to their reading of this psalm.

Ask class members to share what they have written in response to the three questions in the Student section (pages 289-290). This will involve very personal sharing. Be respectful and concerned about each response and serious about class members helping one another reach their discipleship goals.

3. This would be a great time to ask your pastor or other staff person to speak to the class about ministry opportunities within the church. Ask him to suggest ways graduates can put the things they have learned to work in serving the Lord and the church.

4. If you are presenting graduation certificates to recognize successful completion of this course, either do so now or arrange for a special ceremony—perhaps in a worship service of your church. If the latter, announce the details in this class.

5. If you do all of the above, arrange for a longer than usual time for this lesson and announce it ahead of time. Don't spoil it by being rushed!

Thank you for your faithful service in teaching this course!

Instructor Section Notes

1) Flavius Josephus, *Wars of the Jews*, Book VI, Chapter I.

2) Tim Dowley, *Eerdmans' Handbook to the History of Christianity* (Grand Rapids: Eerdmans Publishing Co., 1977), 69.

3) Bruce L. Shelley, *Church History in Plain Language* (Nashville: Nelson Reference, 1996) 61.

4) Andrew Fuller, *Gospel Worthy of All Acceptation*, 2nd ed. (Philadelphia: Anderson and Meehan, 1820).

5) Shelley, 375.

6) New World Dictionary, s.v. "Apologetics."

7) Robert Blatchford, *God And My Neighbour* (Chicago: Charles H. Kerr Publishing Co., 1911).

8) "Meet Your Self," Talks given by Sri Swami Venkatesananda (Uttaranchal, India: The Divine Life Society, 1970).

9) Clark Pinnock, *Set Forth Your Case* (Chicago: Moody Press, 1971).

10) James Sire, *The Universe Next Door,* 4th ed. (Downers Grove: InterVarsity Press, 2004).

LESSON 30

Guarding Your Heart

Congratulations! You are about to complete seven months of study in seven vital subjects relating to the Christian life. This is a major accomplishment for which you need to be (and will be) commended. It reflects your sincere desire to be a faithful servant of Christ.

Your investment of time, money, and energy to achieve this milestone brings you to a place far beyond the "average" Christian in terms of understanding our faith, our history, and our culture. The Lord will use you in special ways because of this preparation.

However, the caution we extend to you at this time is: ***Don't stop now!*** Depending upon where you were in your Christian life at the beginning of this course, the material we studied may either be a good review, entirely new information, or (most likely) a combination of both. Whatever the situation, please recognize that what you have learned is part of the *beginning,* not the end, of your discipleship experience. We are never fully equipped because the process of growth in discipleship is life-long.

Even if it were possible to learn everything there is to know about the Christian life (a totally absurd notion), we would still need to keep learning about the constantly changing culture around us. To be a faithful servant of Christ, we need to be ministering to and within that culture.

In the early years of this third millennium, we find ourselves living in a time of cultural change that is unprecedented. Never has change taken place so quickly. With these rapid changes, many church leaders warn that the church stands in a time of great crisis.

One such church leader is George Barna, who in his professional life is a highly successful marketing consultant, having done research for major secular organizations and businesses as well as Christian organizations, such as Focus on the Family and the Billy Graham Evangelistic Association. He is also a committed Christian with a heart for the Lord's work. He has written several books about the church's effectiveness in the world, including *Frog in the Kettle; Marketing the Church,* and *User Friendly Churches.* We mention all of this just to establish the fact that George Barna probably is in a position to evaluate the church's position in our culture better than most of us because of his extensive research.

Therefore, Barna's recent book, *The Second Coming of the Church,* deserves our careful attention. In it, Barna says "Having devoted the last eighteen years of my life to studying the American people, their churches, and the prevailing culture, I've concluded that within the next few years America will experience one of two outcomes: either massive spiritual revival or total moral anarchy. As a committed Christian, I am urgently praying for revival. As a rational social scientist confronted with a warehouse full of behavioral and attitudinal data...well, the prospects are not encouraging." [25]

That is a frightening evaluation. Barna explains that research clearly shows there is very little difference between "born-again Christians" and the rest of the people in our culture *in the way they live.* Christians claim to have a different worldview than the secular culture around them, but they don't demonstrate that in real life. Consequently, Barna contends a culture that is desperately hungry for spiritual reality is not finding it in the church.

You, as a graduate of *Foundations of Faith*, are in a position to provide leadership to the church in this time of crisis if you continue in the things you have been taught. We will probably not be the kind of leaders who stand before hundreds or thousands with a public ministry. God does not call many of those. But we can be effective in our place of ministry, and we can help change *our* world—the situation immediately around us. We carry a greater than average responsibility to do this because Jesus said, "From everyone who has been given much, much will be demanded" (Luke 12:48).

So what does God require of us?

Below is a list of five characteristics that we think should be a part of the life of every disciple of the Lord Jesus, especially graduates of the *Foundations of Faith*. Please review them carefully and use them as a "checklist" of your own life. In the next class session we will talk about each of these and suggest ways to implement them more fully.

1. Confess Jesus as Lord and Savior

This is the starting point of the Christian life, but it is also a continual public confession. Bear in mind that there is no ritual or formula for beginning the Christian life. Some people assume you have to say exactly the right words or do something (like going down the aisle in an invitation) to be saved. There is no requirement in Scripture except: "Believe in the Lord Jesus, and you will be saved" (Acts 16:31); and "...if you confess with your mouth, 'Jesus is Lord,' and believe in your heart that God raised him from the dead, you will be saved" (Rom. 10:9). Note that the action is genuine ("in your heart"), and it is public ("confess with your mouth").

Sadly, many people assume making a public confession is all there is to being a Christian. That is a tragic misconception. Jesus calls us to discipleship, not merely to "make a decision." Our public confession of Jesus as Lord and Savior is the *beginning* of a wonderfully exciting spiritual adventure that *never ends!*

2. Possess a life-changing faith

The person who truly confesses Christ in the world will experience a transformation in conduct and attitude. If that doesn't happen, his commitment to Christ is not real. The Bible is clear about this. "Faith by itself, if it is not accompanied by action, is dead" (Jas. 2:17).

Sometimes changes are gradual. Sometimes they are dramatically sudden. But every true disciple of Jesus is different from the world, and the difference shows.

3. Feed regularly on God's Word

One of the primary evidences of new life in Christ is a desire to study the Bible, both individually and in groups. This should be expected because if we truly "love the Lord our God with all our heart," we will want to read His letters.

As an assignment for next week, read Psalms 1 and 119. Start early in the week because Psalm 119 is the longest chapter in the Bible!

Because being continually nourished by the Word of God is such a powerful source of spiritual life, the enemy of our souls attacks us most viciously at this point. Consistent Bible study and meditation is one of the most difficult disciplines for us to maintain. For this reason, we will concentrate on that discipline in the next class session and give some practical suggestions for finding victory in this area of our spiritual life.

4. Actively participate in the life of the church

Remember that the term "church" in Scripture refers to the people who belong to Christ. It is not synonymous with an organization, denomination, etc. Therefore, *everyone* who belongs to Christ, regardless of which denomination he may be from, is part of the Church. To such persons we extend Christian fellowship and brotherly love.

In addition to the "church universal" referred to above, Scripture also uses the term "church" to refer to the local body of believers. We are commanded to be faithful in our participation to this group (Heb. 10:25). We desperately need one another for mutual encouragement and learning.

UNIT VII

There are four major functions that should be a part of our regular participation in the local church. They include:

1) *Instruction*. God does not give anyone *all* the information necessary for a complete understanding of His will. The Holy Spirit often speaks to us through others. Some are especially gifted as teachers and counselors. Therefore, in addition to individual study, we need to receive instruction from others within the fellowship of the local church.

2) *Worship*. God calls us to regular and consistent worship of Him within the company of His people.

3) *Fellowship*. Mutual caring for each other is a vital part of the Christian life. To accomplish this, we need to really know each other– our successes and our failures. We need to "rejoice with those who rejoice" and "mourn with those who mourn" (Rom. 12:15).

4) *Service*. Serving God together multiplies our effectiveness and demonstrates the love of God to the world. Many ways to serve the Lord are open to us (Rom. 12:6-8), but this service is best accomplished when it is shared within the body of Christ.

5. Demonstrate a godly concern for others

Anyone who is genuinely in Christ will share Christ's concern for the world. This includes caring for the spiritual, emotional, and physical well-being of both those who are part of the body of Christ and those who are not.

Unfortunately, it is hard to rid ourselves of worldly attitudes. Barna points out that the church is still one of the most segregated institutions in America. The segregation is ethnic, economic, and social. The church of the first century was not like this. One of its great strengths was the unusual way "the ground was level at the foot of the cross." Kings and peasants, slaves and their owners, were all equal in Christ. This was a radical idea, contrary to the practice of its culture. It had a powerful impact on first century society.

In addition to being one in Christ in the above sense, a disciple's concern is global. Christians should be the most knowledgeable people about world conditions and other cultures. Our top priorities should be sending the Gospel to every nation and tongue, not "comfortable pews" and "good entertainment." Our major concern should be people, not things.

In preparation for our next session, write a sentence or two in response to each of the following questions. Be prepared to share your responses with the class.

1) Where do you see yourself in your spiritual journey? At the beginning? Well along the way? Satisfied? Dissatisfied?

2) What changes do you plan to make to "guard your heart" and grow in Christian discipleship?

UNIT VII

3) Of the changes mentioned above, which do you anticipate will be the most difficult to maintain? How can other class members help you reach your goal?

Congratulations on your accomplishment. You have "completed the course!" God will reward you for your diligent and faithful study.

Student Section Notes

1) Hugh Ross, *The Creator and the Cosmos,* (Colorado Springs: NavPress, 1993). 16-17.

2) Archibald G. Brown, cited in Robert Lee, *The Outlined Bible*, an outline and Analysis of every book in the Bible, from a presentation at the Mildmay Conference Hall Bible School, London (London: Fleming H. Revell, nd), 66.

3) Josephus Flavius, *Wars of the Jews,* Book V, Chapter 13, Josephus Complete Works (Grand Rapids: Kregel Publications, 1960), 570.

4) Polycarp, cited in *The American Cyclopedia,* (NY: D. Appleton & Co., 1883), 685.

5) Wycliffe, cited in Bruce Shelley *Church History in Plain Language,* (Dallas TX: Word Publishing Co., 1995), 227.

6) Luther, cited in J.H. Merle D'Aubigne' *The Life and Times of Martin Luther,* (Chicago: Moody Press, 1985), 31.

7) Luther, cited in Shelley, 239.

8) Charles V, cited in D'Aubigne', 433.

9) Luther, cited in D'Aubigne', 433.

10) Roger Williams, cited in *Eerdmans' Handbook to Christianity in America,* (Grand Rapids, MI: Wm. B. Eerdmans' Publishing Co, 1983), 48.

11) Wesley, cited in Shelley, 335.

12) Edwards, cited in Shelley, 346.

13) Paul Lee Tan, *Encyclopeida of 7700 Illustrations, Signs of the Times,* (Rockville, MD: Assurance Publishers, 1979), 1239.

14) George Smoot, cited in Fred Heeren, *Show Me God.* (Wheeling, IL: Day Star Publications, 1997), 139.

15) Fred Hoyle, *Engineering and Science,* (November, 1981) cited in Heeren, 205.

16) John Stuart Mill, *Three Essays on Religion,* (NY: Greenwood Press, 1969 Reprint of original publication by Henry Holt & Co, 1874), 28-29.

17) Bertrand Russell, *Why I Am Not a Christian,* (NY: Simon & Schuster, 1957) 17.

18) D.A. Carson, cited in Lee Strobel, *A Case for Christ,* (Grand Rapids, MI: Zondervan, 1998), 165.

19) Kenneth Scott LaTourette, cited in Vernon C. Grounds *The Reason for Our Hope,* (Chicago: Moody Press, 1945), 40.

20) Napoleon, cited by Grounds, 37.

21) Phillip Schaff, cited by Grounds, 40.

22) C.S. Lewis, *Mere Christianity,* (NY: Macmillan Publishing Co., 1960), 56.

23) Peter Kreeft and Ronald K. Tacelli, *Handbook of Christian Apologetics,* (Downers Grove, IL: InterVarsity Press, 1994), 159.

   Ibid: Chart modified from Kreeft and Tacelli. 171.

24) D. James Kennedy, *Why I Believe,* (Nashville: Word Publishing Co, 1999), 2.

25) George Barna, *The Second Coming of the Church,* (Nashville: Word Publishing Co., 1998), 1.

Certificate of Completion

This certifies that _____ has successfully completed the Foundations of Faith series. Congratulations on your accomplishment. May God reward your diligent and faithful study.

_____
Course Instructor

_____
Date

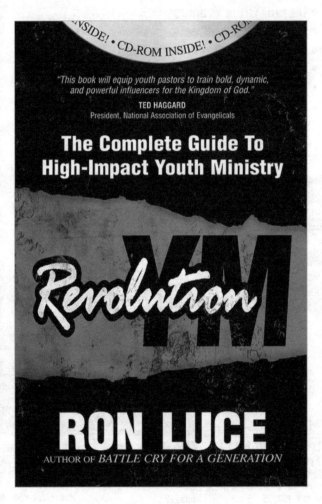

Pick Up 'n' Do Series:
Quick and Easy Lessons to *Pick Up 'n' Do* for Children's Ministry!

Features and Benefits:

- Cost-effective and totally class efficient
- An entire quarter of Sunday School (twelve lessons) in one book!
- Completely reproducible
- 40 Minutes to 1 1/2 hours of solid bible teaching
- In-depth Bible teaching and serious discipleship without hours of preparation or lots of staff
- Recruit older kids to teach younger ones – fewer adult volunteers necessary

- Large Group/Small/Group lesson format
- Instant Bible dramas
- Copy 'n' go handouts
- Optional hands-on workshops
- Lively puppet skits
- Serious discipleship
- Stretch lessons with the easy-to-do crafts, science or food activities

Collect all 6 Titles!

NEW!

Jesus 4U!
ISBN-13: 978-0-7814-4069-1
ISBN-10: 0-78144-069-6
Item#: 103326
Paperback • $19.99

Take Two Tablets and Call Moses!
ISBN-13: 978-0-7814-4067-7
ISBN-10: 0-78144-067-X
Item#: 103324
Paperback • $19.99

Survivor Bible-Style!
ISBN-13: 978-0-7814-4068-4
ISBN-10: 0-78144-068-8
Item#: 103323
Paperback • $19.99

Let's Hear it for the Fruit of the Spirit!
ISBN-13: 978-0-7814-4066-0
ISBN-10: 0-78144-066-1
Item#: 103325
Paperback • $19.99

King Davey and the Royal Tunes!
ISBN-13: 978-0-7814-4377-7
ISBN-10: 0-78144-377-6
Item#: ??
Paperback • $19.99

Rise and Shin
ISBN-13: 978-0-781
ISBN-10: 0-78144-
Item#: ??
Paperback • $19.9

To order, visit www.cookministries.com,
call 1-800-323-7543, or visit your favorite local bookstore.

COOK
COMMUNICATIONS
MINISTRI